Convivial Poems

Giovanni Pascoli

CONVIVIAL POEMS

BY

GIOVANNI PASCOLI

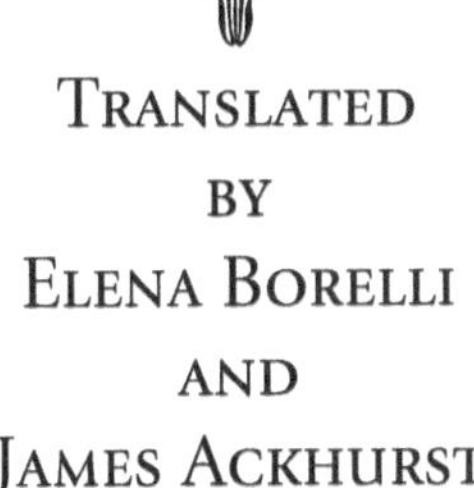

TRANSLATED

BY

ELENA BORELLI

AND

JAMES ACKHURST

ITALICA PRESS
NEW YORK & BRISTOL
2022

ITALICA PRESS, INC.
99 Wall Street, Suite 650
New York, New York 10005

Italica Press Poetry in Translation Series
Revised Printing 2025

Library of Congress Cataloging-in-Publication Data

Names: Pascoli, Giovanni, 1855-1912, author. | Borelli, Elena, translator. | Ackhurst, James, 1982-
translator. | Pascoli, Giovanni, 1855-1912.

Poemi conviviali. | Pascoli, Giovanni, 1855-1912. Poemi conviviali. English.

Title: Convivial poems / Giovanni Pascoli ; translated by Elena Borelli and James Ackhurst.

Description: New York : Italica Press, 2022. | Series: Italica Press poetry in translation | Italian and
English. | Summary: "A new Italian/English dual-language edition of Giovanni Pascoli's "Poemi
conviviali," originally published in 1904"-- Provided by publisher.

Identifiers: LCCN 2022011513 (print) | LCCN 2022011514 (ebook) | ISBN 9781599104355
(hardcover) | ISBN 9781599104362 (trade paperback) | ISBN 9781599104379 (kindle edition) |
ISBN 9781599104386 (adobe pdf)

Subjects: LCSH: Pascoli, Giovanni, 1855-1912--Translations into English. | LCGFT: Poetry.

Classification: LCC PQ4835.A3 P513 2022 (print) | LCC PQ4835.A3 (ebook) |
DDC 851/.912--dc23/eng/20220314

LC record available at https://lccn.loc.gov/2022011513

LC ebook record available at https://lccn.loc.gov/2022011514

Cover Image: Young man singing and playing the kithara. Terracotta
amphora ca. 490 B.C. Attributed to the Berlin Painter. Metropolitan Museum
of Art (56.171.38), Fletcher Fund, 1956.

For a Complete List of
Italica Poetry in Translation
Visit our Web Site at
www.ItalicaPress.com

About the Translators

Elena Borelli teaches Italian and Intercultural Studies at King's College London, UK. Her research focuses on the culture and literature of the late nineteenth century in Europe, and she has published extensively on the notion of desire and issues of translation and reception during that time, as well as on the poets Giovanni Pascoli and Gabriele D'Annunzio. She is also a translator, producing (together with James Ackhurst) translations from contemporary and modern poets for the *Journal of Italian Translation*.

James Ackhurst is a writer and translator based in Wellington, New Zealand. He has published translations (produced with Elena Borelli) in the *Journal of Italian Translation* and poems, stories, and criticism in *takahe, Turbine, Poetry New Zealand, Snorkel, Pericles at Play, Poetry Salzburg Review, Quadrant* and *The Pantograph Punch*.

Contents

INTRODUCTION

TRANSLATING GIOVANNI PASCOLI'S *CONVIVIAL POEMS*:
AN ANCIENT LANGUAGE FOR A MODERN SOUL

Giovanni Pascoli's *Convivial Poems (Poemi Conviviali)* owes its name to the literary journal *Il Convito* ("the *Convivium*"), where the poems were first published. *Il Convito* saw the light in 1895 and was founded by Adolfo de Bosis (to whom Pascoli dedicated the first edition of *Convivial Poems* and whom he addresses in the preface), Angelo Conti, and Gabriele D'Annunzio. Adolfo de Bosis was a businessman, as well as a poet in his own right and a translator of English literature; Angelo Conti was an art historian and a philosopher who had inspired the Aesthetic movement in Italy; Gabriele d'Annunzio was the rising star of the Italian literary scene. The journal was emblematic of the particular kind of Modernism gaining currency in Italy at the end of the nineteenth century: one involving a revival of antiquity and a return to one's roots as the true way of being modern.

Within its richly decorated pages, *Il Convito* espoused the idea that pursuing beauty in art and literature was the way out of the swamp of bourgeois industrialism and socialism affecting Italy both at the cultural and political level. Beauty, in fact, was to be found in classical and pagan ideals and in the artistic forms at the origins of Western civilization, which had been sullied and forgotten in what D'Annunzio describes as his contemporary "grey democratic deluge."[1] The founders of *Il Convito* also called for the active participation

---

1.   This description of Italy's society comes from the pages of D'Annunzio's most successful novel, *The Child of Pleasure*, published in 1889 (*Il Piacere*, Milano: Mondadori, 1988, p.34).

of intellectuals in the political life of the country: as heralds
of beauty and custodians of the classical values, poets and
artists were to be the true priests of modernity. *Il Convito*
was a short-lived experiment, lasting barely two years in its
original form. However, during that time, it showcased the
works of prominent artists and fervent nationalists such as
Enrico Nencioni and Edoardo Scarfoglio, as well almost all
of Pascoli's "convivial" poems. In 1904, Pascoli collected
them and published them under this name, and in 1905, he
issued a second and final edition which featured the extra
poem "The Twins."

When he was invited to contribute to *Il Convito*, Pascoli
was a poet and a classicist who had already won critical
acclaim for both his Italian and Latin poetry. Therefore,
his artistic profile perfectly suited the purpose of *Il Convito*.
However, Pascoli shared very little of D'Annunzio's
enthusiasm for the pagan values à la Nietzsche, his elitist
cult of beauty, and his spite for the bourgeoisie. The preface
of *Convivial Poems* is a declaration of his distance from the
intellectuals of *Il Convito*, whom he nonetheless appreciated
for their revival of classical antiquity. For Pascoli, the ideal
of beauty does not evoke the superiority of the pagan
Übermensch envisioned by D'Annunzio. Beauty, like poetry
and art, is a balm for human sorrow, or, as Freud would
observe in *Civilization and Its Discontents*, a mild narcotic
to ease the pain of existence.[2] Since one of the curses of
mankind is relentless desire — as the greed and lust that
generate discord among people — Pascoli imagines that art
could do to mankind what he felt it could do to him: help
sublimate eros and violence into images of eternal beauty.

---

2.   Sigmund Freud, *Civilization and Its Discontents* (first published in 1930),
translated and edited by James Strachey (New York and London: Norton, 1961),
p. 30: "People who are receptive to the influence of art cannot set too high a
value on it as a source of pleasure and consolation in life. Nevertheless, the
mild narcosis induced in us by art can do no more than bring about a transient
withdrawal from the pressure of vital needs...."

In *Convivial Poems*, Pascoli weaves a history of antiquity, which begins with the ancient Greek poets, such as Sappho and Homer, and continues until Alexander the Great and the Roman Empire, terminating with the birth of Christ. The poems often elaborate upon lesser-known episodes from Greek mythology and literature, but major characters, such as Ulysses/Odysseus, are given considerable space. The first poem, "Solon," has Sappho articulate the relationship between eros and its inner death drive on the one hand and poetry on the other, which has the power to immortalize every object of human desire. The second poem, "The Blind Man of Chios," beautifully juxtaposes the figure of the blind poet — Homer — with that of the young maid Nausicaa in the *Odyssey*. Here poetry is both a curse, as it deprives one of a normal life, and the ultimate gift: in describing the inner landscape of the poet, Pascoli writes lines of an almost psychedelic quality. The next three poems are inspired by minor characters and storylines from the *Iliad*: Achilles' last moments; the death of Memnon, the son of the goddess Aurora; and Helen of Troy's supreme and deadly beauty on the night of the city's downfall. Ulysses is the protagonist of two poems: "The Sleep of Odysseus" and the lengthy "The Last Voyage." The twenty-four cantos of "The Last Voyage" narrate Odysseus' attempt to re-enact his adventurous journey home after the war. In this poem, Pascoli imagines how Odysseus, dissatisfied with his life in Ithaca, gathers his old companions to return to the places they encountered on their voyage home. This new adventure is in fact a journey inward, founded on an impossible desire to re-live his youth. In "The Poet of the Helots," Pascoli strongly rejects the aristocratic mentality of D'Annunzio and the other aesthetes, as he celebrates work as another antidote to the pain of existence. The poem was inspired by a passage of Hesiod's *Works and Days*, in which the author recounts his voyage to the island of Euboea, where he participated in a poetry contest and won a tripod. Probably in the second century AD, this episode inspired a short anonymous narrative called *The Contest of Homer and Hesiod*. Here, Hesiod beats Homer, as he sings of agriculture in times of peace, instead of exalting war and violence. The title of the poems refers to the helots, the lowest rank in Spartan society, and those who were tasked with working the land. In the poems "Ate," "The Courtesan," and "Mother," Pascoli explores the various dimensions of violence and its link with eros and love. In the "Poems of Psyche," the notions of metempsychosis and the soul's immortality take us back to late antiquity, when these notions paved the way for the advent of Christianity. The exquisite poem "Alexandros" puts into play another fundamental human drive: young Alexander's relentless desire for knowledge in his explorations beyond the borders of the known world. Alexander's figure appears also in the poem "Gog and Magog," where, through his masterful use of onomatopoeic language, Pascoli evokes the fear of beast-like hordes of barbarians threatening civilization. The last two poems narrate the advent of Christ, which would call time on the classical world.

Pascoli's poems display a thorough knowledge of classical literature, not only of its content but also of its genres. Indeed, in his poems, Pascoli variously attempts to replicate the metres of ancient Greek poetry, from the elegy to the epyllion, and the philosophical prose of Plato's dialogues, among others. Obscure etymologies and lesser-known versions of myths spark the poet's imagination: for instance, the legendary name of Sappho's lover, Phaon, which means "setting sun," inspires Pascoli to write Sappho's love song, a sapphic ode inside the poem "Solon" where the beloved is compared to a glorious sunset. However, it would be wrong to read *Convivial Poems* as a mere exercise in erudition. Here, Pascoli narrates compelling stories that appeal to the modern reader both for their exquisite and original imagery, at times reminiscent of Pre-Raphaelite paintings, and for their timeless exploration of the human condition. The characters speak an ancient language but embody passions and sorrows as seen through a modern eye: they are driven by desire, they are soothed by beauty and music, and they are consoled by the secular immortality granted by poetry, which Pascoli sees as the only possible religion of modernity.

The task of rendering *Convivial Poems* into another language is particularly daunting. The original Italian is already artificially antiqued, as it is supposed to reproduce some of the features of ancient Greek: there are loan words from the Homeric poems and words that translate epithets and formulaic sentences, such as "swift-footed Achilles"; the spelling of names is purposefully archaic; the syntax at times follows the structure of epic lines with their accumulation of coordinate clauses introduced by "and," to suggest an endless iteration of objects and actions. This archaic language, often structured according to the rhythm of ancient metric forms, is ruptured by images of striking modernity, which betray the influences of Symbolism and Decadentism. As some critics have acknowledged,[3] Pascoli's poems are filled with eerie and uncanny images, such as mysterious female figures awaiting the heroes at the threshold between life and death, wondrous marine landscapes, serene celestial vaults, but also infernal vortexes of Dantean inspiration. Furthermore, even in *Convivial Poems*, Pascoli deploys the usual combinations of the two semantic areas of language that Gianfranco Contini identified in the poet's other works, the post- and the pre-grammatical levels.[4] The post-grammatical level involves the use of very specialized jargon, which normally does not appear in poems, concerning objects of everyday life or flora and fauna. In *Convivial Poems*, this lexicon appears in the philologically accurate descriptions of ancient equipment

3.   See for instance Maria Truglio, *Beyond the Family Romance: The Legend of Pascoli* (Toronto: Toronto University Press, 2007), in which the author explores Pascoli's poetic imagery in the light of Freud's category of the uncanny: something homey yet strange and disquieting.
4.   Gianfranco Contini, *La Letteratura Italiana Otto Novecento* (Florence: Sansoni, 1974), pp.143–45.

and tools. On the other hand, the pre-grammatical level entails a phonematic and onomatopoetic use of human, animal, and ancient languages; a musical use of language rooted in the pure pleasure of sound.

Pascoli's poetic language forces the translator to make choices, since it is often not possible to combine faithfulness to the original metre with the semantic richness and the multilingualism of *Convivial Poems*. Our metric solutions are diverse. In certain cases, like in "The Birds of Memnon" or "Gog and Magog," we adopted a fixed rhyming scheme, which, albeit different from the original, still exposes the reader to the predictable, epic-like rhythm of those poems. When tackling other poems such "Anticlos," we preferred a prose-like translation, keeping the narrative style of the loose hendecasyllables in the original and preserving the epic flavor in the syntax and semantic choices of the lines. In poems like "The Lyre of Achilles" or "The Sleep of Odysseus," we created — whenever possible — lines of four beats, which provide the English reader with the same familiar rhythm that the hendecasyllable presents to the Italian ear. Once or twice, we tried to mirror the metre of Pascoli's lyric passages more precisely, as in "The Old Men of Kea" and, above all, in "Solon," where the sapphic stanzas are faithfully reproduced. Lastly, in "Alexandros," we reproduced the hendecasyllables with lines of exactly eleven syllables.

We chose to translate the poems into modern English with very little use of obsolete words or syntactical alterations to the common word order. However, we kept the Homeric formulas and the quotations from Greek literature. The result is a flowing language, which preserves the flair of ancient literature but is very palatable to the modern reader. We endeavored to provide our translation with some of the key features of Pascoli's poetic language: the frequent use of alliterations, the onomatopoetic language, the wordplay with etymology, the archaic spelling of names, and the accuracy of the botanical and historical lexicon. At the same time, we wanted to make the poems as accessible as possible to the English readers without too much technical jargon obscuring the meaning. We chose accessible synonyms for many of the objects mentioned in the poems. Additionally, we added a few explanatory notes as well as a glossary to identify characters or geographical locations that might not be immediately obvious to the reader. Pascoli often refers to minor episodes in classical history and literature, so we thought that adding the background of a particular story or myth would facilitate comprehension. Far from providing a critical apparatus or a philological reconstruction of Pascoli's work, we simply aim at increasing the reading enjoyment of these beautiful poems.

Convivial Poems is one of the highest poetic achievements of Italian Modernism. Surprisingly, this book has so far remained relatively unknown to an English readership, in strong contrast to other works by Pascoli such as *Myricae* or *Canti di Castelvecchio*, which have attracted the attention of famous poets and translators such as Seamus Heaney, Geoff Brock, or Taije Silverman. The only other complete translation of *Poemi Conviviali*, by Egidio Lunardi and Robert Nugent, dates back to 1979. Selected poems from this collection have been translated by Deborah Brown, Geoffrey Brock, and Taije Silverman. *Convivial Poems* has so far encountered the same destiny as the rest of Pascoli's "erudite" poetry: *Primi Poemetti* or the medieval *Canzoni di Re Enzio* or the beautiful *Poemata Christiana* in Latin. We hope that our translation will allow more readers to appreciate the incredible modernity of Pascoli's ancient world: not a world of neoclassic purity and idealized perfection, but a world of shadows and conflicting desires, which deeply resonates in our own society.

— Elena Borelli

CONVIVIAL POEMS

Preface

Adolfo, your *Convito* is not over yet. It began in January 1895 and occurred each month of that year, in Rome. How did it happen that I was called to be part of that "lively bunch of militant energies, which was to rescue beauty and ideals from the dirty wave of vulgarity inundating the whole of that privileged land where Leonardo created his imperious women and Michelangelo his indomitable heroes?"

I started in January of that year, and in December of the same year, I would turn forty. Every day, from January to December, was spent teaching. I had seen Rome only once, and only briefly, and distracted by other preoccupations. I was economizing, as our Mother Italy sees fit that the lives of those who educate our children and little brothers be poor and miserable. I was among those.

You don't feed animals with the grass growing so lush and verdant among the graves: you burn that. I was cultivating my sadness for it to be of some use to my fellow humans, and I am still doing so: to tell them the words that matter more than every other, that besides the unescapable evils of life, which we cannot remedy, there are other, true evils that we can very easily abolish. How? By practicing contentment. We desire much, but we only need a little to be happy. When you are thirsty, you think that a whole amphora would not quench your thirst, but a cup is enough. And this is the added misfortune of human nature: the thirsty ones, since they believe a whole amphora is not enough for them, they keep it all to themselves, excluding the other thirsty people, only to drink but a cup of its contents. Even worse, they break the amphora so that no one else can drink apart from them. And far worse, after drinking, they spill the liquid so that thirst and hate grow in the others. And the worst of all, they kill each other, the thirsty ones, so that no one drinks. O stolid ones, drink a little water each and have the good amphora filled up again for those who will come!

This is the reason why I say that whatever little joy humans can have comes from having fewer things, and I am sincere, dear Adolfo. I had the chance of trying the perks of having only little, because a great deal was stolen from me, and I was not able to rescue very much of it. "The perks of having fewer things," I said.… But truly, how much less can you ask than having those who gave birth to you by your side, so long as nature allows it? Enough, let's change subject. So, I rescued a little bit of what was taken from me. And I am joyful for it, as I should be. Therefore, I am honest when I describe the joy of living in a clean house, albeit modest, of sitting at a table covered with a clean tablecloth, rough as it may be, of growing some flowers, of hearing the birds sing.… But those who are deep into the history of literature call this honest attitude "Arcadian.…"[1] I am (…) an Arcadian. Besides

1.   In one of my not-so-successful books, entitled *My Thoughts on Humanity* (Messina: Muglia, 1903), in "The Little Child," I discuss this disease, which is not the disease of literature, as written in the first edition of *Convivial Poems*, but of the history of said literature, as I corrected it in this second edition. "We divide poetry by century and school, we call it Arcadian, Romantic, classical, Veristic, Naturalistic, and so on.… We state that poetry progresses, decays, is created, dies, resurrects, and dies again. In truth, poetry is such a wondrous thing that if you write a true poem, it will be of the same quality of a poem written four thousand years ago. Why? Because mankind improves its way of speaking every year, every century and millennium, but began with the same whimpers everywhere in the world. The psychological essence is the same in the children of all kinds of people. A child is a child everywhere. Therefore, there is no Arcadian, Romantic, or classical poetry, nor Italian, Greek or Sanskrit poetry, but poetry, only poetry…and non-poetry. There is adulteration, sophistication, imitation of poetry, and this one has many names. There are people who imitate birds: they sound like birds, but they are not birds, they are bird watchers. I cannot tell you how useless the history of such idleness is.…

And further on [in my book]: "In Italy we think and discuss too much. That school was better, that one was worse. We need to go back to that one, renounce that one. No: all schools of poetry are bad, and we should not fixate on any of them. There is no poetry but poetry. The scholars then, when one writes a true poem on a flock of sheep, say that that poet is an Arcadian; and because another poet in a true poem exaggeratedly magnifies something, they call it 17th-century style; those scholars are silly and pedantic in equal manner.

being an idle fantasy, mine would be a soft, emasculated attitude, which, if not promptly curbed, would end up infecting the body of the nation. Wouldn't it have the same ruinous effects, I say, as the ones produced in Japan by the pure contemplation of birds and flowers? The love for one's little home, small garden, and simple tatami? Silly people! I don't believe much in the power of poetry, and even less in the power of mine: but if there is a power, it will be that of comforting, exalting, and helping people persevere and be serene. It will give people strength: because I put strength in my poetry, as I had nothing but strength in my soul made so bare by tragedy; a strength almost invisible and inaudible without any pomp or fanfare: nothing but strength.

To sum up, I was never locked away in a "solitary garden," although I was secluded, remote, and unknown, when you and Gabriele D'Annunzio invited me to join those "militant energies."

O Gabriele, my elder and younger brother! Already seven years earlier, Gabriele had written words of praise for some of my sonnets. As he entered my native land of Romagna, on a horse, with his regiment, he was intoning (to the Italian people) some of my verses:

SUNNY ROMAGNA, SWEET LAND!

The young man, full of grace and glory, was trying every moment of his bright and flourishing life to steal his elder and younger brother away from the desert, the silence and sadness in which he dwelled. For my part, I may have sometimes forgotten, in my restlessness, the kind gesture

---

Any subject can be contemplated by the deep eyes of the inner child; any small thing can appear enormous in those eyes. You only have to judge (since you have a passion for judging) if the eyes were indeed those of the inner child; and leave aside Arcadia and the 17th century.

Additionally: "Schools constrain us. They are like thin iron wires, stretching across the trees in Matilda's forest: as we make flowers, we are constantly at risk of falling because of them. As I said: if one delights in the beauty of the countryside, they call them Arcadian...."

But I will let them talk.

of the prodigy: but I went back to it many times, in love and admiration. I go back to it now, more grateful than ever, now that I collect and dedicate to you, Adolfo, king of the banquet, these poems of mine, which first appeared in *Il Convito* and that Gabriele liked. Will others like them? One can only hope. Or will they share the same destiny as another work of mine for *Il Convito, Minerva Oscura,* which then generated two more volumes, *Sotto il Velame* and *La Mirabile Visione,* and the *Prolusione al Paradiso,* and will perhaps generate more?

I would not mind much if these poems had the same fate as those volumes. Those volumes were derided, mocked, insulted, and slandered, but they will live on. I will die: they won't. This I believe and know. Dante, the genius of our people, will point his children to them.[2]

Before that day, which will come much sooner for me than for you or Gabriele, don't we want to complete *Il Convito* and create the last of its twelve volumes? We will recount there what we hoped and dreamed, what we sowed and harvested, what we leave and what we abandon. O Adolfo, you will not be (I am not speaking of Gabriele, as he's *blissful*) merrier or less sad than me! Do you know why? The reason is in this book. Read "The Old Men of Kea." Both left their life rather content: but one more and the other less. The latter had nothing in his house, as the fruit of his life, other than a few Isthmian or Nemean garlands of dry and green parsley (this one had dried up, too!). The other had these garlands and children and children of children. You are this one, Adolfo: Panthis, who received the gifts of the three Graces.

Pisa, 30 June 1904
Giovanni Pascoli

2.   Pascoli hoped that his books of Dantean criticism would be successful at least after his death – as they were poorly received by the academic community at the time of their publication. In this sentence, Pascoli imagines that the spirit of Dante will one day encourage Italians (his children) to read those books.

NON OMNES ARBUSTA IUVANT

Solon

SOLON

SOLON

Triste il convito senza canto, come
tempio senza votivo oro di doni;
ché questo è bello: attendere al cantore
che nella voce ha l'eco dell'Ignoto.
Oh! nulla, io dico, è bello più, che udire
un buon cantore, placidi, seduti
l'un presso l'altro, avanti mense piene
di pani biondi e di fumanti carni,
mentre il fanciullo dal cratere attinge
vino, e lo porta e versa nelle coppe;
e dire in tanto grazïosi detti,
mentre la cetra inalza il suo sacro inno;
o dell'auleta querulo, che piange,
godere, poi che ti si muta in cuore
il suo dolore in tua felicità.

— Solon, dicesti un giorno tu: Beato
chi ama, chi cavalli ha solidunghi,
cani da preda, un ospite lontano.
Ora te né lontano ospite giova
né, già vecchio, i bei cani né cavalli
di solid'unghia, né l'amore, o savio.
Te la coppa ora giova: ora tu lodi
più vecchio il vino e più novello il canto.
E novelle al Pireo, con la bonaccia
prima e co' primi stormi, due canzoni
oltremarine giunsero. Le reca
una donna d'Eresso — Apri: rispose;
alla rondine, o Phoco, apri la porta.-
Erano le Anthesterïe: s'apriva
il fumeo doglio e si saggiava il vino.

Entrò, col lume della primavera
e con l'alito salso dell'Egeo,
la cantatrice. Ella sapea due canti:
l'uno, d'amore, l'altro era di morte.

Solon

Sad is the songless banquet, like
temples without votive gold:
sweet it is to hear the singer whose
voice can sing the Unknown.
Nothing is better, I say, than
hearing a singer peacefully
sitting by a full table,
golden bread and meat,
while the boy holds the crater
and fills the cups with good wine;
stringing together fine verses
as the lyre sings holy hymns;
enjoying the plaintive song
of the flute, as inside your heart
sorrow turns into joy.

"Solon, you said that happy are
those who love, have fine horses,
hunting dogs, foreign guests.
No faraway guests anymore,
horses nor dogs, old man,
no lover to please you, wise one.
Now your joy is a wine that's aged
and a song that's new."
Two new songs came to Athens,
with the calm sea and the first birds:
songs by a woman from Lesbos.[1]
"Phocus, open the door —
let the swallow come in."
It was the Feast of Flowers;
time to taste the new wine.

She came with the light of springtime,
with the salty breath of the sea,
the singer who knew the two songs:
one love song and one about death.

1. Sappho.

Entrò pensosa; e Phoco le porgeva
uno sgabello d'auree borchie ornato
ed una coppa. Ella sedé, reggendo
la risonante pèctide; ne strinse
tacita intorno ai còllabi le corde;
tentò le corde fremebonde, e disse:

Splende al plenilunïo l'orto; il melo
trema appena d'un tremolio d'argento…
Nei lontani monti color di cielo
sibila il vento.

Mugghia il vento, strepita tra le forre,
su le quercie gettasi… Il mio non sembra
che un tremore, ma è l'amore, e corre,
spossa le membra!

M'è lontano dalle ricciute chiome,
quanto il sole; sì, ma mi giunge al cuore,
come il sole; bello, ma bello come
sole che muore.

Dileguare! e altro non voglio: voglio
farmi chiarità che da lui si effonda.
Scoglio estremo della gran luce, scoglio
su la grande onda,

dolce è da te scendere dove è pace:
scende il sole nell'infinito mare;
trema e scende la chiarità seguace
crepuscolare.

La Morte è questa! il vecchio esclamò. Questo,
ella rispose, è, ospite, l'Amore.
Tentò le corde fremebonde e disse:

Togli il pianto. È colpa! Sei del poeta
nella casa, tu. Chi dirà che fui?
Piangi il morto atleta: beltà d'atleta
muore con lui.

Solemnly she came and took
a golden stool carved all around,
settled on it with a cup of wine,
took up the lyre, and tightened
the strings on the levers, then she plucked
the trembling strings and sang:

"Gardens shine in silvery moonlight. Apple
trees resound a silvery ring the whole night.
Through the mountains blue as the sky is a soft
          whispering wind blows,

moaning on, then hollering through the canyons,
through the levelled oaks.… But the wind is softer
running through me. Nevertheless, it's love, strong,
          wringing my strength out.

He's as far from me, from my glistening hair,
as the sun, that's true, but he gets to my heart
like the sun: a beautiful man, yes, like a
          beautiful sunset.

Fade away — that's all that I want at this point,
turning into light that flows out from his sun.
Farthest rock in dazzling splendor, out there
          proud in the sea-wave,

sweet to climb right down where the calm is: as the
sun goes down in infinite ocean, a peace
follows on — that peace after sunset, that peace
          trailing the day's end."

"Death!" the old man cried.
"Love," she said, and plucked
her trembling strings and sang:

"Cry no more, at home with the poet — it's a sin!
Who will tell men who you once were? You cry for
athletes passing, ah, but an athlete's beauty
          dies with the athlete.

SOLON   II

Muore la virtù dell'eroe che il cocchio
spinge urlando tra le nemiche schiere;
muore il seno, sì, di Rhodòpi, l'occhio
del timoniere;

ma non muore il canto che tra il tintinno
della pèctide apre il candor dell'ale.
E il poeta fin che non muoia l'inno,
vive immortale,

poi che l'inno (diano le rosee dita
pace al peplo, a noi non s'addice il lutto)
è la nostra forza e beltà, la vita,
l'anima, tutto!

E chi voglia me rivedere, tocchi
queste corde, canti un mio canto: in quella,
tutta rose rimireranno gli occhi
Saffo la bella.

Questo era il canto della Morte; e il vecchio
Solon qui disse: Ch'io l'impari, e muoia.

Like the hero's courage in battle, driving
onward through the enemy's ranks — that dies too.
So the heaving breast of the maiden dies, the
                    plots of the helmsman.

But a song lives on through the lyre. It lives on,
spreading the truth, opening up its bright wings.
As the song lasts, so does the poet also
                    live on, immortal.

Don't, then, tear your clothes in a useless mourning.
That's not our style. Song is our strength, our beauty.
Song is all life, song is our soul, a song is
                    all that there is.

If you want to see me again, just touch these
strings and sing my songs, and at once, I'll be there,
eyes upon me as when I flowered on Lesbos,
                    beautiful Sappho."

This was the song of Death.
He said: "I will learn it and die."

Il cieco di Chio

THE BLIND MAN OF CHIOS

Il cieco di Chio

O Deliàs, o gracile rampollo
di palma, ai piedi sorto su del Cyntho,
alla corrente del canoro Inopo;
figlia di Palma; e di qual dono io mai
posso bearti il giovanetto cuore?
Ché all'invito de' giovani scotendo
gl'indifferenti riccioli del capo,
gioia t'hai fatto del vegliardo grigio
cui poter falla e desiderio avanza.
E lui su le tue lievi orme adducevi
all'opaca radura ed al giaciglio
delle stridule foglie, in mezzo ai pini
sonanti un fresco brulichìo di pioggia
presso la salsa musica del mare.
Né già la bianca tua beltà celasti
a gli occhi della sua memore mano:
non vista ad altri, che a lui cieco e, forse,
al solitario tacito alcïone.

O Deliàs, e già finì la gara
de' tunicati Iàoni: già tace
il vostro coro, grande meraviglia,
in cui nessuna di te meglio scosse
i procellosi crotali d'argento.
Ed il nocchiero su la nave nera
l'albero drizza, ed in su trae le pietre,
le gravi pietre su cui dondolando
dorme la nave nel loquace porto.
Ora un nocchiero addimandai: Nocchiero,
vago per l'onde come smergo ombroso,
dài ch'alla nave il pio cantore ascenda?
cieco uomo, e vive nella scabra Chio.

The Blind Man of Chios

Delias, delicate flower of palm,
born at the base of the Cynthus mountain
by the stream of the singing Inopus!
Dryad![1] Is there a gift I may give you
to fill with bliss your young maiden's heart?
With a scornful toss of your curly locks,
you refused the young men who wanted you.
Instead, you found joy in the arms of a man
whose potency fails, while desire still lasts.
You led me by way of your dainty footsteps
to a shrouded glade where you sleep on a bed
of stridulous leaves in the shade of pine trees,
which sway and swarm with the sound of cool rain
and join in the rhythm of the salty sea.
You didn't conceal your naked white beauty
from my hand, memorizing the map of your body,
known by me and me only, or perhaps
also by a silent halcyon in the heavens.

O Delias! The game is now over
for the tunic-clad Ionians,[2] and so is the song
of your choir of maidens, a marvelous thing,
and nobody shook the rainy tambourine
better than you, nor with more grace.
Proudly the helmsman on the stern of the ship
raises the mast and pulls up the anchor stones,
the heavy stones on which the ship sleeps,
swaying and rocking in the noisy harbor.
Then I asked him, "Helmsman," I said,
"you who wander the waves like a lonely bird,
will you accept a poet on board?
A blind one, from Chios, a savage isle.

1.   We have translated "figlia di Palma" ("daughter of a palm tree") as dryad,
which conveys the beauty of the young woman's slender body.
2.   The Ionians, a major tribes of ancient Greece, introduced the chiton, a
tunic that fastens at the shoulder, which was worn both by Greek and Roman
men and women.

Così te veda un ospite all'approdo.
Tanto io gli dissi. Egli assentì; ché grande
è del cantore, ben che nudo e cieco,
la grazia in uno ardor di venti, in una
ai cuori alati ritrosia di calma.

E di qual dono, o Deliàs, partendo,
né so per dove, su la nave nera,
posso bearti il giovanetto cuore?
Ché non possiedo, fuor della bisaccia
lacera, nulla, e dell'eburnea cetra.
E il canto, industre che pur sia, non m'offre
se non un colmo calice ed un tocco
di pingue verro e, terminato il canto,
una lunga nel cuore eco di gioia.
Io cieco vo lungo l'alterna voce
del grigio mare; sotto un pino io dormo,
dai pomi avari: se non se talora
m'annunziò, per luoghi soli, stalle
di mandrïani un subito latrato;
o, mentre erravo tra la neve e il vento,
la vampa da un aperto uscio imrovvisa
nella sua casa mi svelò la donna
che fila nel chiaror del focolare.

Pur non già nulla dar non può, sì molto,
il cieco aedo; e quale a me tu dono,
negato a tutti, della tua bellezza,
offristi, donna; né maggior potevi;
tale a te l'offro, né potrei maggiore.
Cieco non ero, e ciò pascea con gli occhi,
che rumino ora bove paziente;
e il fior coglievo delle cose, ch'ora
nella silenzïosa ombra mi odora.
Era per aspri gioghi il mio cammino,
degli uomini vetusti, antelunari.
Nacquero sopra le montagne nere,
che ancor la luna non correa su quelle:

And may you be welcome wherever you go."
So I spoke, and he gave his consent,
as the power of poets is great, even when
poor and blind: in the fury of winds,
in the deadly calm that winged hearts hate.

    Is there a gift I may give you, Delias,
sailing away now for I know not where,
to fill with bliss your young maiden's heart?
For I have nothing but a ragged old bag,
no possessions, except my white lyre,
and my song, good as it is, can barely
refill my cup with wine and my plate
with meat, and when the song is over,
the music fills my heart with joy.
Blind as I am, I follow the changing
voice of the sea. I often sleep
under barren pine trees, and every now and then
the howling of dogs announces my presence
in lonely places, in shepherds' stables.
Or as I walk in the wind and snow,
a door slams open and inside I see,
in the dimming light of the fireplace blazing,
a woman weaving and weaving alone.

    But it's not nothing he can give,
the sightless singer. The gift of your beauty
denied to all but myself was great.
There's no greater gift you could give.
So what I offer is the best I can.
There was a time my eyes could see
the things that I now chew over like an ox:
when I used to graze on the flowers of life
whose scent still wafts through the soundless darkness.
Once I wandered on the rugged paths
of a country older than the moon.
Its people were reared on those dark high mountains
before the moon could shine on them.

nacque dopo essi, e palpitò per loro
gemiti strani. Era un meriggio estivo:
io sentiva negli occhi arsi il barbaglio
della via bianca, e nell'orecchio un vasto
tintinnìo di cicale ebbre di sole.

Ed ecco io vidi alla mia destra un folto
bosco d'antiche roveri, che al giogo
parea del monte salir su, cantando
a quando a quando con un improvviso
lancio discorde delle mille braccia.
Entrai nel bosco abbrividendo, e molto
con muto labbro venerai le ninfe,
non forse audace violassi il musco
molle, lambito da' lor molli piedi.
E giunsi a un fonte che gemea solingo
sotto un gran leccio, dentro una sonora
conca di scabra pomice, che il pianto
già pianto urgea con grappoli di stille
nuove, caduchi, e ne traeva un canto
dolce, infinito. Io là m'assisi, al rezzo.
Poi, non so come, un dio mi vinse: presi
l'eburnea cetra e lungamente, a prova
col sacro fonte, pizzicai le corde.

Così scoppiò nel tremulo meriggio
il vario squillo d'un'aerea rissa:
e grande lo stupore era de' lecci,
ché grande e chiaro tra la cetra arguta
era l'agone, e la vocal fontana.
Ogni voce del fonte, ogni tintinno,
la cava cetra ripetea com'eco;
e due diceva in cuore suo le polle
forse il pastore che pascea non lungi.
Ma tardo, al fine, m'incantai sul giogo
d'oro, con gli occhi, e su le corde mosse
come da un breve anelito; e li chiusi,
vinto; e sentii come il frusciare in tanto

It came later and rose above them
with strange cries. Then a summer's high noon:
my eyes ablaze with the dazzling glare
of a white road, my ears filled
with the constant rattle of sun-drunk cicadas.

On my right, I saw a dense dark forest
of ancient oaks, which seemed to climb
the slope, and they almost sang, if you listened,
raising and swaying their thousand arms.
With a silent shiver, I entered the forest.
With a silent prayer, I worshipped the nymphs,
daring to touch the lush green grass
on which the goddesses had placed their feet.
I reached a spring that wept so sadly
under a holly oak into a hollow
made of weathered ancient stone. It wept,
it wept and wept, distilling teardrops,
which bloomed and fell, writing a song,
endless and sweet. I sat in the shade.
A god possessed me, I don't know how:
I took my lyre, I plucked the strings,
I played a contest with the singing spring.

And so in the haze of a hot afternoon,
heavenly music erupted in the air,
and the holly oaks looked on, struck dumb
at the contest sounding high and clear
between my lyre and the singing fountain.
The water twinkled and the fountain sang.
The hollow lyre then echoed back.
If a shepherd had happened to pass nearby,
he'd have thought there were two springs instead of one.
Long I lingered there and stared,
transfixed: the hill was aglow, the strings
pulsed — so it seemed — with living breath.
I closed my eyes and heard the whisper

di mille cetre, che piovea nell'ombra;
e sentii come lontanar tra quello
la meraviglia di dedalee storie,
simili a bianche e lunghe vie, fuggenti
all'ombra d'olmi e di tremuli pioppi.

Allora io vidi, o Deliàs, con gli occhi,
l'ultima volta. O Deliàs, la dea
vidi, e la cetra della dea: con fila
sottili e lunghe come strie di pioggia
tessuta in cielo; iridescenti al sole.
E mi parlò, grave, e mi disse: Infante!
qual dio nemico a gareggiar ti spinse,
uomo con dea? Chi con gli dei contese,
non s'ode ai piedi il balbettìo dei bimbi,
reduce. Or va, però che mite ho il cuore:
voglio che il male ti germogli un bene.
Sarai felice di sentir tu solo,
tremando in cuore, nella sacra notte,
parole degne de' silenzi opachi.
Sarai felice di veder tu solo,
non ciò che il volgo víola con gli occhi,
ma delle cose l'ombra lunga, immensa,
nel tuo segreto pallido tramonto.

Disse, e disparve; e, per tentar che feci
le irrequïete palpebre, più nulla
io vidi delle cose altro che l'ombra,
pago, finché non m'apparisti al raggio
della tua voce limpida, o fanciulla
di Delo, o palma del canoro Inopo,
sola tu del mio sogno anche più bella,
maggior dell'ombra che ti serpeggia
nel mio segreto pallido tramonto.
Ora a te sola ridirò le storie
meravigliose, che sentii quel giorno
come vie bianche lontanar tra i pioppi.
E quale il tuo, che non maggior potevi,

of a thousand strings like a sudden rainfall
in a shadowy glade, and somewhere behind that,
a thousand labyrinthine stories
spreading out like long white roads
shaded by rows of elms and poplars.

That was the last thing I saw with my eyes,
Delias: I saw the goddess before me,
the goddess, Delias, her lyre with strings
as long and thin as bars of rain.
With a fearsome face she spoke to me:
"Which evil spirit possessed you, my child,
to challenge a god? Those who do,
don't often live to hear the sound
of babies babbling at their feet.
But carry on, I have a soft heart.
I want this sin to seed something good.
In your solitude, you will be able to hear
with a quaking heart in the sacred night
words that spring from the darkest silence.
In your loneliness, you will be able to see
not what vulgar eyes desecrate
but the tall, unending shadow of things
in your pallid private sundown."

So she spoke and vanished, and however
I strained my restless eyes, the only
thing that I could see was unending
shadow. Content, though, until you came
under the halo of your silvery voice,
maiden from Delos, slender palm
from the singing Inopus,
the only one fairer than my dreams,
greater than the the shadow you cast
in my pallid private sundown.
Now I will tell you, and you only,
the enchanting stories that I heard that day
like white roads disappearing among the poplars.
Your gift was the greatest you could give,

tale il mio dono, né potrei maggiore;
ché il bene in te qui lascerò, come ape
che punge, e il male resterà più grave,
grave sol ora, al tuo cantor, cui diede
la Musa un bene e, Deliàs, un male!

so what I offer is the best I can:
I'll leave what's good right here in you,
like a bee and its sting, but the hurt will remain
with me, worse, and worse now
for your bard, to whom the goddess gave
a blessing, Delias, and a curse.

La cetra d'Achille

THE LYRE OF ACHILLES

I

I re, le genti degli Achei vestiti
di bronzo, tutti, sì, dormian domati
dal molle sonno, e i loro cavalli sciolti
dal giogo, avvinti con le briglie ai carri,
pascean, soffiando, il bianco orzo e la spelta.
Dormivano i custodi anche de' fuochi,
abbandonato il capo sugli scudi
lustri, rotondi, presso i fuochi accesi,
al cui guizzare balenava il rame
dell'armi, come nuvolaglia a notte,
prima d'un nembo. Domator di tutto
teneva il sonno i Panachei chiomanti,
mirabilmente, nella notte ch'era
l'ultima notte del Pelide Achille;
e in cuore ognuno lo sapea, nel cielo
e nella terra, e tutti ora sbuffando
dalle narici il rauco sonno, in sogno
lo vedean fare un grande arco cadendo,
e sollevare un vortice di fumo;
ma in sogno senz'altro fragor cadeva,
simile ad ombra; e senza suono, a un tratto,
i cavalli e gli eroi misero un ringhio
acuto, i carri scosser via gli aurighi,
mentre laggiù, sotto Ilio, alta e feroce
la bronzea voce si frangea, d'Achille.

II

Dormian, sì, tutti; e tra il lor muto sonno
giungeva un vasto singhiozzar dal mare.
Piangean le figlie del verace Mare,

THE LYRE OF ACHILLES

I

Sleep had tamed the kings
and all the bronze-clad Greeks.[1]
Their mighty horses, unyoked,
tied by their reins to the chariots,
ate white barley and spelt.
The guards were asleep as well,
their heads on their shiny round shields
by the flames of the fires that blazed
and flashed in the copper spears
like storm clouds before the storm.
Sleep had conquered them all,
binding the long-haired Greeks
with a spell, that night, which would be
Achilles' last night on earth.
And the sky and the earth both knew it:
each of them in their deep
raucous slumber had seen him
tumble and fall in slow motion
in a whirlwind of smoky dust,
the soundless surreal fall
of shadows in dreams. And horses
whinnied and hounds snarled:
the charioteers all stood up,
while in the distance, under
the walls of glorious Troy,
high and wild, the bronze
voice of Achilles rang out.

II

The whole of the army was sleeping,
and behind their silent sleep,
the sea's enormous sobbing.
The waves in the sea were weeping

1.   The poem is set during the last year of the Trojan War, right after Hector's
death at the hands of Achilles.

nel nero Ponto, l'ancor vivo Achille,
lontane, ch'egli non ne udisse il pianto.
Ed altre, sì, con improvviso scroscio
ululando montavano alla spiaggia,
per dirgli il fato o trarlo a sé; ma in vano:
fuggian con grida e gemiti e singhiozzi
lasciando le lor bianche orme di schiuma.
Ma non le udiva, benché desto, Achille,
desto sol esso; ch'egli empiva intanto
a sé l'orecchio con la cetra arguta,
dedalea cetra, scelta dalle prede
di Thebe sacra ch'egli avea distrutta.
Or, pieno il cuore di quei chiari squilli,
non udiva su lui piangere il mare,
e non udiva il suo vocale Xantho
parlar com'uomo all'inclito fratello,
Folgore, che gli rispondea nitrendo.
L'eroe cantava i morti eroi, cantava
sé, su la cetra già da lui predata.
Avea la spoglia, su le membra ignude,
d'un lion rosso già da lui raggiunto,
irsuta, lunga sino ai pie' veloci.

for Achilles, unheard by him
still alive and still far away,
daughters of the Black Sea;[2]
others with a sudden crash
climbed crying onto the shore
to tell him his fate or else
to gather him to them,
in vain. They fled with cries
and groans and sobs, leaving
behind white prints of foam.
But he, Achilles, didn't
hear them though he was awake:
his ears were filled with the sound
of a silvery lyre he took
from the spoils of holy Thebes
when he had sacked the city.[3]
His heart was so full with its clear
notes that he didn't hear
the sea crying for him,
nor Xanthos, his golden horse
whisper to Lightning, his twin,[4]
who whinnied back in answer.
He sang of dead heroes
and of himself on the lyre
which he had once seized.
And over his naked limbs
there hung the pelt of a lion
which he had once hunted,
tawny, and bristling, and reaching
down to his swift feet.

2.   The Nereids.
3.   At the time of the Trojan War, Hypoplacian Thebes was populated by
Cilicians and ruled by King Eetion. Eetion's daughter, Andromache, was given in
marriage to Hector, son of King Priam of Troy. The Greeks, led by Achilles, sacked
the city during the latter part of the war, killing Eetion, his wife, and their sons.
4.   Xanthos and Balios were Achilles' two horses. Xanthos refers to the golden
colour of the horse's mane, Balios means "flash" or "lightning" and alludes to
the horse's speed.

III

Così le glorie degli eroi consunti
dal rogo, e sé con lor cantava Achille,
desto sol esso degli Achei chiomanti:
ecco, avanti gli stette uno, canuto,
simile in vista a vecchio dio ramingo.
E gli fu presso e gli baciò le mani
terribili. Sbalzò attonito Achille
su, dal suo seggio, e il morto lion rosso
gli raspò con le curve unghie i garretti.
E gli volgeva le parole alate:
"Vecchio, chi sei? donde venuto? Sembri,
sì, nell'aspetto Priamo re, ma regio
non è il mantello che ti para il vento.
Chi ti fu guida nella notte oscura?
Parla, e per filo il tutto narra, o vecchio.
E gli parlava rispondendo il vecchio:
No, non ti sono io re, splendido Achille;
un dio felice non mi fu l'auriga:
io da me venni. Tutti, anche i custodi
dormono presso il crepitar dei fuochi.
Tu solo vegli; e non udii, venendo,
ch'esili stridi dagli eroi sopiti,
e che un sommesso brulichio dai morti.
E nella sacra notte a me fu guida
un suono, il suono d'una cetra, o Achille.

IV

Lo guardò scuro e gli rispose Achille:
Tu non m'hai detto il caro nome, e donde
vieni e perché? Non forse tu notturno
vieni, alle navi degli Achei ricurve,

III

He sang the glory of heroes
dead and gone and his own,
the only Achaean still awake.
Suddenly an old man appeared
before him, gray-haired,
like some ancient vagrant god.
And he came up next to him
and kissed his fearsome hands.
Achilles, astonished, stood up
with the rough red lion-pelt
rubbing rough on his calves,
and the words he spoke had wings:
"Who are you, and from where,
resembling the king of Troy
in all but your ragged cloak?
Tell me, old man, who led you
here through the darkened night?"
The old man replied to him:
"I'm not a king, Achilles.
No god has guided me here.
I came on my own to your camp
where all the guards are sleeping
by the crackling of the fires,
and you alone are awake.
I didn't hear a sound
other than the lonely snores
of warriors as they slept
and the muffled whisper of the dead.
And the only guide I had
through this sacred night
was the sound of a lyre, Achilles."

IV

Achilles's face went dark.
"You haven't told me your name,
nor where you've come from, or why.
Have you come by night
among the Greeks' curved ships

per dono grande, ad esplorare, o vecchio?
E gli parlava rispondendo il vecchio:
Io sono aedo, o pieveloce Achille,
caro ai guerrieri, non guerriero io stesso.
Io nacqui sotto la selvosa Placo,
in Thebe sacra, già da te distrutta.
Da te non vengo a liberarmi un figlio
cui lecchi il sangue un vigile tuo cane;
il figlio, no; recando qui sul forte
plaustro mulare tripodi e lebeti
e pepli e manti e molto oro nell'arca.
Non a me copia, non a te n'è d'uopo;
ché tu sei già del tuo destino, e tutti
lo sanno, il cielo, l'infinito mare,
la nera terra, e lo sai tu ch'hai dato
ai cari amici le tue prede e i doni
splendidi; ansati tripodi, cavalli,
muli, lustranti buoi, donne ben cinte,
e grigio ferro, e reso Ettore al padre
e la tua vita al suo dovere… Oh! rendi
dunque all'aedo la sua cetra, Achille!

V

Disse, e sporgea la mano alla sua cetra
bella, dedalea, ma l'argenteo giogo
era dai peli del lion coperto.

looking to find some major
bounty, perhaps, old man?"
The old man replied to him:
"I'm a bard, quick-footed Achilles,
cherished by the heroes,
but not one of them myself.
Born beneath Mount Placos
in holy Thebes, which you sacked.
I haven't come to ransom
the corpse of a son whose blood
your wakeful dog is lapping,
driving my strong chariot
here, lugging tripods and cauldrons,
robes and cloaks and gold.
I don't have the wealth,
and you don't have the need.
You know your fate already,
everyone knows it:
the sky, the endless sea,
the black earth; and you
know yourself that you've
given to your dear friends
spoils you've won in battle,
precious gifts — bronze
tripods, horses and mules,
glistening oxen, women
wrapped up like presents, gray
iron. And you know you've given
Hector back to his father,[5]
and your life to duty.… So why not
give your lyre to me?"

V

He spoke and reached for the lyre,
but the silvery lyre was covered
by the lion's heavy pelt.

5.   Achilles had agreed to return Hector's corpse to Priam, father of the Trojan
warrior and king of Troy.

E il cuor d'Achille mareggiava, come
il mare in dubbio di spezzar la nave,
piccola, curva. E poi parlava, e disse:
Te'; riporgendo al pio cantor la cetra;
non sì che, urtando nel pulito seggio,
non mettesse, tremando, ella uno squillo.
Poi tacque, in mano dell'aedo, anch'ella.
Allora, stando, il pari a un dio Pelide
udì ringhiare i suoi grandi cavalli,
intese Xantho favellar com'uomo,
e parlar della sua morte al fratello,
Folgor, che gli rispondea nitrendo.
Allora udí su lui piangere il mare,
piangere le figlie del verace Mare,
lui, così bello, così nel fiore;
e molte con un improvviso scroscio
venir per trarlo via con sé; ma in vano.
E vide nella sacra notte il fato
suo, che aspettava alle Sinistre Porte,
come l'auriga asceso già sul carro,
la sferza in pugno, che all'eroe si volge,
sopragiungente nel fulgor dell'armi.

VI

E il vecchio disse le parole alate:
Lascia ch'io vada senza indugio, e porti

And Achilles' heart swelled up
like the sea swells when it has
in mind whether to break
some tiny, curved ship.
And then he spoke: "Here,"
he said, handing the lyre
over to the reverent bard.
It fell on the polished seat,
emitting a silvery ring.
Then, in the hands of the bard,
the lyre went quiet.
It was then that Achilles heard
his two great horses neigh,
Xantho telling stories
just like a man,
talking about his death
to Lightning, his brother,
who answered with a whinny.
He heard the sea crying for him,
the sea's real daughters,
for him, so great, in his prime;
heard many with a sudden
crash reach out to drag him
away with them, in vain.
And in the sacred night,
he saw his destiny
beside the Sinister Gates,[6]
waiting like a charioteer,
holding his whip in his hand,
who then turns to the hero as he jumps
on board in the blaze of his armor.

VI

The poet's words had wings:
"Let me go without
delay, and let me take

---

6. The Skaian Gate, Troy's south gate, also called the Dardanian Gate.

meco la cetra, che non forse il cuore
nero t'inviti a piangere, su questa
cetra di glorie, l'ancor vivo Achille.
Lascia che pianga e mare e terra e cielo;
tu no. Non devi inebbriar di canto
tu, divo Achille, l'animo sereno
che sa, non devi a te celare il fato
non che ti volle ma che tu volesti.
Restaci grande, o Peleiade Achille!
Noi, canteremo. Noi ti te diremo
che, sì, piangevi, ma lontano e solo,
e che dicevi il tuo dolore all'onde
del mare ed alle nuvole del cielo.
E noi diremo che una dea non vista
a frenar la tua fosca ira veniva,
e ti prendea per la criniera rossa,
rossa criniera che così sconvolta
poi ti lisciava un'altra dea non vista,
nel tuo dolore; e che obbedivi a voci
dell'infinito o cielo o mare: avanti,
spingendo con un grande urlo d'auriga
verso la morte l'immortal tuo Xantho.
    Disse e disparve nell'ambrosia notte.

VII

    E stette Achille ad ascoltare i ringhi
de' suoi cavalli, e più lontano il pianto

the lyre with me in case
your melancholy heart
brings you to mourn over
this lyre for songs of glory,
Achilles, before your death.
The sea and earth and sky
shall weep, but you must not.
Don't drown in song, godlike
Achilles, your high mind,
which knows — you mustn't hide it
from yourself — that fate didn't choose you:
you chose it. Be still
that great man, Peleus' son.
We, for our part, we will
sing. We'll say of you
that yes, you cried, but far
away and on your own;
that you told your pain to the waves
of the sea and the clouds of the sky.
And we'll say that a goddess nobody
saw came to curb
your dreadful anger and that
she held you by your red mane,
which another goddess nobody
saw combed for you,
frazzled as it was, in your pain.
We'll say you listened to voices
from the infinite sea and sky,
as you drove onward, with the great
shout of a charioteer,
towards death your deathless steed."
He said these words, then vanished
into the sacred night.

VII

Achilles stood to hear
the neighs of his horses,
and further off,

delle Nereidi, e dentro i lor singhiozzi
sentì più trista, sì ma più sommessa,
la voce della sua cerulea madre.
Anche sentì tra il sonno alto del campo
passar con chiaro tintinnìo la cetra,
di cui tentava il pio cantor le corde;
mentre i cavalli sospendean, fremendo,
di dirompere il bianco orzo e la spelta.
Passava il canto tra la morte e il sogno:
qualche avvoltoio, sorto su dai morti,
gli eroi viventi ventilava in fronte.
Lontanò ella sotto il cielo azzurro,
e poi vanì. Né più la intese Achille.
Né gli restava, oltre i cavalli e il carro
da guerra e le stellanti armi, più nulla,
se non montare sopra i due cavalli,
fulgido, in armi, come Sole, andando
al suo tramonto. Quando udì vicino
un singulto: Briseide su la soglia
stava, e piangeva, la sua dolce schiava.
Ed egli allora si corcò tenendo
lei tra le braccia, con su lor la pelle
del lion rosso; ed aspettò l'aurora.

the weeping of the Nereids,
and among their sobs
sadder, yes, but quieter,
the voice of his sea-green mother.
He also heard, in the deep
sleep of the camp, the lyre
passing, sounding clear.
The bard was trying its strings
while the horses lifted their snouts
from their barley and their spelt.
The music passed between death
and dream; here and there a vulture
rose up from the corpses, fanning
the living heroes.
The music grew more distant
under the blue sky
and then it disappeared.
Achilles heard it no more.
Nothing more was left him
but his horses, his battle-chariot,
and his glittering arms.
Nothing more was left
but to climb onboard behind
his two horses, gleaming,
in his armor, like the sun,
heading towards the sunset.
Then he heard a sob:
Briseis was standing at
the threshold, weeping, his sweet
slave. And Achilles went
to sleep with her, holding
her in his arms, the red
lion-pelt over them,
waiting for the dawn.

Le Memnonidi

THE BIRDS OF MEMNON

Le Memnonidi

Ecco apparì l'Aurora che la terra
nera toccava con le rosee dita.

I

Disse: — Uccidesti il figlio dell'Aurora:
non rivedrai né la sua madre ancora!

E sì, t'amavo come un suo fratello.
Tu fulvo, ei nero; nero sì, ma bello:

tu come rogo che divampa al vento,
ei come rogo che la pioggia ha spento:

Memnone amato! E tu dovevi amare
lui nato in cielo figlio tu del mare!

L'azzurro mare ama la terra nera;
il giorno ardente ama l'opaca sera;

l'opera, il sonno; ama il dolor la morte…
Va dunque, Achille, alle Sinistre Porte!

II

Io sì t'amava, e ti ricordo, molle
della mia guazza la criniera fulva,
nella lontana Ftia ricca di zolle:

nei boschi, invasi dall'odor di lauro,
del Pelio: lungo lo Sperchèo, tra l'ulva
pesta dall'ugne del tuo gran Centauro.

Io ti mostrava là su l'alte nevi
i foschi lupi che notturni a zonzo
fiutaron l'antro dove tu giacevi:

The Birds of Memnon

And there was Aurora, touching the earth,
the black earth, with her rosy fingers.

I

She said to him, "You killed my son.
You won't see his mother ever again!

And yes, I loved you, as if you both were mine:
your features fair, his dark but fine;

you like a fire that the wind has kindled,
and he, a fire that in the rain has dwindled.

Beloved Memnon! Oh sea-born one,[1]
you should have loved my sky-born son!

As blue seas love black shores,
bright day the darkling night adores,

labor sleep, so death is sorrow's mate.
Go then, Achilles, to the Sinister Gate![2]

II

And I did love you, and I remember you,
your tawny mane wet with my dew
in far-off, fertile Phthia,

in Pelion's laurel-scented wood,
the grass on which your centaur trod,[3]
along the Spercheios River.

I showed you from a snowy height
the dark wolves roaming at night,
sniffing the cave where you lay.

1.   Achilles was the son of the sea goddess Tethys.
2.   See page 37, note 6.
3.   Achilles was reared by the centaur Chiron.

e tu gettavi contro loro incauto
la voce ch'ora squilla come bronzo,
allor sonava come lidio flauto.

Io ti vedeva predatore impube
correre a piedi, immerso nella tua
anima azzurra come in una nube;

io rosseggiando, e con la bianca falce
la luna smorta, vedevam laggiù
correre un uomo dietro una grande alce.

III

E meco c'era Memnone, che un urlo
dal ciel mandava ai piedi tuoi veloci.
Tu li credevi di laggiù le voci
forse della palustre oca o del chiurlo.

Perché t'amava anch'esso, il tuo fratello
crepuscolare, che poi te protervo
seduto sopra il boccheggiante cervo,
circondava de' suoi strilli d'uccello.

Or egli è pietra, e ben che nera pietra,
il figlio dell'Aurora ha le sue pene,
ché quando io sorgo, e piango, ei dalle vene
rivibra un pianto come suon di cetra…

forse sospesa a un ramo, quale io credo
d'udire ancora, qui tra i pini e i cedri,
che al primo sbuffo de' miei due polledri
vibrò chiamando il suo perduto aedo.

IV

E quando io sorgo, le Memnonie gralle
fanno lor giochi, quali intorno un rogo,
non come aurighi con Ferèe cavalle
sbalzano in alto sotto il lieve giogo,
con la lucida sferza su le spalle;

How fearlessly did you then shout!
A voice that piped like a Lydian flute
but which clangs like bronze today.

I saw you, boy hunter, running there
wrapped in a soul as blue as the air
as if you were wrapped in a cloud.

And I turned red, and the moon was wan,
a white sickle, and we watched a man
hunting a gigantic elk.

III

And Memnon was with me on that peak,
crying out for your swift feet.
Down where you were it sounded to you
like the call of a goose or maybe a curlew.

Because Memnon, Achilles, loved you too,
your dusky brother, and that hot afternoon
he garlanded you with his cries of a bird
as you stood in your pride over a wheezing hart.

Now he is stone, the darkest stone,
but he still suffers even so.
And when I arise and weep, he resounds
with mourning like a harp that sounds…

a harp, perhaps, that's hanging from a tree
like the one that I think I still hear
up here in the pines, which at my horses' snort
rings out a call for the absent bard.

IV

When I arise, the stilts are there
as if around a pyre's blazes:
not like Pheraean charioteers,
their steeds straining against their traces
and the shining lash they have to bear,

THE BIRDS OF MEMNON   47

e né come unti lottatori ignudi
che si serrano a modo di due travi,
e né come aspri pugili coi crudi
cesti allacciati intorno ai pugni gravi;
ma come eroi, con l'aste e con gli scudi.

Quasi al fuoco d'un rogo, al mio barlume
ecco ogni eroe contro un eroe si slancia:
lottano in mezzo alle rosate schiume
del lago, e il molle becco è la lor lancia,
e non ferisce sul brocchier di piume.

Guarda le innocue gralle irrequiete,
là, con lo scudo ombelicato e il casco!
negli acquitrini dove voi mietete
lanuginose canne di falasco,
per tetto della casa alta, d'abete.

V

Ei piange, e vede la mia mano ch'apre
rosea, di monte in monte, usci e cancelli;
apre, toccando lieve i chiavistelli,
alle belanti pecore, alle capre;

anche al fanciullo che la verga toglie,
curva, e si lima i cari occhi col dosso
dell'altra mano: anche al villano scosso
di mezzo ai sogni dall'industre moglie;

anche all'auriga che i cavalli aggioga
al carro asperso ancor del sangue d'ieri,
mentre l'eroe, già stretti gli stinieri,
prende lo scudo per l'argentea soga:

scudo rotondo, di lucente elettro,
grande, con le città, con le capanne,
e greggi e mandre, e corbe d'uva e manne
di spighe, e un re pei solchi, con lo scettro.

nor like naked, oiled-up wrestlers
fitted together like two planks of wood,
nor like boxers, aggressive, their heavy fists
bound with some wrapping, rough and crude,
but like heroes with their shields and spears.

As if around a pyre's crown,
these heroes meet as my light leaks
like rosy ripples over the lake,
their lances are their pliant beaks
that cannot pierce their shields of down.

Watch the harmless restive birds
jousting with their feathered arms
down in the marshes, where men harvest
pliant reeds to build their farms
with roofs of twigs on beams of fir.

V

And as my rosy hand unlocks
the doors and gates, my son weeps;
my hand that gently frees the flocks,
through hill and dale, of goats and sheep,

and wakes the boy, who picks up his stick
and with his fingers rubs his eyes,
and wakes the shepherd from the thick
of tranquil dreams in which he lies,

and the charioteer, who yokes
his horses still wet with yesterday's blood,
while the booted, helmeted hero takes
up his shield by the silver rod:

a large, round shield of bright copper,
carved with cities, cattle, flocks,
grapes and wheat piled in stacks,
and among the furrows, a king with a sceptre.

VI

Ma te non più porterò via, divino
eroe, sul carro, col rotondo scudo
ch'ha suon di tibie, e dolce canta, ai lino:

dall'altra parte tornerò del cielo,
a sera, e te con altri ignudi ignudo
io parerò tenendo un aureo stelo;

un aureo stelo con in cima un astro;
e parerò le vostre esili vite,
come un pastore, con quel mio vincastro:

un gregge d'ombre, senza i folti velli
color viola. E per le vie muffite
v'udrò stridire come vipistrelli.

La bianca Rupe tu vedrai, dov'ogni
luce tramonta, tu vedrai le Porte
del Sole e il muto popolo dei Sogni.

E giunto alfine sosterai nel Prato
sparso dei gialli fiori della morte,
immortalmente, Achille, affaticato.

VII

Dove dirai: Fossi lassù garzone,
in terra altrui, di povero padrone;

VI

But I won't carry you away anymore
in my chariot, hero, with your shield so round,
which rings like a flute and sings a hymn.[4]

From the other side, when the day is done,
I'll appear to you and the other fallen
holding up a golden stem,

a golden stem with a star at the top.
And I will guide your feeble souls
the way a shepherd guides a flock,

a flock of shades, shorn of their coats
of violet. Down the mouldy ways,
I'll hear you squeaking away like bats.

You will see the White Rock,[5]
where every light goes down, the Gates
of the Sun,[6] the dream-world's voiceless folk.

And once arrived, you'll linger,
weary now until forever,
on fields strewn with the flowers of death.

VII

And you'll wish you were a lad,
a poor servant, poorly clad,

4.   A reference to Achilles' shield in *Iliad* 18.570. Among other images on the
shield, there is the figure of a boy playing a lyre and intoning a holy song, *ai
linon,* in ancient Greek.
5.   From *Odyssey* 24.11: the cliff on the island of Lefkada was seen as the
farthest limit of the horizon, on which the sun would set. In the *Odyssey,* this
place is called "the rock of light." Pascoli translates it as "the white rock" after
the name of the island (Lefkada means "white"). This is also the rock where,
according to the legend, Sappho committed suicide by throwing herself into
the sea. This episode is also mentioned in the poem "Solon."
6.   The Gates of the Sun and the fields, mentioned in the next stanza, are all
mythical places at the entrance of Hades, the underworld, as indicated in *Odyssey*
24.12–13.

ma pur godessi, al sole ed alla luna,
la dolce vita che ad ognuno è una;

e i miei cavalli fossero giovenchi,
che lustro il pelo, i passi hanno sbilenchi;

e ritrovassi, nell'uscir dal tetto,
per asta dalla lunga ombra, il pungetto;

e rimirassi, nell'uscir dal clatro,
per carro dal sonante asse, l'aratro:

l'aratro pio che cigola e lavora
nella penombra della nuova aurora! —

Diceva, e già nel cielo era appassita:
venne il Sole, e s'alzò l'urlo di guerra.

and you could still see the sun,
have your life (we get just one!),

and your horses were but cattle,
fed and fat, not good for battle,

and a goad outside your door,
not a high, long-shadowed spear,

and outside your gate a plough,
not a chariot with a bow:

a plough that always creaks and moans
every day when the sun dawns!"

So she spoke and left the sky.
The Sun brought forth the war-like cry.

Antìclo

ANTICLOS

I

E con un urlo rispondeva Antìclo,
dentro il cavallo, a quell'aerea voce;
se a lui la bocca non empìa col pugno
Odisseo, pronto, gli altri eroi salvando;
e ognun chiamando tuttavia per nome
la voce alata dileguò lontano;
fin ch'all'orecchio degli eroi non giunse
che il loro corto anelito nel buio;
come già prima, quando già lì fuori
impallidiva il vasto urlìo del giorno,
l'urlìo venato da virginei cori,
che udian dietro una nera ombra di sonno;
nel lungo giorno; e poi languì, ché forse
era già sera, e forse già sul mare
tremolava la stella Espero, e forse
la luna piena già sorgea dai monti;
ed allora una voce ecco al cavallo
girare attorno, che sonava al cuore
come la voce dolce più che niuna,
come ad ognuno suona al cuor sol una.

II

Era la donna amata, era la donna
lontana, accorsa, in quella ora di morte,
da molta ombra di monti, onda di mari:
sbalzò ciascuno quasi a porre il piede
su l'inverdita soglia della casa.
Ma tutti un cenno di Odisseo contenne:

ANTICLOS[1]

I

Inside the wooden horse, Anticlos cried out
in response to that heavenly voice he heard —
or he would have cried out, if Odysseus hadn't
covered his mouth, saving the heroes,
till, still calling out those heroes' names,
that winged voice faded into the distance,
and finally, all that could be heard
was the short breathing of the heroes,
just like before, when they were entranced
by the enormous hubbub of the waning day,
by the crystalline singing of choruses of girls,
which they listened to behind a cloud of sleep.
Then it disappeared, because maybe it was night,
and the Evening Star was already shivering
over the sea. Maybe it was night
with a full moon rising out of the hills.
Then there it was, a voice that circled
the wooden horse and that sounded like
the voice that each man most wanted to hear —
every heart has a voice it longs for most.

II

It was the woman that each of them loved,
the far-off, unreachable woman they loved,
suddenly appearing from across the sea waves
and the dark mountains in that fateful hour,
and each man jumped like he was placing a foot
on the mossy doorstep of his home.
A look from Odysseus reined them all in,

1.   Pascoli draws inspiration from a few lines of the *Odyssey* (4.274–89) where a warrior named Anticlos is mentioned. The Greeks are inside the wooden horse, waiting to be taken into Troy. The Trojans send Helen to the horse, so she can advise them about the strange object. Once there, she calls each of the warriors imitating their wives' voices , thus trying to lure them from the horse. The Greeks are not fooled, except for Anticlos, who desperately wants to answer that female voice, believing it is his wife's voice.

Antìclo, no. Poi ch'era forte Antìclo,
sì, ma per forza; e non avea la gloria
loquace a cuore, ma la casa e l'orto
d'alberi lunghi e il solatìo vigneto
e la sua donna. E come udì la voce
della sua donna, egli sbalzò d'un tratto
su molta onda di mari, ombra di monti;
udì lei nelle stanze alte il telaio
spinger da sé, scendere l'ardue scale;
e schiuso il luminoso uscio chiamare
lui che la bocca aprì, tutta, e vi strinse
il grave pugno di Odisseo Cent'arte;
e sentì nella conca dell'orecchio
sibilar come raffica marina:
Helena! Helena! è la Morte, infante!

III

Ma quella voce gli restò nel cuore;
e quando uscì con gli altri eroi — la luna
piena pendeva in mezzo della notte —
gli nereggiava di grande ira il cuore;
e per tutto egli uccise, arse, distrusse.
Gittò nel fuoco i tripodi di bronzo,
spinse nel seno alle fanciulle il ferro;
ché non prede voleva; egli voleva
udir, tra grida e gemiti e singulti,
la voce della sua donna lontana.
Ma era nella sacra Ilio il nemico
di gloria Antìclo, non in Arne ancora,
fertile d'uva, o in Aliarto erboso:
e in un vortice rosso Ilio vaniva
a' piè del plenilunïo sereno.
Morti i guerrieri, giù nelle macerie
fumide i Danai ne battean gl'infanti,
alle lor navi ne rapian le donne:
e d'Ilio in fiamme al cilestrino mare,
dalle Porte al Sigeo bianco di luna,
passavano con lunghi ululi i carri.

all but Anticlos. Anticlos was a force —
but only because he was forced to be.
No tales of glory babbled in his heart,
just slender cypresses, a sunny vineyard,
and his woman, whose voice he now heard, and he
was there, across the dark mountains, across
the sea waves, and she was pushing the loom away
and coming down the stairs, the door
was opening, and he opened his lips —
and the heavy hand of Odysseus shut them,
the man with a hundred tricks and ways.
Then he heard in the seashell of his ear
a harsh whisper, like a cold sea breeze:
"It's Helen, Helen — death, you fool!"

III

But the voice stayed with him, and when, with the others,
he left the horse — the full moon hanging
in the middle of the night — the heart within him
was blackening with rage. Everywhere he went
he killed, burnt down, destroyed. He tipped
the sacred tripods into the fire,
drove his sword through maidens' breasts.
He didn't want captives. All he wanted
was to hear, through screams and cries and groans,
the voice of the woman he loved, his own.
But now he, enemy of glory,
was in holy Troy and not in Arne,
rich in grapes, or in Haliartus
leafy, and Troy went down in a
whirlpool of blood while the moon looked on
serenely. The warriors dead, the children
were thrown onto the smoking rubble.
The women were dragged to the waiting ships,
and from Troy in flames to the sky-blue sea,
through the Sigean Gates, white in the moonlight,
the chariots passed. And the cries went on.

IV

Ma non ancora alle Sinistre Porte
Antìclo eroe dalla città giungeva.
Lì l'auriga attendeva il suo guerriero
insanguinato; e oro e bronzo, il carro,
e la giovane schiava alto gemente.
Voto era il carro, solo era l'auriga:
legati con le briglie abili al tronco
del caprifico, in cui fischiava il vento,
i due cavalli battean l'ugne a terra,
fiutando il sangue, sbalzando alle vampe.
Ma non giungeva Antìclo: egli giaceva
sul nero sangue, presso l'alta casa
di Deifobo. E dentro eravi ancora
fremere d'ira, strepere di ferro:
poi che, intorno all'amante ultimo, ancora
gli eroi venuti con le mille navi,
Locri, Etoli, Focei, Dolopi, Abanti,
contendean ai Troiani Helena Argiva;
tutti per lei si percotean con l'aste
i vestiti di bronzo e i domatori
di cavalli; e le loro aste, stridendo,
rigavano di lunghe ombre le fiamme.

V

Ma pensava alla sua donna morendo
Antìclo, presso l'atrïo sonoro
dell'alta casa. E divampò la casa
come un gran pino; ed al bagliore Antìclo
vide Lèito eroe sul limitare.
Rapido a nome lo chiamò: gli disse:
Lèito figlio d'Alectryone, trova
nell'alta casa il vincitore Atride,
di cui s'ode il feroce urlo di guerra.
Digli che fugge alle mie vene il sangue
sì come il vino ad un cratere infranto.
E digli che per lui muoio e che muoio
per la sua donna, ed ho la mia nel cuore.

IV

But Anticlos didn't pass through those gates
nor any other in the walls of Troy.
His charioteer waited for him
in the gilded chariot with a fresh young slave
wailing wildly, and the horses, their reins
tied to a fig-tree the wind whistled through,
stamped their hooves on the dusty ground,
sniffed at the blood, and reared at the flames.
But Anticlos did not come. He lay
in a dark pool of blood, in the high house
of Deiphobos, son of Priam.
And over him there raged still
the lust of battle, the clash of bronze,
since, in the fatal footsteps of Deiphobos,
the warriors who came in a thousand ships
from Locris, Aetolia, Phocis, Dolopia, Euboea,
still fought with the Trojans over Argive Helen,
still struck at each other with their shadowed spears —
the bronze-clad, the tamers of horses —
as their spears clashed and their long shadows
stood out like scars on a city in flames.

V

But Anticlos thought of his woman
as he lay there dying in the sonorous hall
of that great house, which now went up
like a tottering pine devoured by flame.
And through the flash, Anticlos
saw Leitus standing in the doorway.
Immediately he called to him:
"Leitus, son of Alectryon,
find Menelaus, the conqueror,
whose mighty cry of war I hear.
Tell him the blood leaks from my veins
like wine out of a broken jug.
Tell him that I'm dying for him
and for his woman, though I have mine

Che venga la divina Helena, e parli
a me la voce della mia lontana:
parli la voce dolce più che niuna,
come ad ognuno suona al cuor sol una.

VI

Disse, e la casa entrò Lèito, e seguiva
tra le fiamme il feroce urlo di guerra,
che come tacque, egli trovò l'Atride
poggiato all'asta dalla rossa punta,
dritto, col piede sopra il suo nemico.
E contro gli sedeva Helena Argiva,
tacita, sopra l'alto trono d'oro;
e lo sgabello aveva sotto i piedi.
E Lèito disse al vincitore Atride:
uno mi manda, da cui fugge il sangue
sì come il vino da cratere infranto:
Antìclo, che muore per te, che muore
per la tua donna, ed ha la sua nel cuore.
Oh! vada la divina Helena, e parli
a lui la voce della sua lontana,
la voce dolce forse più che niuna,
e come suona forse al cuor sol una.

VII

E così, mentre già moriva Antìclo,
veniva a lui con mute orme di sogno
Helena. Ardeva intorno a lei l'incendio,
su l'incendio brillava il plenilunio.
Ella passava tacita e serena,
come la luna, sopra il fuoco e il sangue.
Le fiamme, un guizzo, al suo passar, più alto;
spremeano un rivo più sottil le vene.
E scrosciavano l'ultime muraglie,
e sonavano gli ultimi singulti.
Stette sul capo al moribondo Antìclo
pensoso della sua donna lontana.
Tacquero allora intorno a lei gli eroi

in my heart. Tell him to bring Helen
to speak to me in the voice of my woman,
the voice that I most want to hear.
Every heart has a voice that it longs for most."

VI

So he spoke, and Leitus passed through the house
tracking that mighty cry of war,
and when it went quiet, he found Menelaus
leaning on a spear that ended in a wound,
with his foot on the corpse of his enemy.
And there sat Helen, silently,
high on a throne of solid gold,
her feet upon a golden footstool.
Leitus said to Menelaus,
"Someone, whose blood is leaking
like wine out of a broken jug, sent me.
Anticlos, who's dying for you
and for your woman, though he has his
in his heart. So please, let Helen go
to speak to him in the voice of his woman,
the voice that he most wants to hear.
Every heart has a voice that it longs for most."

VII

So it was that as Anticlos
lay dying, Helen came to him,
silently as a dream. Around her
the conflagration blazed, and above
the conflagration shone the moon.
And she passed silently, serenely
as the moon, over the blood and flames.
The flames soared higher as she passed.
The blood cooled in the dying veins.
The last houses came crashing down.
Men's last gasps hung in the air.
She stood over Anticlos where he lay dying,
thinking of his woman far away.
The warriors fell silent, hoarse from the war-cry.

rauchi di strage, e le discinte schiave.
E già la bocca apriva ella a chiamarlo
con la voce lontana, con la voce
della sua donna, che per sempre seco
egli nell'infinito Hade portasse;
la rosea bocca apriva già; quand'egli
— No — disse: — voglio ricordar te sola. —

The slave-girls fell silent in their torn robes,
and her mouth was just about to open
with that far-away voice, the voice of his woman,
so that he could carry it with him to Hades.
Her lips were opening when Anticlos said, "Stop!
I want to remember you alone."

IL SONNO DI ODISSEO

THE SLEEP OF ODYSSEUS

Il sonno di Odisseo

I

Per nove giorni, e notte e dì, la nave
nera filò, ché la portava il vento
e il timoniere, e ne reggeva accorta
la grande mano d'Odisseo le scotte;
né, lasso, ad altri le cedea, ché verso
la cara patria lo portava il vento.
Per nove giorni, e notte e dì, la nera
nave filò, né l'occhio mai distolse
l'eroe, cercando l'isola rupestre
tra il cilestrino tremolìo del mare;
pago se prima di morir vedesse
balzarne in aria i vortici del fumo.
Nel decimo, là dove era vanito
il nono sole in un barbaglio d'oro,
ora gli apparse non sapea che nero:
nuvola o terra? E gli balenò vinto
dall'alba dolce il grave occhio: e lontano
s'immerse il cuore d'Odisseo nel sonno.

II

E venne incontro al volo della nave,
ecco, una terra, e veleggiava azzurra
tra il cilestrino tremolìo del mare;
e con un monte ella prendea del cielo,
e giù dal monte spumeggiando i botri
scendean tra i ciuffi dell'irsute stipe;
e ne' suoi poggi apparvero i filari
lunghi di viti, ed a' suoi piedi i campi
vellosi della nuova erba del grano:
e tutta apparve un'isola rupestre,
dura, non buona a pascere polledri,
ma sì di capre e sì di buoi nutrice:
e qua e là sopra gli aerei picchi

The Sleep of Odysseus[1]

I

Nine days and nights the black ship
sailed, carried on by winds
and by its helmsman's hand.
Odysseus had the wheel
and never let it out of his hands,
for he was sailing home.
Nine days and nights the black ship
sailed, and his eyes never stopped
looking out for his homeland
in the blue haze of the sea,
eager to see the smoke rise
from its chimneys once again.
The tenth day, a dark something
emerged out of the golden blaze
where the ninth sun had vanished:
cloud or land? Odysseus' eyelids
went down with the sunrise,
and his heart was plunged into sleep.

II

Someone's homeland was coming towards him
steadfast, sailing up to the ship
in the blue haze of the ocean,
touching heaven with its peaks,
stormy rivers down its cliffs,
bushes, woods, and weeds,
long green vineyards on its hills,
long lush fields of wheat and grain,
greening still with their new grass.
It was a hard land of stone,
not good for breeding horses,
suited though to goats and cattle.
On its misty mountain tops,

---

1. The poem is based on *Odyssey* 10.28–55. While sailing to Ithaca, Odysseus falls asleep. His companions open a jar that was a gift of Aeolus and unleash the winds that divert their journey homeward.

morian nel chiaro dell'aurora i fuochi
de' mandrïani; e qua e là sbalzava
il mattutino vortice del fumo,
d'Itaca, alfine: ma non già lo vide
notando il cuore d'Odisseo nel sonno.

III

Ed ecco a prua dell'incavata nave
volar parole, simili ad uccelli,
con fuggevoli sibili. La nave
radeva allora il picco alto del Corvo
e il ben cerchiato fonte; e se n'udiva
un grufolare fragile di verri;
ed ampio un chiuso si scorgea, di grandi
massi ricinto ed assiepato intorno
di salvatico pero e di prunalbo;
ed il divino mandrïan dei verri,
presso la spiaggia, della nera scorza
spogliava con l'aguzza ascia un querciolo
e grandi pali a rinforzare il chiuso
poi ne tagliò coi morsi aspri dell'ascia;
e sì e no tra lo sciacquìo dell'onde
giungeva al mare il roco ansar dei colpi,
d'Eumeo fedele: ma non già li udiva
tuffato il cuore d'Odisseo nel sonno.

IV

E già da prua, sopra la nave, a poppa,
simili a freccie, andavano parole
con fuggevoli fremiti. La nave
era di faccia al porto di Forkyne;
e in capo ad esso si vedea l'olivo,
grande, fronzuto, e presso quello un antro:
l'antro d'affaccendate api sonoro,
quando in crateri ed anfore di pietra
filano la soave opra del miele:
e si scorgeva la sassosa strada
della città: si distinguea, tra il verde

shepherds put their fires out
at the first light of the dawn.
Smoke went up the morning sky
over Ithaca, but he missed it
since his heart was swimming in sleep.

III

Winged words were flying
on the prow of the slim ship,
like birds squawking feebly.
The ship passed by Crow's Peak
and its well-encircled spring.
A frail grunting of hogs,
a large circle of tall stones
like a hedgerow around
a pear tree and a hawthorn.
Eumeus, the swineherd,
on the beach was peeling off
the bark of a dark young oak.
He cut the trunk with his axe
to make a fence for the trees,
and the thud of the axe mixed
with the crashing of seawaves
on the shore. But Odysseus missed it,
since his heart was lost in sleep.

IV

Words like arrows on the prow
and the poop went flying fast,
fleeting and trembling. The ship
faced the port of Phorcys,
with its olive tree on top,
a big leafy tree by a cave
filled up with the buzz of bees
as they weave their threads of gold
into pots and stony urns.
One could see the stony path
to the city, a white well

d'acquosi ontani, la fontana bianca
e l'ara bianca, ed una eccelsa casa:
l'eccelsa casa d'Odisseo: già forse
stridea la spola fra la trama, e sotto
le stanche dita ricrescea la tela,
ampia, immortale… Oh! non udì né vide
perduto il cuore d'Odisseo nel sonno.

V

E su la nave, nell'entrare il porto,
il peggio vinse: sciolsero i compagni
gli otri, e la furia ne fischiò dei venti:
la vela si svoltò, si sbatté, come
peplo, cui donna abbandonò disteso
ad inasprire sopra aereo picco:
ecco, e la nave lontanò dal porto;
e un giovinetto stava già nel porto,
poggiato all'asta dalla bronzea punta:
e il giovinetto sotto il glauco olivo
stava pensoso; ed un veloce cane
correva intorno a lui scodinzolando:
e il cane dalle volte irrequïete
sostò, con gli occhi all'infinito mare;
e com'ebbe le salse orme fiutate,
ululò dietro la fuggente nave:
Argo, il suo cane: ma non già l'udiva
tuffato il cuore d'Odisseo nel sonno.

VI

E la nave radeva ora una punta
d'Itaca scabra. E tra due poggi un campo
era, ben culto; il campo di Laerte;
del vecchio re; col fertile pometo;
coi peri e meli che Laerte aveva
donati al figlio tuttavia fanciullo;
ché lo seguiva per la vigna, e questo
chiedeva degli snelli alberi e quello:
tredici peri e dieci meli in fila

surrounded by green trees,
a white altar, and a house —
Odysseus's noble house where
tired fingers weaved and weaved
an endless cloth, immortal,
on a web. But he missed it
since his heart was drowned in sleep.

V

But when the ship was docking,
the sailors opened Aeolus'
goatskins, and winds raged out.
The sail unwrapped and tightened
like a woman's dress put out
to dry in a windy spot,
and the ship sailed away
from land where a young lad
stood leaning on a spear,
pensive under a silver
olive tree, with his swift dog
wagging its tail and running
in circles. The dog stopped
at once and stared at the sea.
He sniffed the track of the ship
and howled at it a while,
Argos the dog. But Odysseus missed it
since his heart was immersed in sleep.

VI

And the ship coasted a tip
of the rocky island where
old King Laertes' field was.
A fertile orchard it was,
of pear and apple trees,
the King gave his son as a boy,
who followed him in the vineyard
asking the name of each tree.
Thirteen pear trees, ten of apples,

stavano, bianchi della lor fiorita:
all'ombra d'uno, all'ombra del più bianco,
era un vecchio, poggiato su la marra:
il vecchio, volto all'infinito mare
dove mugghiava il subito tumulto,
limando ai faticati occhi la luce,
riguardò dietro la fuggente nave:
era suo padre: ma non già lo vide
notando il cuore d'Odisseo nel sonno.

VII

Ed i venti portarono la nave
nera più lungi. E subito aprì gli occhi
l'eroe, rapidi aprì gli occhi a vedere
sbalzar dalla sognata Itaca il fumo;
e scoprir forse il fido Eumeo nel chiuso
ben cinto, e forse il padre suo nel campo
ben culto: il padre che sopra la marra
appoggiato guardasse la sua nave;
e forse il figlio che poggiato all'asta
la sua nave guardasse: e lo seguiva,
certo, e intorno correa scodinzolando
Argo, il suo cane; e forse la sua casa,
la dolce casa ove la fida moglie
già percorreva il garrulo telaio:
guardò: ma vide non sapea che nero
fuggire per il violaceo mare,
nuvola o terra? e dileguar lontano,
emerso il cuore d'Odisseo dal sonno.

in a row, white in their blossom.
In the shade of the whitest,
an old man leaned on its cane
staring at the endless sea,
where the stormy waves roared,
shading his eyes with his hand.
His father! But he missed him
since his heart was swimming in sleep.

VII

As the winds pushed the ship
away, he opened his eyes,
the hero, only to see
the smoke rise up from his home,
Eumaeus within his fenced enclosure,
his father in his field staring
at the sea, bent on his cane,
perhaps his son with his spear
looking out to the ship,
and Argos, his loyal dog,
running and wagging his tail,
and his home and his wife,
weaving her cloth at the loom.
All he saw was a dark something
fading on the wine-colored sea.
Cloud or land? And then it disappeared again,
just as his heart was waking from sleep.

L'ultimo viaggio

THE LAST VOYAGE

L'ultimo viaggio

I. La pala

Ed il timone al focolar sospese
in Itaca l'Eroe navigatore.
Stanco giungeva da un error terreno,
grave ai garretti, ch'egli avea compiuto
reggendo sopra il grande omero un remo.
Quelli cercava che non sanno il mare
nè navi nere dalle rosse prore,
e non miste di sale hanno vivande.
E già più lune s'erano consunte
tra scabre rupi, nel cercare in vano
l'azzurro mare in cui tuffar la luce;
né da gran tempo più sentiva il cielo
l'odor di sale, ma l'odor di verde:
quando gli occorse un altro passeggero,
che disse; e il vento che ululò notturno,
si dibatteva, intorno loro, ai monti,
come orso in una fossa alta caduto:
"Uomo straniero, al re tu muovi? Oh! tardo!
Al re, già mondo è nel granaio il grano.
Un dio mandò quest'alito, che soffia
anc'oggi, e ieri ventilò la lolla.
Oggi, o tarda opra, vana è la tua pala".
Disse; ma il cuore tutto rise accorto
all'Eroe che pensava le parole
del morto, cieco, dallo scettro d'oro.
Ché cieco ei vede, e tutto sa pur morto:
tra gli alti pioppi e i salici infecondi,
nella caligo, egli, bevuto al botro
il sangue, disse: "Misero, avrai pace
quando il ben fatto remo della nave
ti sia chiamato un distruttor di paglie".
Ed ora il cuore, a quel pensier, gli rise.
E disse: "Uomo terrestre, ala! non pala!
Ma sia. Ben ora qui fermarla io voglio

THE LAST VOYAGE

I. The Spade

    And he hung his ship's wheel above the fire
in Ithaca, the seafaring hero.
He was tired out from a long journey,
an overland journey, hard on his feet,
carrying his oar on his shoulder
and looking for an inland folk
with no black ships or red bows,
whose food has no taste of the sea.
And many a moon had died off
on rough cliffs, trying to plunge
its light in the depths of the sea;
and the sky had lost the flavor of
the sea and smelled instead of grass,
when he met a man along the road,
who said to him (as the night wind howled,
caged in the mountains round about
like a bear that had fallen into a deep pit):
"Stranger, you're late! The king's silo
is already full of well-stored wheat.
A god sent us this wind, which
tore the husk from the grain.
Your shovel is no longer needed."
The hero smiled a secret smile,
Tiresias' words in his mind,
the dead prophet, all-knowing,
who, among poplars and willows,
and mist, having drunk the blood
of the sacrifice, had said:
"Wretched one, you will find peace
when your oar is mistaken for a shovel."
And he smiled a secret smile.
"It's a blade, not a spade, inlander!
But I want to plant it down here,

nella compatta aridità del suolo.
Un fine ha tutto. In ira a un dio da tempo
io volo foglia a cui s'adira il vento".
E l'altro ancora ad Odisseo parlava:
"Chi, donde sei degli uomini? venuto
come, tra noi? Non già per l'aere brullo,
come alcuno dei cigni longicolli,
ma scambiando tra loro i due ginocchi.
Parlami, e narra senza giri il vero".

II. L'ala

E rispose l'Eroe molto vissuto:
"Tutto ti narro senza giri il vero.
Sono, a voi sconosciuti, uomini, anch'essi
mortali sì, ma, come dei, celesti,
che non coi piedi, come i lenti bovi,
vanno, e con la vicenda dei ginocchi,
ma con la spinta delle aeree braccia,
come gli uccelli, ed hanno il color d'aria
sotto sé, vasto. Io vidi viaggiando
sbocciar le stelle fuor del cielo infranto,
sotto questi occhi, e il guidator del Carro
venir con me fischiando ai buoi lontano,
e l'auree rote lievi sbalzar sulla
tremola ghiaia della strada azzurra.
Né sempre l'ali noi tra cielo e cielo
battiamo: spesso noi prendiamo il vento:
a mezzo un ringhio acuto, per le froge
larghe prendiamo il vano vento folle,
che ci conduca, e con la forte mano
le briglie io reggo per frenarlo al passo.
Ma un dio ce n'odia, come voi la terra
odia, che voi sostenta sì, ma spezza.
Ch'ha tutto un fine. Or tu fa che un torello
dal re mi venga, ed un agnello e un verro;
che qui ne onori quell'ignoto iddio".

into the solid dry land.
There's an end to everything. For far too long
I was a leaf blown about by the gods' wrath."
The man replied to Odysseus:
"Who are your people, and how did you get here?
Surely not borne on the bare winds
like a long-necked swan but, like the rest of us,
by putting one foot in front of the other.
Tell me the truth without digressions."

II. The Blade

And the wayfarer hero responded:
"I won't stray from the truth.
There's a people unknown to you,
mortal as well, but celestial,
not moving the way of slow oxen,
one foot in front of the other,
but by force of aerial blades,
like birds, with the color of
the vast air below. I saw
a million stars blooming
in that broken sky and the Ploughman
appear and whistle to his oxen,
the golden wheels of his cart
leaping off the shimmering
gravel of that blue way.
But we don't always beat wings.
At times, we catch a strong wind,
wild and crazy like a horse,
snorting with fuming nostrils.
We rein him in and hold him
firmly so that he carries us.
But the gods also hate us, like the earth
hates you. It feeds you, then breaks you.
There's an end to everything. Let the king give
a young bull, a pig, and a lamb
to honor the unknown god."

E l'altro ancora rispondea stupito:
"L'ignoto è grande, e grande più, se dio.
Or vieni al re, che raddolcito ha il cuore
oggi, che il grano gli avanzò le corbe".
Così l'eroe divino in una forra
selvosa il remo suo piantò, la lieve
ala incrostata dalla salsa gromma.
Al dio sdegnato per il suo Ciclope,
egli uccise un torello ed un agnello
e terzo un verro montator di scrofe;
e poi discese, e insieme a lui più lune
vennero, e l'una dopo l'altra ognuna
sé, girando tra roccie aspre, consunse.
L'ultima, piena tremolò sul mare
riscintillante, e su la bianca sabbia,
piccola e nera gli mostrò la nave,
e i suoi compagni, ch'attendean guardando
a monte, muti. Ed ei salpò. Sbalzare
vide ancora le rote auree del Carro
sopra le ghiaie dell'azzurra strada:
rivide il fumo salir su, rivide
Itaca scabra, e la sua grande casa.
Dove il timone al focolar sospese.

III. Le gru nocchiere

E un canto allora venne a lui dall'alto,
di su le nubi, di raminghe gru.
Sospendi al fumo ora il timone, e dormi.
Le Gallinelle fuggono lo strale

And the other answered in awe:
"Great is the unknown, and it's greater
still if it's divine.
Come to the king — his heart
is cheerful now that the harvest
has filled his sacks with grain."
And so the godlike hero
planted his oar in the woody ravine,
a wing crusted with salt.
To quench the wrath of Poseidon,
he killed a young bull and a lamb
and then a huge boar,
a real sow-mounter.
Then he went down to the sea,
and many moons went with him,
then exhausted themselves
wandering around the sharp rocks.
The last, a full moon, sparkled
on the shimmering waves
and then on the white sand
and on a small black ship
and its sailors waiting in silence.
So he set sail and saw
again the golden wheels
of the Ploughman's cart leaping
off its shimmering way.
And he saw smoke rising from the chimneys
of rocky Ithaca again.
He saw again his great house
where he hung his wheel by the fire.

III. The Navigator Cranes

And a song came down from the sky,
from cranes wandering in the clouds.
"Hang your wheel by the fire and sleep.
Orion's dart has scattered the Hens,

già d'Orïone, e son cadute in mare.
Rincalza su la spiaggia ora la nave
nera con pietre, che al ventar non tremi,
Eroe; ché sono per soffiare i venti.
L'alleggio della stiva apri, che l'acqua
scoli e non faccia poi funghir le doghe,
Eroe; ché sono per cader le pioggie.
Sospendi al fumo ora il timone, e in casa
tieni all'asciutto i canapi ritorti,
ogni arma, ogni ala della nave, e dormi.
Ché viene il verno, viene il freddo acuto
che fa nei boschi bubbolar le fiere
che fuggono irte con la coda al ventre:
quando a tre piedi, il filo della schiena
rotto a metà, la grigia testa bassa,
il vecchio va sotto la neve bianca;
e il randagio pitocco entra dal fabbro,
nella fucina aperta, e prende sonno
un poco al caldo tra l'odor di bronzo.
Navigatore di cent'arti, dormi
nell'alta casa, o, se ti piace, solca
ora la terra, dopo arata l'onda.-
Questo era canto che rodeva il cuore
del timoniere, che volgea la barra
verso un approdo, e tedio avea dell'acqua;
ché passavano, agli uomini gridando
giunto il maltempo, venti nevi pioggie,
e lo sparire delle stelle buone;
e tra le nubi esse con fermo cuore,
gittando rauche grida alla burrasca,
andavano, e coi remi battean l'aria.

IV. *Le gru guerriere*

   Dicean, — Dormi — al nocchiero — Ara, al villano,
di su le nubi, le raminghe gru.
— Ara: la stanga dell'aratro al giogo

and they have plunged into the sea.
Drag your ship onto the shore,
secure it, so that it won't move
as the autumn winds blow, hero.
Let the water flow from your boat
so that the wood won't go mouldy
as the autumn rains fall, hero.
Hang your wheel by the fire, keep
ropes, spars, and wings well dry
in the warmth of your house, and sleep.
As winter comes, its bitter cold
haunts the wild beasts in the wood,
makes them shiver, howl, and run
away, with their tails tucked under their bellies.
Leant on his cane, his backbone
broken, his gray head bent down,
an old man walks as the snow falls:
a homeless pauper, he enters into
a smithy and then dozes off
by the heat of the irony fire.
Sleep now, sailor, in your high-built house,
or, if you prefer, plough the land
now that you have ploughed the sea."
This was the song biting his heart,
as he steered the wheel of his boat
to the dock, tired of navigating,
as the cranes announced bad weather,
and winds and rains and snow came,
and the favorable stars disappeared.
The mighty cranes up in the clouds,
with their raucous screams in the storm,
flew on, beating the air with their oars.

IV. The Warrior Cranes

They said, "Sleep" to the soldier,
"Plough" to the farmer, from the clouds.
"Plough. Tie the plough to the yoke

lega dei bovi; ché tu n'hai, ben d'erbe
sazi, in capanna, o figlio di Laerte.
Fatti col cuoio d'un di loro, ucciso,
un paio d'uose, che difenda il freddo,
ma prima il dentro addenserai di feltro;
e cucirai coi tendini del bove
pelli de' primi nati dalle capre,
che a te dall'acqua parino le spalle;
e su la testa ti porrai la testa
d'un vecchio lupo, che ti scaldi, e i denti
bianchi digrigni tra il nevischio e i venti.
Arare il campo, non il mare, è tempo,
da che nel cielo non si fa vedere
più quel branchetto delle sette stelle.
Sessanta giorni dopo volto il sole,
quando ritorni il conduttor del Carro,
allor dolce è la brezza, il mare è calmo;
brilla Boote a sera, e sul mattino
tornata già la rondine cinguetta,
che il mare è calmo e che dolce è la brezza.
La brezza chiama a sé la vela, il mare
chiama a sé il remo; e resta qua canoro
il cuculo a parlare al vignaiolo.-
Questo era canto che mordeva il cuore
a chi non bovi e sol avea l'aratro;
ch'egli ha bel dire, Prestami il tuo paro!
Son le faccende, ed ora ogni bifolco
semina, e poi, sicuro della fame,
ode venti fischiare, acque scrosciare,
ilare. E intanto esse, le gru, moveano
verso l'Oceano, a guerra, in righe lunghe,
empiendo il cielo d'un clangor di trombe.

V. Il remo confitto

E per nove anni al focolar sedeva,
di sua casa, l'Eroe navigatore:

of your oxen, the grass-fed steers
in your barn, son of Laertes.
Kill one ox and make yourself
breeches against the great cold,
filled inside with fur and felt.
Use the oxen's tendons to stitch
the soft skins of kids and lambs
into a coat for the rainy days.
Cover your head with the head of an old
wolf — he'll keep you warm as his teeth
snarl among the winter winds.
It's time to plough the land, not the sea,
as that little flock of seven stars
has now vanished from the heavens.
Sixty days after the solstice,
when the Ploughman comes back into the sky,
then the breeze is soft, and the sea is calm.
The Ploughman shines in the evening sky,
and the swallows are back and chirp in the morning
since the breeze is soft, and the sea is calm.
The wind calls out for sails, the sea
calls out for oars, and the cuckoo sings
to the workers toiling in the vineyards."
This was the song eating the heart
of those who had ploughs but no oxen,
who might well say, "Lend me a pair!"
That's the task, and now every
churl sows seed and later, secure
from hunger, listens to the wind blowing,
the rain falling, content. Meanwhile,
the cranes, still at war, move towards
the ocean in long lines, filling
the air with the clamor of trumpets.

V. The Oar in the Ground

For nine years, he sat by the fire
in his house, the seafaring hero.

ché più non gli era alcuno error marino
dal fato ingiunto e alcuno error terrestre.
Sì, la vecchiaia gli ammollia le membra
a poco a poco. Ora dovea la morte
fuori del mare giungergli, soave,
molto soave, e né coi dolci strali
dovea ferirlo, ma fiatar leggiera
sopra la face cui già l'uragano
frustò, ma fece divampar più forte.
E i popoli felici erano intorno,
che il figlio, nato lungi alle battaglie,
savio reggeva in abbondevol pace.
Crescean nel chiuso del fedel porcaio
floridi i verri dalle bianche zanne,
e nei ristretti pascoli più tanti
erano i bovi dalle larghe fronti,
e tante più dal Nerito le capre
pendean strappando irsuti pruni e stipe,
e molto sotto il tetto alto giaceva
oro, bronzo, olezzante olio d'oliva.
Ma raro nella casa era il convito,
né più sonava l'ilare tumulto
per il grande atrio umbratile; ché il vecchio
più non bramava terghi di giovenco,
né coscie gonfie d'adipe, di verro;
amava, invano, la fioril vivanda,
il dolce loto, cui chi mangia, è pago,
né altro chiede che brucar del loto.
Così le soglie dell'eccelsa casa
or d'Odissèo dimenticò l'aedo
dai molti canti, e il lacero pitocco,
che l'un corrompe e l'altro orna il convito.
E il Laertiade ora vivea solingo
fuori del mare, come il vecchio remo
scabro di salsa gromma, che piantato
lungi avea dalle salse aure nel suolo,

No longer did fate enjoin his wandering
across the oceans or over the earth.
Old age, it is true, was softening his limbs
little by little. Now death would come,
not on the sea, but gently, so gently,
not wounding him with its arrows,
but breathing lightly on a flame
that the tempest had lashed time and again,
only making it leap up higher.
And his people were flourishing around him,
with his son, born far from battles,
ruling wisely in abundant peace.
His loyal swineherd would breed him
plump hogs with snow-white fangs,
and in their well-enclosed pastures,
grazed his large-headed cattle,
herds of goats up the Niritos
fed on bushes and wild grass,
and under his high roof, he had
gold and bronze and fragrant oil.
But banquets were rare in that house,
no more roaring laughter echoed
in the shadowy hall since the king
was old with no hunger for meat,
for beef, or greasy pork legs.
He sought oblivion — in vain —
in the lotus flowers. Whoever eats them
is satisfied and no longer
craves to graze on anything else.
So poets forsook the high house,
which was now Odysseus',
and beggars too, who can be the ruin
of banquets or their ornament.
The son of Laertes lived secluded,
far from the sea, like an old oar
encrusted with salt, planted in the earth,
far away from the salty winds of the sea,

e strettolo, ala, tra le glebe gravi.
E il grigio capo dell'Eroe tremava,
avanti al mormorare della fiamma,
come là, nella valle solitaria,
quel remo al soffio della tramontana.

VI. Il fuso al fuoco

E per nove anni ogni anno udì la voce,
di su le nubi, delle gru raminghe
che diceano — Ara- che diceano — Dormi-;
ed alternando squilli di battaglia
coi remi in lunghe righe battean l'aria:
-mentre noi guerreggiamo, ara, o villano;
dormi, o nocchiero, noi veleggeremo.-
E il canto il cuore dell'Eroe mangiava,
chiuso alle genti come un aratore
cui per sementa mancano i due bovi.
Sedeva al fuoco, e la sua vecchia moglie,
la bene oprante, contro lui sedeva,
tacita. E per le fauci del camino
fuligginose, allo spirar de' venti
umidi, ardeano fisse le faville;
ardean, lievi sbraciando, le faville
sul putre dorso dei lebeti neri.
Su quelle intento si perdea con gli occhi
avvezzi al cielo il corridor del mare.
E distingueva nel sereno cielo
le fuggitive Pleiadi e Boote
tardi cadente e l'Orsa, anche nomata
il Carro, che lì sempre si rivolge,
e sola è sempre del nocchier compagna.
E il fulgido Odisseo dava la vela
al vento uguale, e ferme avea le scotte,
e i buoni suoi remigatori stanchi
poneano i remi lungo le scalmiere.
La nave con uno schioccar di tela

a wing stuck fast in the heavy clods.
And the gray head of the hero trembled
in front of the whispering of the fire,
as out there, in the solitary valley,
the old oar trembled in the north wind.

VI. The Spindle

Every year for nine years
he heard the cry of the wandering cranes:
"Plough," they said, and then "Sleep,"
alternating their battle-cry
as they stroked the air in long lines.
"While we row, you plough, churl.
While you sleep, sailor, we'll spread our sails."
This was the song biting his heart,
the hero, lonely as a farmer
without any oxen to pull his plough.
He sat by the fire, and his old wife,
hard-working Penelope, sat beside him
quietly. And in the sooty maw
of the fireplace, at the breath
of the clammy winds, fixed sparks
blazed. On the mucky bottoms of the black
cauldrons, sparks, waving gently,
blazed. Engrossed by them, his eyes
used to reading the skies, the old
sea-wanderer drifted off.
And he made out in the limpid night
the fugitive Pleiades and the slow-turning
Ploughman and the Bear, also known as
the Chariot, which always turns around
and is the seaman's one true friend.
Brilliant Odysseus was giving sail
to an even wind, holding the sheets
while his brave sailors, tired out,
laid their oars along the gunwales.
The ship with a shake of her sails seemed to run

correa da sé nella stellata notte,
e prendean sonno i marinai su i banchi,
e lei portava il vento e il timoniere.
L'Eroe giaceva in un'irsuta pelle,
sopra coperta, a poppa della nave,
e, dietro il capo, si fendeva il mare
con lungo scroscio e subiti barbagli.
Egli era fisso in alto, nelle stelle,
ma gli occhi il sonno gli premea, soave,
e non sentiva se non sibilare
la brezza nelle sartie e nelli stragli.
E la moglie appoggiata all'altro muro
faceva assiduo sibilare il fuso.

VII. La zattera

E gli dicea la veneranda moglie:
"Divo Odisseo, mi sembra oggi quel giorno
che ti rividi. Io ti sedea di contro,
qui, nel mio seggio. Stanco eri di mare,
eri, divo Odisseo, sazio di sangue!
Come ora. Muto io ti vedeva al lume
del focolare, fissi gli occhi in giù".
Fissi in giù gli occhi, presso la colonna,
egli taceva: ché ascoltava il cuore
suo che squittiva come cane in sogno.
E qualche foglia d'ellera sul ciocco
secco crocchiava, e d'uno stizzo il vento
uscia fischiando; ma l'Eroe crocchiare
udiva un po' la zattera compatta,
opera sua nell'isola deserta.
Su la decimottava alba la zattera
egli sentì brusca salire al vento
stridulo; e l'uomo su la barca solo
era, e sola la barca era sul mare:
soli con qualche errante procellaria.

all by herself through the thick-starred night.
The rowers found sleep along the benches
as the wind and the helmsman carried her.
The hero lay covered on a rich pelt
on the poop of the ship, and behind his head,
the sea shattered into a million pieces
with long crashes and quick flashes of light.
His gaze was fixed on the stars,
but sweet sleep was weighing on his eyes,
since all he could hear was the whistling
of the wind in the sails and the rigging,
and his wife leant against the wall
keeping her spindle whistling.

VII. The Raft

His venerable wife then said to him:
"Godlike Odysseus, it seems like today,
the day I saw you again.
I was sitting opposite you, here
in my chair. You were tired of the sea,
godlike Odysseus. You'd had your fill
of blood. Like now. I saw you by
the light of the fire. You didn't say a word.
Your gaze was fixed on the ground before you."
His gaze was fixed on the ground before him.
He didn't say a word. He was listening to
his heart yelping like a dreaming dog.
Some leaves on one of the logs creaked,
and all of a sudden, the wind cried,
but the hero heard his raft creak,
the raft he'd built on that desert island.
On the eighteenth dawn, he felt the raft
rear up briskly in a shrill wind,
a man all alone on a raft,
a raft all alone on the sea,
alone except for a few stray birds.

E di là donde tralucea già l'alba,
ora appariva una catena fosca
d'aeree nubi, e torbide a prua l'onde
picchiavano; ecco e si sventò la vela.
E l'uomo allora udì di contro un canto
di torte conche, e divinò che dietro
quelle il nemico, il truce dio del mare,
venìa tornando ai suoi cerulei campi.
Lui vide, e rise il dio con uno schianto
secco di tuono che rimbombò tetro;
e venne. Udiva egli lo sciabordare
delle ruote e il nitrir degli ippocampi.
E volavano al cielo alto le schiume
dalle lor bocche masticanti il morso;
e l'uragano fumido di sghembo
sferzava lor le groppe di serpente.
Soli nel mare erano l'uomo e il nume
e il nume ergeva su l'ondate il torso
largo, e scoteva il gran capo; e tra il nembo
folgoreggiava il lucido tridente.
E il Laertiade al cuore suo parlava,
ch'altri non v'era; e sotto avea la barra.

VIII. Le rondini

E per nove anni egli aspettò la morte
che fuor del mare gli dovea soave
giungere; e sì, nel decimo, su l'alba,
giunsero a lui le rondini, dal mare.
Egli dormia sul letto traforato
cui sosteneva un ceppo d'oleastro
barbato a terra; e marinai sognava
parlare sparsi per il mare azzurro.
E si destò con nell'orecchio infuso
quel vocìo fioco; ed ascoltò seduto:
erano rondini, e sonava intorno
l'umbratile atrio per il lor sussurro.

And from where the dawn was breaking through,
there now appeared a chain of clouds,
angry waves beat down on the raft,
and the favouring wind went out of the sails.
And then he heard a song, that man,
the song that sings from the coils of seashells,
and he knew that behind them his enemy
Poseidon, fell god of the sea,
was coming home to his sea-blue lands.
The god saw him, and he laughed with a dry
crack of thunder, which echoed grimly.
He was coming nearer. Odysseus heard
waves slapping against his wheels
and the neighing of seahorses. And foam from their mouths
chewing the bit was flying up to the high
sky, and the slanted whip of the storm
slashed at their saddled serpentine backs.
God and man were all alone on the sea,
and the god was rising, his broad torso
lifting clear of the waves. He shook his great head,
and his bright trident shone through the mists.
And the son of Laertes was talking to his heart,
since there was no-one else around,
and his gaze was fixed on the tiller behind him.

VIII. The Swallows

For nine years he awaited that death,
which was supposed to come over him softly,
far from the sea, and in the tenth year,
at dawn, the swallows arrived from the sea.
He was sleeping on his great carved bed
scooped from the stump of an olive tree
with roots in the ground, and he dreamt
of sailors talking, scattered in
the blue sea. He woke up,
those faint voices still in his ears.
He sat on the edge of his bed and listened.
Swallows! The shadowy hall rang

E si gittò sugli omeri le pelli
caprine, ai piedi si legò le dure
uose bovine: e su la testa il lupo
facea nell'ombra biancheggiar le zanne.
E piano uscì dal talamo, non forse
udisse il lieve cigolìo la moglie;
ma lei teneva un sonno alto, divino,
molto soave, simile alla morte.
E il timone staccò dal focolare,
affumicato, e prese una bipenne.
Ma non moveva il molto accorto al mare,
subito, sì per colli irti di quercie,
per un vïotterello aspro, e mortali
trovò ben pochi per la via deserta;
e disse a un mandriano segaligno,
che per un pioppo secco era la scure;
e disse ad una riccioluta ancella,
che per uno stabbiolo era il timone:
così parlava il tessitor d'inganni,
e non senz'ali era la sua parola.
E poi soletto deviò volgendo
l'astuto viso al fresco alito salso.
Le quercie ai piedi gli spargean le foglie
roggie che scricchiolavano al suo passo.
Gemmava il fico, biancheggiava il pruno,
e il pero avea ne' rosei bocci il fiore.
E di su l'alto Nerito il cuculo
contava arguto il su e giù de l'onde.
E già l'Eroe sentiva sotto i piedi
non più le foglie ma scrosciar la sabbia;
né più pruni fioriti, ma vedeva
i giunchi scabri per i bianchi nicchi;
e infine apparve avanti al mare azzurro
l'Eroe vegliardo col timone in collo

with their hubbub. And he threw a goatskin over
his shoulders, lashed his stiff leather
boots to his feet, and on his head,
a wolf bared its white teeth to the shadows.
And he stood up from the bed slowly
just in case the slight shaking
woke his wife, but she was held
by a deep sleep, the sleep of the gods,
a blissful sleep, a sleep like death.
He took the smoky ship's rudder down
from above the fireplace, and he picked up his axe.
But, always alert, he didn't make
for the sea, not directly. Instead,
he headed down a hillside bristling with oaks,
down a steep little path, and few men he came
across on that godforsaken way.
He told a bony herdsman that
his axe was for a dried-out poplar;
and he told a curly-haired maiden
that the rudder was for a fence.
So he spoke, the weaver of tricks,
and the words he spoke were not without wings.
Alone at last he changed his course,
turned his sly face towards the salt sea.
The oaks were scattering leaves at his feet,
which crinkled with every step he took.
The fig was sprouting, the blackthorn blossoming,
the pear held its flowers in their pink buds.
And from on high the shrill cuckoo
counted the toing and froing of the waves.
And already the hero felt under his feet
the crunch no longer of leaves, but of sand.
No more white blackthorns did he see, but white
shells stuck in the reeds of the shore.
And finally, he appeared at the blue sea,
the wise old hero, carrying the rudder

e la bipenne; e l'inquieto mare,
mare infinito, fragoroso mare,
su la duna lassù lo riconobbe
col riso innumerevole dell'onde.

IX. Il pescatore

Ma lui vedendo, ecco di subito una
rondine deviò con uno strillo.
Ch'ella tornava. Ora Odisseo con gli occhi
cercava tutto il grigio lido curvo,
s'egli vedesse la sua nave in secco.
Ma non la vide; e vide un uomo, un vecchio
di triti panni, chino su la sabbia
raspare dove boccheggiava il mare
alternamente. A lui fu sopra, e disse:
"Abbiamo nulla, o pescator di rena?
Ben vidi, errando su la nave nera,
uomo seduto in uno scoglio aguzzo
reggere un filo pendulo sul flutto;
ma il lungo filo tratto giù dal piombo
porta ai pesci un adunco amo di bronzo
che sì li uncina; e ne schermisce il morso
un liscio cerchio di bovino corno.
Ché l'uomo, quando è roso dalla fame,
mangia anche il sacro pesce che la carne
cruda divora. Io vidi, anzi, mortali
gittar le reti dalle curve navi,
sempre alïando sui pescosi gorghi,
come le folaghe e gli smerghi ombrosi.
E vidi i pesci nella grigia sabbia
avvoltolarsi, per desìo dell'acqua,
versati fuori della rete a molte
maglie; e morire luccicando al sole.
Ma non vidi senz'amo e senza rete
niuno mai fare tali umide prede,
o vecchio, e niuno farsi mai vivanda

and an axe. And the restless sea,
the sea without end, the thunderous sea,
recognized him up there on top of the dune
with the unmeasurable laughter of a million waves.

IX. The Fisherman

But suddenly there was a swallow
that saw him and turned away with a cry
and then wheeled round. And now Odysseus
scanned the whole gray coast
searching for his beached ship.
He didn't see it, but he saw
an old man in rags on the beach,
bent over the sand so he could dig it
where the sea was rasping as it came and went.
Odysseus went up to him and said:
"Nothing, have we, fisher of sand?
I have definitely seen from my black ship
a man sitting on a pointy rock,
holding a droopy line over the waves,
but the long line, dragged down by the sinker,
still delivers to the fish a curved bronze hook,
and that snares them. And a smooth ring
of cow horn stops them biting the line.
And so man, when hunger gnaws him,
eats the fish, the sacred fish
that devours raw flesh. I've also
seen mortals casting nets from their curved ships
even as they glide over the fishy deep
like coots or shadowy mergansers.
And I've seen fish on the gray sand,
writhing out of want of water,
having been poured out of thick-meshed nets.
I've seen them die, flashing in the sun.
But I have never seen anyone without a hook or a net
catching this sort of wet quarry, old man.
And I've never seen anyone making a meal

di tali scabre chiocciole dell'acqua,
che indosso hanno la nave, oppur dei granchi,
che indosso hanno l'incudine dei fabbri".
E il malvestito al vecchio Eroe rispose:
"Tristo il mendico che al convito sdegna
cibo che lo scettrato re gli getta,
sia tibia ossuta od anche pingue ventre.
Ché il Tutto, buono, ha tristo figlio: il Niente.
Prendo ciò che il mio grande ospite m'offre,
che dona, cupo brontolando in cuore,
ma dona: il mare fulgido e canoro,
ch'è sordo in vero, ma più sordo è l'uomo".
Or al mendico il vecchio Eroe rispose:
"O non ha la rupestre Itaca un buono
suo re ch'ha in serbo molto bronzo e oro?
che verri impingua, negli stabbi, e capre?
cui molto odora nei canestri il pane?
Non forse il senno d'Odisseo qui regge,
che molto errò, molto in suo cuor sofferse?
e fu pitocco e malvestito anch'esso.
Non sai la casa dal sublime tetto,
del Laertiade fulgido Odisseo?"

X. La conchiglia

Il malvestito non volgeva il capo
dal mare alterno, ed al ricurvo orecchio
teneva un'aspra tortile conchiglia,
come ascoltasse. Or all'Eroe rispose:
"O Laertiade fulgido Odisseo,
so la tua casa. Ma non io pitocco
querulo sono, poi che fui canoro
eroe, maestro io solo a me. Trovai

out of such unpalatable sea-snails,
snails, which carry around their own ship,
or of crabs, which carry around their own anvil."
The beggar answered the old hero:
"Sad is the beggar who at the banquet
disdains the food a sceptered king
throws to him, whether it's a bony shank
or some fatty belly. Having it all,
you see, has a grim result: having
nothing. I take whatever my great host
gives. He gives it with his dark heart thundering,
but he gives nonetheless – the sea gives,
splendid and sonorous. An indifferent sea,
it's true — but is man any less?"
And now the old hero answered the beggar:
"But doesn't rocky Ithaca have
its good king with his stores of bronze
and gold? Who has stables stuffed with fattening
pigs and goats and baskets loaded
with fragrant bread? Doesn't that wise
Odysseus rule here, who wandered
for so long and suffered so much
in his heart? He was a beggar
and outcast, too. Do you know, by chance,
the whereabouts of the high-roofed house
of glorious Odysseus, son of Laertes?"

X. The Seashell

But the beggar did not turn his gaze
from the changeable sea. He was holding
a coiled shell to his curved ear
as if he was listening. He answered the hero:
"Glorious Odysseus, son of Laertes,
I know your house. But I am no
whiny beggar. I was once
a hero and a singer, my own master,

sparsi nel cuore gl'infiniti canti.
A te cantai, divo Odisseo, da quando
pieno di morti fu l'umbratile atrio,
simili a pesci quali il pescatore
lasciò morire luccicando al sole.
E vedo ancor le schiave moriture
terger con acqua e con porose spugne
il sangue, e molto era il singulto e il grido.
A te cantavo, e tu bevendo il vino
cheto ascoltavi. E poi t'increbbe il detto
minor del fatto. Ascolto or io l'aedo,
solo, in silenzio. Chè gittai la cetra,
io. La raccolse con la mano esperta
solo di scotte un marinaio, un vecchio
dagli occhi rossi. Or chi la tocca? Il vento".
Or all'Aedo il vecchio Eroe rispose:
"Terpiade Femio, e me vecchiezza offese
e te: chè tolse ad ambedue piacere
ciò che già piacque. Ma non mai che nuova
non mi paresse la canzon più nuova
di Femio, o Femio; più nuova e più bella:
m'erano vecchie d'Odisseo le gesta.
Sonno è la vita quando è già vissuta:
sonno; chè ciò che non è tutto, è nulla.
Io, desto alfine nella patria terra,
ero com'uomo che nella novella
alba sognò, nè sa qual sogno, e pensa
che molto è dolce a ripensar qual era.
Or io mi voglio rituffar nel sonno,
s'io trovi in fondo dell'oblio quel sogno.
Tu verrai meco. Ma mi narra il vero:
qual canto ascolti, di qual dolce aedo?
Ch'io non so, nella scabra isola, che altri
abbia nel cuore inseminati i canti".
E il vecchio Aedo al vecchio Eroe rispose:
"Questo, di questo. Un nicchio vile, un lungo
tortile nicchio, aspro di fuori, azzurro

my heart strewn with songs without end.
I sang to you, god-like Odysseus,
when your shadowy hall was full of corpses
like fishes that the fisherman
has left to die there flashing, in the sun.
I still see your slave girls, hours from death,
wiping the blood with water and porous
sponges. They sobbed and wailed. I sang for you,
and you listened in silence, drinking your wine.
But soon you tired of songs that were less
than deeds done. And now I listen,
alone, in silence. I threw
my harp away. It was picked up
by an old sailor with red eyes
and fingers fit only for rigging. And now
who plays the thing? Only the wind."
The aged hero replied to the poet:
"Phemius, old age has insulted us both,
robbing us of the pleasures
that we once enjoyed. Never
did one of your new songs appear to me
anything but new. Newer each time,
and finer! But the deeds of Odysseus
got old. Life that's already been lived
is sleep. It's everything or nothing.
I, at last awake in my fatherland,
was like a man at dawn who's dreamed
a dream that he can't quite remember,
though it's sweet to linger on it.
Now I want to plunge back into that sleep
so I might find that dream again
in oblivion. You'll come with me.
But tell me the truth: what song do you hear,
and who sings it? Because I don't know
anyone else on this stony island
whose heart has been seeded with so many songs."
And the aged poet to the aged hero:
"This, from this. A humble shell,
a long, coiled shell, rough on the outside

di dentro, e puro, non, Eroe, più grande
del nostro orecchio; e tutto ha dentro il mare,
con le burrasche e le ritrose calme,
coi venti acuti e il ciangottìo dell'acque.
Una conchiglia, breve, perché l'oda
il breve orecchio, ma che il tutto v'oda;
tale è l'Aedo. Pure a te non piacque".
Con un sorriso il vecchio Eroe rispose:
"Terpiade Femio, assai più grande è il mare!"

XI. La nave in secco

E il vecchio Aedo e il vecchio Eroe movendo
seguian la spiaggia del sonante mare,
molto pensando, e là, sul curvo lido,
piccola e nera, apparve lor la nave.
Vedean la poppa, e n'era lunga l'ombra
sopra la sabbia; nè molt'alto il sole.
E sopra lei bianchi tra mare e cielo
galleggiavano striduli gabbiani.
E vide l'occhio dell'Eroe che fresca
era la pece: e vide che le pietre
giaceano in parte, chè placato il vento
già non faceva più brandir la nave;
e vide in giro dagli scalmi acuti
pender gli stroppi di bovino cuoio;
e vide dal righino alto di poppa
sporger le pale di ben fatti remi.
Gli rise il cuore, poi che pronta al corso
era la nave; e le moveva intorno,
come al carro di guerra agile auriga
prima di addurre i due cavalli al giogo.
E venuto alla prua rossa di minio,
sopra la sabbia vide assisi in cerchio
i suoi compagni, tutti volti al mare
tacitamente; e si godeano il sole,
e la primaverile brezza arguta
s'udian fischiare nelle bianche barbe.

and blue inside, and pure; no larger,
hero, than one of our ears, and yet
it has the whole sea inside
with its raucous storms and bashful calms,
its cutting winds and babble of waters.
A sea-shell – small, so that a small ear
can hear, but hear everything:
that's the poet's craft. Which for you got old."
The hero answered with a smile:
"The sea, dear Phemius, is a little bit larger!"

XI. The Grounded Ship

The hero and the poet walked pensively
along the shore of the sounding sea.
And there, tucked inside the bay,
a ship appeared, slender and black.
They saw its stern, its long shadow
cast on the sand by the setting sun.
And over it, stridulous white seagulls
floated between the sky and the sea.
The keen eye of the hero saw
that the pitch was fresh and the stones
lay on one side, for the wind
had abated and no longer shook the ship.
He saw cowhide ropes on the side
of the ship, hanging from the oarlocks.
He saw the blades of the well-made oars
jut from the high-water mark of the stern.
He secretly smiled: the ship was ready
to sail. And he circled her
like a charioteer circles his chariot
before he yokes his two horses.
He went up to the crimson prow,
and his old companions were there,
sitting on the sand, staring at the sea,
listening to the cool springtime wind
blow through their white beards.

Sedean come per uso i longiremi
vecchi compagni d'Odisseo sul lido,
e da dieci anni lo attendean sul mare
col tempo bello e con la nuova aurora.
E veduta la rondine, le donne
recavano alla nave alte sul capo
l'anfore piene di fiammante vino
e pieni d'orzo triturato gli otri.
E prima che la nuova alba spargesse
le rose in cielo, essi veniano al mare,
i longiremi d'Odisseo compagni,
reggendo sopra il forte omero i remi,
ognuno il suo. Poi su la rena assisi
stavano, sotto la purpurea prora,
con gli occhi rossi a numerar l'ondate,
ad ascoltarsi il vento nelle barbe,
ad ascoltare striduli gabbiani,
cantare in mare marinai lontani.
Poi quando il sole si tuffava e quando
sopra venia l'oscurità, ciascuno
prendeva il remo, ed alle sparse case
tornavan muti per le strade ombrate.

XII. *Il timone*

Ed ecco, appena il vecchio Eroe comparve,
sorsero tutti, fermi in lui con gli occhi
Come quando nel verno ispido i bovi
giacciono, avvinti, innanzi al lor presepe;
sdraiati a terra ruminano il pasto
povero, mentre frusciano l'acquate;
se con un fascio d'odoroso fieno
viene il bifolco, sorgono, pur lenta-
mente, nè gli occhi stolgono dal fascio:
così sorsero i vecchi, ma nessuno
gli andava, stretto da pudor, più presso.
Ed egli, sotto il teschio irto del lupo,
così parlò tra lo sciacquìo del mare:

They sat on the beach like they used to,
his old friends with their long oars.
Ten years they had waited for him
in the fair weather and the spring morning.
As the first birds came, their wives
carried down to the ship casks
brimming with flaming red wine
and goatskins full of crushed barley.
Before the spring dawn could spread
its roses all over the sky, the oarsmen
would come to the beach, Odysseus' friends,
with their oars on their shoulders,
each his own. They sat on the sand
under the cinnabar prow,
red-eyed, counting the sea waves,
feeling the wind in their beards,
hearing the stridulous seagulls
and far-off sailors sing on the sea.
Each day, when the sun set in the sea
and darkness prevailed, all would take
their oars and return to their scattered homes
as the roads quickly filled with shadows.

XII. The Rudder

When the old hero appeared,
they all stood up, their eyes fixed on him.
As when oxen in the rough winter
lie down, tied up before their manger,
and slowly chew their humble meal
while the rain comes whooshing down,
and if a cowherd brings a bundle
of fragrant hay, they slowly get up,
their eyes fixed upon the hay,
the old men rose too, but they were all
far too shy to go near him.
The hero then spoke from under
the rough wolfskin on his head,
and his words mixed with the crashing waves:

"Compagni, udite ciò che il cuor mi chiede
sino da quando ritornai per sempre.
Per sempre? chiese, e, No, rispose il cuore.
Tornare, ei volle; terminar, non vuole.
Si desse, giunti alla lor selva, ai remi
barbàre in terra e verzicare abeti!
Ma no! Nè può la nera nave al fischio
del vento dar la tonda ombra di pino.
E pur non vuole il rosichìo del tarlo,
ma l'ondata, ma il vento e l'uragano.
Anch'io la nube voglio, e non il fumo,
il vento, e non il sibilo del fuso,
non l'ozïoso fuoco che sonnacchia,
ma il cielo e il mare che risplende e canta.
Compagni, come il nostro mare io sono,
ch'è bianco all'orlo, ma cilestro in fondo.
Io non so che, lasciai, quando alla fune
diedi, lo stolto che pur fui, la scure;
nell'antro a mare ombrato da un gran lauro,
nei prati molli di viola e d'appio,
o dove erano cani d'oro a guardia,
immortalmente, della grande casa,
e dove uomini in forma di leoni
battean le lunghe code in veder noi,
o non so dove. E vi ritorno. Io vedo
che ciò che feci è già minor del vero.
Voi lo sapete, che portaste al lido
negli otri l'orzo triturato, e il vino
color di fiamma nel ben chiuso doglio,
che l'uno è sangue e l'altro a noi midollo.
E spalmaste la pece alla carena,
ch'è come l'olio per l'ignudo atleta;
e portaste le gomene che serpi
dormono in groppo o sibilano ai venti;
e toglieste le pietre, anche portaste
l'aerea vela; alla dormente nave,
che sempre sogna nel giacere in secco,

"Friends, hear what my heart has asked
ever since I settled in Ithaca forever.
Forever? My heart said no. I longed
to return, yes, but not to end it all,
as if oars could take root in the woods
and become the green firs they once were!
Nor can the black ship cast again
the round shadow of a pine tree,
nor does she miss the gnawing of woodworms
but loves the wave, the wind, and the storm.
I too want clouds, not the smoke of the hearth;
the wild wind, not the whir of the spindle;
not the idle fireplace snoring,
but the sky and the sea that dazzles and sings.
Friends, you see, I am like our sea,
white on the edge, but blue deep down.
I don't know what I forsook when,
like a fool, I hung my axe with ropes.
In the seaside cave shaded by laurels,
in the soft fields of violet and celery,
or where golden dogs were watching
over the palace, eternally,
or where men, turned into lions,
wagged their tails upon seeing us.
I forgot where else, but I'll go back.
I see that my deeds fade from my memory.
As well you know, because you brought
your crushed barley poured into goatskins,
and flaming red wine in sealed casks,
one is our blood, the other's our marrow.
And you smeared the hull of the ship with pitch
as a naked athlete oils his skin,
and carried the hawsers, which are like snakes
sleeping in knots or hissing in the wind.
You cleared off the stones, and you carried
the light sails to the ship asleep,
who dreams while she lies grounded.

portaste ognun la vostra ala di remo;
e ora dunque alla ben fatta nave
che manca più, vecchi compagni? Al mare
la vecchia nave: amici, ecco il timone".
Così parlò tra il sussurrìo dell'onde.

XIII. La partenza

Ed ecco a tutti colorirsi il cuore
dell'azzurro color di lontananza;
e vi scorsero l'ombra del Ciclope
e v'udirono il canto della Maga:
l'uno parava sufolando al monte
pecore tante, quante sono l'onde;
l'altra tessea cantando l'immortale
sua tela così grande come il mare.
E tutti al mare trassero la nave
su travi tonde, come su le ruote;
e avvinsero gli ormeggi ad un lentisco
che verzicava sopra un erto scoglio;
e già salito, il vecchio Eroe nell'occhio
fece passar la barra del timone;
e stette in piedi sopra la pedagna.
Era seduto presso lui l'Aedo.
E con un cenno fece ai remiganti
salir la nave ed impugnare il remo:
sedevano essi con ne' pugni il remo.
Egli tagliò la fune con la scure.
E cantava un cuculo tra le fronde,
cantava nella vigna un potatore,
passava un gregge lungo su la rena
con incessante gemere d'agnelli,
ricciute donne in lavatoi perenni
batteano a gara i panni alto cianciando
e dalle case d'Itaca rupestre
balzava in alto il fumo mattutino.
E i marinai seduti alle scalmiere
facean coi remi biancheggiar il flutto.

You brought your winged oars too.
What else does she, this well-made ship,
need, my dear friends? Let's sail it!
Hold the wheel, my loyal friends!"
His words mixed with the murmur of waves.

XIII. Departure

And everyone's heart suddenly turned
the blue color of the far horizon.
They saw the shadow of the Cyclops.
They heard the sorceress' song.
The giant played his pipe as he grazed
as many sheep as the waves in the sea.
Circe sang as she wove a cloth
as immortal and wide as the sea.
They dragged the ship to the shore
on rounded beams, as if they were wheels,
and tied the mooring ropes to a lentisk
that grew green on a pointy rock.
The hero, already on board,
made the tiller pass through the eye
of the rudder. He stood on the stretcher,
and the poet sat beside him.
With a nod, he had the sailors
climb aboard the ship and grip the oars.
Then he cut the hawser with his axe.
A cuckoo sang in the trees,
a pruner sang in his vineyard,
a flock of sheep crossed the beach
with the incessant bleating of lambs.
Women with curly hair chattered,
rinsing their clothes in old washhouses.
The morning smoke leaped high
from the houses of stony Ithaca.
The sailors seated at their oarlocks
made the waves white with foam.

E Femio vide sopra un alto groppo
di cavi attorti la vocal sua cetra,
la cetra ch'egli avea gittata, e un vecchio
dagli occhi rossi lieto avea raccolta
e portata alla nave, ai suoi compagni;
ed era a tutti, l'aurea cetra, a cuore,
come a bambino infante un rondinotto
morto, che così morto egli carezza
lieve con dita inabili e gli parla,
e teme e spera che gli prenda il volo.
E Femio prese la sua cetra, e lieve
la toccò, poi, forte intonò la voga
ai remiganti. E quell'arguto squillo
svegliò nel cuore immemore dei vecchi
canti sopiti; e curvi sopra i remi
cantarono con rauche esili voci.
— Ecco la rondine! Ecco la rondine! Apri!
ch'ella ti porta il bel tempo, i belli anni.
È nera sopra, ed il suo petto è bianco.
È venuta da uno che può tanto.
Oh! apriti da te, uscio di casa,
ch'entri costì la pace e l'abbondanza,
e il vino dentro il doglio da sé vada
e il pane d'orzo empia da sé la madia.
Uno anc'a noi, col sesamo, puoi darne!
Presto, ché non siam qui per albergare.
Apri, ché sto su l'uscio a piedi nudi!
Apri, ché non siam vecchi ma fanciulli!—

XIV. Il pitocco

Cantavano; e il lor canto era fanciullo,
dei tempi andati; non sapean che quello
e nella stiva in cui giaceva immerso
nel dolce sonno, si stirò le braccia
e si sfregò le palpebre coi pugni

And Phemius saw on a knot of twisted ropes
his old melodious harp, the harp
he had cast aside, which an old man
with red eyes had gladly picked up
and brought back to the ship.
Everyone loved the silvery harp
as a child loves a dead swallow
and caresses the bird's cold body
with clumsy fingers and speaks to it,
hoping it will wake and fly again.
Phemius took his harp, gently plucked
its strings, then played to the beat
of the oars. That silvery voice
reached their oblivious hearts and awoke
songs from their past. Bent over their oars,
they sang again with frail and hoarse voices:
"The swallow! The swallow! Open! The light![1]
It brings fair weather, it brings flowers!
Its back is black, but its breast is white
and comes from someone with power.
Open yourself, door, open yourself!
Let peace and abundance come in!
And wine will fill our kilderkin,
and bread will fill our shelf!
Give us one sesame loaf. Hurry,
for we are not here for the night.
We stand barefoot at your doorstep,
no longer old men, but young boys!"

XIV. The Beggar

They sang, and their song was childlike,
of a time gone by, as they knew no other.
In the hold where he lay asleep,
Irus the beggar stretched his arms
and rubbed his eyes with his fists.

1.   Here Pascoli inserts the translations of two traditional Greek songs, "The Song
of the Swallow" (from Rhodes) and "The Song of the Swallow" (from Samos). Bits
of the first song are also included in the first of *Convivial Poems,* "Solon."

Iro, il pitocco. E niuno lo sapeva
laggiù, qual grosso baco che si chiude
in un irsuto bozzolo lanoso,
forse a dormire. Ché solea nel verno
lì nella nave d'Odisseo dormire,
se lo cacciava dalla calda stalla
l'uomo bifolco, o s'ei temeva i cani
del pecoraio. Nella buona estate
dormia sotto le stelle alla rugiada.
Ora quivi obliava la vecchiaia
trista e la fame: quando il suono e il canto
lo destò. Dentro gli ondeggiava il cuore:
— Non odo il suono della cetra arguta?
Dunque non era sogno il mio, che or ora
portavo ai proci, ai proci morti, un messo:
ed ecco nell'opaco atrio la cetra
udivo, e le lor voci esili e rauche.
Invero udiva il tintinnio tuttora
e il canto fioco tra il fragor dell'onde,
qual di querule querule ranelle
per un'acquata, quando ancor c'è il sole.
E tra sé favellava Iro il pitocco:
— O son presso ad un vero atrio di vivi?
e forse alcuno mi tirò pel piede
sino al cortile, poi che la mascella
sotto l'orecchio mi fiaccò col pugno?
Come altra volta, che Odisseo divino
lottò con Iro, malvestiti entrambi.
Così pensando si rizzò sui piedi
e su le mani, e gli fiottava il capo,
e movendo traballava come ebbro
di molto vino; e ad Odisseo comparve,
nuotando a vuoto, ed ai remigatori,
terribile. Ecco e s'interruppe il canto,
e i remi alzati non ripreser l'acqua,
e la nave da prua si drizzò, come
cavallo indomito, e lanciò supino,

Nobody knew he was down there
like an enormous silkworm dozing
inside a fuzzy, woolly cocoon.
In the winter, he'd taken up the habit
of sleeping in Odysseus' ship
when the farmer kicked him out
of the stable or if he feared
the shepherd's dogs. In the warm summer,
he slept under the star on the dewy grass
where he could forget old age and hunger.
The noise and the singing had woken him.
His heart was pounding inside his chest:
"Do I not hear the sound of the silvery harp?
Did I not dream that I'd carried a message
to Penelope's suitors, but they were dead,
and the harp echoed in the dark hall,
and I heard these voices, frail and hoarse?"
Indeed, he still heard that tinkling sound
and a faint song through the crash of the waves,
faint as the griping of an army of frogs
in a sunshower. He mumbled to himself:
"Am I in a hall full of living men?
Has anyone dragged me by the foot
to the courtyard and broken my jaw
right under my ear with his clenched fist
like the time divine Odysseus, disguised
as a beggar, beat up the beggar Irus?"
Irus quickly got up on his feet.
His head was spinning, he reeled like a drunkard.
He suddenly appeared before Odysseus
and his sailors, paddling in the air,
a dreadful sight. They stopped singing,
raised up their oars from the water,
and the ship reared like a wild horse.
Irus lost his balance and fell on his back

a piè di Femio e d'Odisseo seduti,
Iro il pitocco. E lo conobbe ognuno
quando, abbrancati i lor ginocchi, sorse
inginocchioni, e gli grondava il sangue
giù per il mento dalle labbra e il naso.
E un dolce riso si levò di tutti,
alto, infinito. Ed egli allor comprese,
e vide dileguare Itaca, e vide
sparir le case, onde balzava il fumo:
e le due coscie si percosse e pianse.
E sorridendo il vecchio Eroe gli disse:
"Soffri. Hai qui tetto e letto, e orzo e vino.
Sii nella nave il dispensier del cibo,
e bevi e mangia e dormi, Iro non-Iro".

XV. La procella

E sopra il flutto nove dì la nave
corse sospinta dal remeggio alato,
e notte e giorno, ché Odisseo due schiere
dinumerò degl'incliti compagni;
e l'una al sonno e l'altra era alla voga.
Nel decimo l'aurora mattiniera
a un lieve vento dispergea le rose.
Ei dalla scassa l'albero d'abete
levò, lo congegnò dentro la mastra,
e con drizze di cuoio alzò la vela,
ben torto, e saldi avvinse alle caviglie
di prua li stragli, ma di poppa i bracci.
E il vento urtò la vela in mezzo, e il flutto
rumoreggiava intorno alla carena.
E legarono allora anche le scotte
lungo la nave che correa veloce:
e pose in mezzo un'anfora di vino
Iro il pitocco, ed arrancando intorno
lo ministrava ai marinai seduti;
e sorse un riso. E nove dì sul flutto
li resse in corsa il vento e il timoniere.

at the feet of Odysseus and Phemius.
Everyone recognized the beggar Irus
when he got up and clutched their knees
kneeling before them, blood dripping down
his chin from his nose and lips.
And sweet laughter rose from the crew,
loud and long. Irus understood.
He saw Ithaca disappearing in the distance,
its houses vanishing as smoke leaped up.
He beat his thighs and began to weep.
The old hero smiled and said to him:
"Cheer up. Here you have room and board,
barley and wine. Be our pantryman,
and drink and sleep, Irus no-Irus."

XV. The Storm

For nine days the ship sailed,
propelled by its winged oars,
by night and by day, as Odysseus had
divided the sailors into two groups:
one rowed while the other slept.
On the tenth day, the morning breeze
spread rose petals all over the sky.
He lifted the mast from its block
and set it up inside the mast-hole hatch.
He raised the topsail with halyards
of twisted leather, and he bound the stays
to the prow pegs and the brackets to the stern.
The wind struck the sail in the middle,
the waves roared against the hull.
They then secured the sheets
alongside the ship, which sailed fast.
The beggar Irus placed a big cask
in the middle. He poured wine
for the sailors, hobbling,
and they all laughed. Nine days
the ship sailed with wind and wheel.

Nel decimo tra nubi era l'aurora,
e venne notte, ed una aspra procella
tre quattro strappi fece nella vela;
e il Laertiade ammainò la vela,
e disse a tutti di gettarsi ai remi;
ed essi curvi sopra sé di forza
remigavano. E nove dì sbalzati
eran dai flutti e da funesti venti.
Infine i venti rappaciati e i flutti,
sul far di sera, videro una spiaggia.
A quella spinse il vecchio Eroe la nave,
in un seno tranquillo come un letto.
E domati da sonno e da stanchezza,
dormian sul lido, ove batteva l'onda.
Ma non dormiva egli, Odisseo, pur vinto
dalla stanchezza. Ché pensava in cuore
d'essere giunto all'isola di Circe:
vedea la casa di pulite pietre,
come in un sogno, e sorgere leoni
lenti, e le rosse bocche allo sbadiglio
aprire, e un poco già scodinzolare;
e risonava il grande atrio del canto
di tessitrice. Ora Odisseo parlava:
"Terpiade Femio, dormi? Odimi: il sogno
dolce e dimenticato ecco io risogno!
Era l'amore; ch'ora mi sommuove,
come procella omai finita, il cuore".
Diceva; e nella notte alta e serena
dormiva il vento, e vi sorgea la falce,
su macchie e selve, della bianca luna
già presso al fine, e s'effondea l'olezzo
di grandi aperti calici di fiori
non mai veduti. Ed il gran mare ancora
si ricordava, e con le lunghe ondate
bianche di schiuma singhiozzava al lido.

On the tenth day, the dawn was cloudy.
Night fell, and a sudden storm
made three or four tears in the sails.
Odysseus lowered the sail and
told the crew to start rowing.
Bent over, they rowed and rowed
with all their strength. For nine days,
they were flung about by baleful winds.
When at last the storm abated,
they saw a shore in the twilight.
The hero set sail towards that inlet,
which seemed to them like a bed.
Sleep then conquered the sailors,
who lay exhausted on the wet seashore.
But he could not sleep, Odysseus,
tired as he was, since he thought
he had reached the island of Circe.
As in a dream, he saw her house
of polished stones. Her lions got up
slowly, their red jaws opened
in a yawn, and they wagged their tails.
And then the great hall echoed
with the weaver's song. He said:
"Phemius, son of Therpes, are you sleeping?
I dream that sweet forgotten dream,
love…which stirs my heart still
like a storm when it's almost over."
He spoke, and in the deep starry night,
the wind slept and the moon rose
over woods and meadows, a pale sliver
of moon. All around was the scent
of open calices, of mysterious invisible
flowers. The vast sea remembered,
and with the motion of its frothy waves,
it sighed and sobbed on the shore.

XV. L'isola Eea

E con la luce rosea dell'aurora
s'avvide, ch'era l'isola di Circe.
E disse a Femio, al molto caro Aedo:
"Terpiade Femio, vieni a me compagno
con la tua cetra, ch'ella oda il tuo canto
mortale, e tu l'eterno inno ne apprenda".
E disse ad Iro, dispensier del cibo:
"Con gli altri presso il grigio mar tu resta,
e mangia e bevi, ch'ella non ti batta
con la sua verga, e n'abbi poi la ghianda
per cibo, e pianga, sgretolando il cibo,
con altra voce, o Iro non-più-Iro".
Così diceva sorridendo, e mosse
col dolce Aedo, per le macchie e i boschi,
e vide il passo donde l'alto cervo
d'arboree corna era disceso a bere:
Ma non vide la casa alta di Circe.
Or a lui disse il molto caro Aedo:
"C'è addietro. Una tempesta è il desiderio,
ch'agli occhi è nube quando ai piedi è vento".
Ma il luogo egli conobbe, ove gli occorse
il dio che salva, e riconobbe il poggio
donde strappò la buona erba, che nera
ha la radice, e come latte il fiore.
E non vide la casa alta di Circe.
Or a lui disse il molto caro Aedo:
"C'è innanzi. La vecchiezza è una gran calma,
che molto stanca, ma non molto avanza".
E proseguì pei monti e per le valli,
e selve e boschi, attento s'egli udisse
lunghi sbadigli di leoni, désti
al lor passaggio, o l'immortal canzone
di tessitrice, della dea vocale.
E nulla udì nell'isola deserta,
e nulla vide; e si tuffava il sole,
e la stellata oscurità discese.

XVI. Aeaea

And with the pink light of dawn,
he saw it was Circe's island.
He then said to his dear Phemius:
"Son of Therpes, accompany me
and bring your harp. She'll hear your mortal song,
and you will learn her immortal hymn."
And to old Irus, pantryman:
"Stay behind, near the gray sea,
eat and drink, lest she touch you
with her staff, and you be given acorns
for food and regret that, grunting
like a hog, Irus no-longer-Irus."
He said these words with a smile and left
with the poet. They crossed woods and meadows,
until they reached a river where a great stag
was drinking, his horns like a tree.
But Circe's house was not there.
His old friend, the poet, said to him:
"It's behind us. Desire is a storm,
which clouds the eyes and gives speed to the feet."
But he recognized the place where
Hermes had rescued him, the hill
where the god had plucked the magic herb
with black roots and milky flowers.
But Circe's high house was not there.
"It's ahead. Old age is like a calm sea:
it makes little progress, although it tires much."
And he passed hills and valleys,
woods and forests, watchful lest he hear
the long yawns of the lions alerted
by their footsteps or the immortal hymn
of the Weaver, divine singer.
He heard nothing on that deserted island,
nor did he see anything. The sun set,
and a starry darkness fell upon them.

E l'Eroe disse al molto caro Aedo:
"Troppo nel cielo sono alte le stelle,
perché la strada io possa ormai vedere.
Or qui dormiamo, ed assai caldo il letto
a noi facciamo; ché risorto è il vento".
Disse, e ambedue si giacquero tra molte
foglie cadute, che ammucchiate al tronco
di vecchie quercie aveva la procella;
e parvero nel mucchio, essi, due tizzi,
vecchi, riposti con un po' di fuoco,
sotto la grigia cenere infeconda.
E sopra loro alta stormìa la selva.
Ed ecco il cuore dell'Eroe leoni
udì ruggire. Avean dormito il giorno,
certo, e l'eccelsa casa era vicina.
Invero intese anche la voce arguta,
in lontananza, della dea, che, sola,
non prendea sonno e ancor tessea notturna.
Né prendea sonno egli, Odisseo, ma spesso
si volgea su le foglie stridule aspre.

XVII. L'amore

E con la luce rosea dell'aurora
non udì più ruggito di leoni,
che stanchi alfine di vegliar, col muso
dormian disteso su le lunghe zampe.
Dormiva anch'ella, allo smorir dell'alba,
pallida e scinta sopra il noto letto.
E il vecchio Eroe parlava al vecchio Aedo:
Prenda ciascuno una sua via: ch'è meglio.
"Ma diamo un segno; con la cetra, Aedo,
tu, che ritrova pur da lungi il cuore.
Ma s'io ritrovi ciò che il cuor mi vuole,
ti getto allora un alalà di guerra,
quale gettavo nella mischia orrenda
eroe di bronzo sopra i morti ignudi,
io; che il cuore lo intenda anche da lungi".

The hero said to his beloved poet:
"The stars are too high in the sky
for me to discern my path.
Let's sleep here, and let's make ourselves
a warm bed, since the wind has risen again."
They both lay down among the fallen leaves,
which the storm had heaped
against the trunks of old oaks.
They seemed, in the leafy heap, like two embers
banked up with a little flame
under gray, barren ashes.
Above them, the trees rustled.
The hero's heart now heard the lions roar.
They had slept through the day,
and Circe's high house was nearby.
Indeed, he heard her silvery voice
in the distance: the goddess, alone,
was awake and wove in the night.
Nor could he sleep, Odysseus,
tossing and turning on the crackling leaves.

XVII. Love

And with the pink light of dawn,
he no longer heard the lions' roar.
Tired of watching, they slept
with their heads between their paws.
She too slept as the dawn wanned,
pale, undressed, on the bed he'd known.
The old hero said to the old poet:
"Best to take each a different path.
But let's give a sign: play your harp,
since its sound can reach my heart anywhere.
And if I find what my heart wants,
I will shout my alala,
the same I once shouted in battle,
in my bronze armor, among naked corpses,
and your heart will hear it wherever you are."

Disse, e taceva dei leoni uditi
nell'alta notte, e della dea canora.
E prese ognuno la sua via diversa
per macchie e boschi, e monti e valli, e nulla
udì l'Eroe, se non ruggir le quercie
a qualche rara raffica, e cantare
lontan lontano eternamente il mare.
E non vide la casa, nè i leoni
dormir col muso su le lunghe zampe,
nè la sua dea. Ma declinava il sole,
e tutte già s'ombravano le strade.
E mise allora un alalà di guerra
per ritrovare il vecchio Aedo, almeno;
e porse attento ad ogni aura l'orecchio
se udisse almeno della cetra il canto;
e sì, l'udì; traendo a lei, l'udiva,
sempre più mesta, sempre più soave,
cantar l'amore che dormia nel cuore,
e che destato solo allor ti muore.
La udì più presso, e non la vide, e vide
nel folto mucchio delle foglie secche
morto l'Aedo; e forse ora, movendo
pel cammino invisibile, tra i pioppi
e i salici che gettano il lor frutto,
toccava ancora con le morte dita
l'eburnea cetra: così mesto il canto
n'era, e così lontano e così vano.
Ma era in alto, a un ramo della quercia,
la cetra arguta, ove l'avea sospesa
Femio, morendo, a che l'Eroe chiamasse
brillando al sole o tintinnando al vento:
al vento che scotea gli alberi, al vento
che portava il singulto ermo del mare.
E l'Eroe pianse, e s'avviò notturno
alla sua nave, abbandonando morto
il dolce Aedo, sopra cui moveva
le foglie secche e l'aurea cetra il vento.

He said nothing of the lions he'd heard
in the night or of the singing goddess.
And each took a different path
through woods, forests, hills, and valleys.
But all he heard was oaks rustling
in rare gusts of wind and the sea
in the distance, singing its eternal song.
He didn't see the house, nor the lions
sleeping with their heads between their paws,
nor his goddess. The sun was already setting,
and all the paths quickly filled with shadows.
Then he shouted his alala
so that he could at least find the old poet
and listened to each gust of wind
so that his heart could hear the harp.
Yes, he heard it. As he moved closer,
he heard its bittersweet song
of love that sleeps in one's heart
and no sooner awakens than dies.
He heard it and could not yet see it
but saw the poet, lying dead
on a thick bed of dry leaves.
Perhaps he still plucked the strings with dead fingers,
as he walked on invisible paths
among barren poplars and willows.
And the tune he played was so mournful
and faint, already fading away.
The harp dangled from the branch of an oak.
The dying poet had hung it there
so that its strings could give a sign to the hero,
gleaming in the sun or tinkling in the wind,
in the wind that stirred the trees
and carried the distant sob of the sea.
And the hero wept as he returned
to the ship, leaving the dead poet
behind. Above him, the wind played
a sad song with the harp and the falling leaves.

XVIII. *L'isola delle Capre*

Indi più lungi navigò, più triste,
E corse i flutti nove dì la nave
or col remeggio or con la bianca vela.
E giunse alfine all'isola selvaggia
ch'è senza genti e capre sole alleva.
E qui vinti da sonno e da stanchezza
dormian sul lido a cui batteva l'onda.
Ma con la luce rosea dell'aurora
vide Odisseo la terra dei Ciclopi,
non presso o lungi, e gli sovvenne il vanto
ch'ei riportò con la sua forza e il senno,
del mangiatore d'uomini gigante.
Ed oblioso egli cercò l'Aedo
per dire a lui: Terpiade Femio, il sogno
dolce e dimenticato io lo risogno:
era la gloria… Ma il vocale Aedo
dormia sotto le stridule aspre foglie,
e la sua cetra là cantava al vento
il dolce amore addormentato in cuore,
che appena desto solo allor ti muore.
E l'Eroe disse ai vecchi remiganti:
"Compagni, udite. Qui non son che capre;
e qui potremmo d'infinita carne
empirci, fino a che sparisca il sole.
Ma no: le voglio prendere al pastore,
pecore e capre; ch'è, così, ben meglio.
È là, pari a un cocuzzolo silvestro,
quel mio pastore. Io l'accecai. Ma il grande
cuor non m'è pago. Egli implorò dal padre,
ch'io perdessi al ritorno i miei compagni,
e mal tornassi, e in nave d'altri, e tardi.
Or sappia che ho compagni e che ritorno

XVIII. Goat Island

Thence he sailed on, sadder.
For nine days the ship rode the waves,
propelled by oars or by sail,
until it reached a wild island
inhabited only by wild goats.
There, vanquished by sleep and fatigue,
they slept on the wet seashore.
But, with the pink light of dawn,
Odysseus saw the land of the Cyclopes,
neither near nor far, and he remembered
how his guile and strength had helped him
win the fight against the man-eating brute.
He unconsciously turned to his poet
to say to him, "Phemius, son of Therpes,
I've dreamed that sweet, forgotten dream,
glory...." But the singing poet
lay dead on the stridulous leaves,
and his harp was singing to the wind
of love that sleeps in one's heart
and no sooner awakens than dies.
The hero called his oarsmen:
"Friends, there are only goats
here, and we could fill our bellies
with good meat until the sun goes down.
But I want to rob the shepherd
of his goats, a glorious deed.
There he is, like a wooded summit,
my shepherd. I blinded him.
But my heart still isn't sated,
for he prayed to his father[2] that I might lose
all my companions on my voyage home,
and that I would come home unhappily,
many years later, in someone else's ship.
He must know that I have my crew now,

2.   The shepherd whom Odysseus remembers is the Cyclops Polyphemus,
son of the god Poseidon.

sopra nave ben mia dal mio ritorno.
Andiamo: a mare troveremo un antro
tutto coperto, io ben lo so, di lauro.
Avessi ancora il mio divino Aedo!
Vorrei che il canto d'Odisseo là dentro
cantasse, e quegli nel tornare all'antro
sostasse cieco ad ascoltar quel canto,
coi greggi attorno, il mento sopra il pino.
E io sedessi all'ombra sua, nel lido!"
Disse, e ai compagni longiremi ingiunse
di salir essi e sciogliere gli ormeggi.
Salirono essi, e in fila alle scalmiere
facean coi remi biancheggiare il flutto.
E giunti presso, videro sul mare,
in una punta, l'antro, alto, coperto
di molto lauro, e v'era intorno il chiuso
di rozzi blocchi, e lunghi pini e quercie
altochiomanti. E il vecchio Eroe parlava:
"Là prendiam terra, ch'egli dal remeggio
non ci avvisti; ch'a gli orbi occhio è l'orecchio;
e non ci avventi un masso, come quello
che troncò in cima di quel picco nero,
e ci scagliò. Rimbombò l'onda al colpo".
Ed accennava un alto monte, tronco
del capo, che sorgeva solitario.

XIX. Il Ciclope

Ecco: ai compagni disse di restare
presso la nave e di guardar la nave.
Ed egli all'antro già movea, soletto,
per lui vedere non veduto, quando
parasse i greggi sufolando al monte.
Ora all'Eroe parlava Iro il pitocco:
"Ben verrei teco per veder quell'uomo
che tanto mangia, e portar via, se posso,
di sui cannicci, già scolati i caci,
e qualche agnello dai gremiti stabbi.

and I return from my land on my own ship.
Let's go. There will be a cave by the sea,
all hidden behind laurel leaves.
If only my poet still lived,
he would sing Odysseus' song
in the cave so that the giant, returning,
would stop and listen, blind as he is,
with his flock and his wooden crook,
and I sitting in his great shadow!"
He said these words and ordered his oarsmen
to board the ship and untie the hawsers.
They got on board, bent over their oars,
and made the waves white with foam.
As they drew near, they saw the cave
on the shore, on a rocky point,
hidden behind laurel leaves, with a fence
of sturdy rocks, tall pine trees,
and oaks. And the hero said:
"Let's touch land here, so he won't spot us —
the ear is a blind man's eye —
and so he won't hurl his stones at us
like the one he cut from the mountain
and threw at us, making the sea rumble.
And he showed them a mountain with its top
cut off, standing out in the distance.

XIX. The Cyclops

He commanded his friends to stay
near the ship and watch over it.
He wanted to reach that cave alone
so he might see, unseen, the giant
as he watched his flock on the mountain.
Irus, the beggar, said to the hero:
"I should like to come too and see
that big glutton and perhaps steal
his cheeses from their drying trays
and some lambs from his crowded folds.

Poi ch'Iro ha fame. E s'ei dentro ci fosse,
il gran Ciclope, sai ch'Iro è veloce
ben che non forte; è come Iri del cielo
che va sul vento con il piè di vento".
L'Eroe sorrise, e insieme i due movendo,
il pitocco e l'Eroe, giunsero all'antro.
Dentro e' non era. Egli pasceva al monte
i pingui greggi. E i due meravigliando
vedean graticci pieni di formaggi,
e gremiti d'agnelli e di capretti
gli stabbi, e separati erano, ognuni
ne' loro, i primaticci, i mezzanelli
e i serotini. E d'uno dei recinti
ecco che uscì, con alla poppa il bimbo,
un'altocinta femmina, che disse:
"Ospiti, gioia sia con voi. Chi siete?
donde venuti? a cambiar qui, qual merce?
Ma l'uomo è fuori, con la greggia, al monte;
tra poco torna, ché già brucia il sole.
Ma pur mangiate, se il tardar v'è noia".
Sorrise ad Iro il vecchio Eroe: poi disse:
"Ospite donna, e pur con te sia gioia.
Ma dunque l'uomo a venerare apprese
gli dei beati, ed ora sa la legge,
benché tuttora abiti le spelonche,
come i suoi pari, per lo scabro monte?"
E l'altocinta femmina rispose:
"Ospite, ognuno alla sua casa è legge,
e della moglie e de' suoi nati è re.
Ma noi non deprediamo altri: ben altri,
ch'errano in vano su le nere navi,
come ladroni, a noi pecore o capre
hanno predate. Altrui portando il male
rischian essi la vita. Ma voi siete
vecchi, e cercate un dono qui, non prede".
Verso Iro il vecchio anche ammiccò: poi disse:
"Ospite donna, ben di lui conosco
quale sia l'ospitale ultimo dono".

Irus is hungry. If the great Cyclops
was there, Irus would be swift,
though he's weak, as swift as Iris,
the wind-footed rider of winds."
The old hero smiled, and together
beggar and king reached the cave.
It was empty, since the shepherd
was grazing his fat flock on the mountain.
Plenty of cheese in the baskets,
lambs and kids in the folds:
one fold for each kind,
the first born, the second born,
and the youngest. A high-girdled woman
came forth from one of the pens,
nursing her child at her breast:
"Guests, joy be with you. Who are you,
and what have you come to barter?
My man is away with the flock,
but he'll soon return, for the sun is hot.
If the wait is too long, eat now."
The hero smiled at Irus and said:
"Joy be with you, too, kind lady.
Has your man learned to worship
the gods and observe human law
although he still inhabits a cave
in a rugged mountain, like all his peers?"
The high-girdled woman replied:
"Guest, every man is a king in his house,
ruling over his wife and children.
But we do not rob each other.
Others landed here from their black ships
and raided all of our flocks.
Others risked their lives to bring
death. But I see that you're old
and seek no spoils, but succor."
The old hero winked at Irus again:
"Woman, I know very well
the succor your man will give us."

Ed ecco un grande tremulo belato
s'udì venire, e un suono di zampogna,
e sufolare a pecore sbandate:
e ne' lor chiusi si levò più forte
il vagir degli agnelli e dei capretti.
Ch'egli veniva, e con fragore immenso
depose un grande carico di selva
fuori dell'antro: e ne rintronò l'antro.
E Iro in fondo s'appiattò tremando.

XX. La gloria

E l'uomo entrò, ma l'altocinta donna
gli venne incontro, e lo seguiano i figli
molti, e le molte pecore e le capre
l'una all'altra addossate erano impaccio,
per arrivare ai piccoli. E infinito
era il belato, e l'alte grida, e il fischio.
Ma in breve tacque il gemito, e ciascuno
suggea scodinzolando la sua poppa.
E l'uomo vide il vecchio Eroe che in cuore
meravigliava ch'egli fosse un uomo;
e gli parlò con le parole alate:
"Ospite, mangia. Assai per te ne abbiamo".
Ed al pastore il vecchio Eroe rispose:
"Ospite, dimmi. Io venni di lontano,
molto lontano; eppur io già, dal canto
d'erranti aedi, conoscea quest'antro.
Io sapea d'un enorme uomo gigante
che vivea tra infinite greggie bianche,
selvaggiamente, qui su i monti, solo
come un gran picco; con un occhio tondo…"
Ed il pastore al vecchio Eroe rispose:
"Venni di dentro terra, io, da molt'anni;
e nulla seppi d'uomini giganti".
E l'Eroe riprendeva, ed i fanciulli
gli erano attorno, del pastore, attenti:

They heard a sudden, tremulous bleat,
a reed pipe called the disbanded
sheep, and a man whistled to them.
In the folds the whimpering
of lambs and kids echoed loud.
The man came and put down a load
of wood with a loud thud,
which echoed inside the cave
and made Irus squat down in terror.

XX. Glory

As the shepherd entered, his woman
came to meet him with their many
children, goats, and sheep.
The flock all massed together, trying
to reach their little ones. Their bleating
was loud with shrill cries and whistles.
But shortly their whining ceased,
as the little ones sucked their mother's teats.
The shepherd saw the old hero, who secretly
wondered why he was not a giant,
and spoke these winged words to him:
"Guest, eat. We have enough for you."
And the hero answered him:
"Host, do tell me. I've come from afar,
a very far land. However, I knew
this cave from the song of wandering poets.
I knew of a huge giant
living among his many white herds,
wild and solitary on the mountains
like a remote peak and one-eyed...."
But the shepherd said: "I came
from the continent a long time
ago, but I've never heard of this giant."
The hero continued, surrounded
by the children who listened in awe:

"che aveva solo un occhio tondo, in fronte,
come uno scudo bronzeo, come il sole,
acceso, vuoto. Verga un pino gli era,
e gli era il sommo d'un gran monte, pietra
da fionda, e in mare li scagliava, e tutto
bombiva il mare al loro piombar giù…"
Ed il pastore, tra i suoi pastorelli,
pensava, e disse all'altocinta moglie:
"Non forse è questo che dicea tuo padre?
Che un savio c'era, uomo assai buono e grande
per qui, Telemo Eurymide, che vecchio
dicea che in mare piovea pietre, un tempo,
sì, da quel monte, che tra gli altri monti
era più grande; e che s'udian rimbombi
nell'alta notte, e che appariva un occhio
nella sua cima, un tondo occhio di fuoco…"
Ed al pastore chiese il moltaccorto:
"E l'occhio a lui chi trivellò notturno?"
Ed il pastore ad Odisseo rispose:
"Al monte? l'occhio? trivellò? Nessuno.
Ma nulla io vidi, e niente udii. Per nave
ci vien talvolta, e non altronde, il male".
Disse: e dal fondo Iro avanzò, che disse:
"Tu non hai che fanciulli per aiuto.
Prendi me, ben sì vecchio, ma nessuno
veloce ha il piede più di me, se debbo
cercar l'agnello o rintracciare il becco.
Per chi non ebbe un tetto mai, pastore,
quest'antro è buono. Io ti sarò garzone".

XXI. Le Sirene

Indi più lungi navigò, più triste.
E stando a poppa il vecchio Eroe guardava
scuro verso la terra de' Ciclopi,
e vide dal cocuzzolo selvaggio
del monte, che in disparte era degli altri,
levarsi su nel roseo cielo un fumo,

"He had one eye on his forehead,
round like a bronze shield or a sun,
red and hollow. His crook was a pine tree,
he used boulders for his slingshot.
He hurled them into the sea, and
the whole sea trembled." The shepherd,
pensive among his children, said
to his high-girdled wife:
"Is this not perhaps what your father told us?
There was a wise old man once,
named Telemus, son of Eurymus,
who saw stones rain in the sea
from the top of the tallest mountain,
where a round flaming eye appeared
and the dark night was full of thunder...."
The wily Odysseus asked the shepherd:
"An eye...who drilled that eye in the night?"
And the shepherd replied: "The eye of the mountain?
Drilled?... Nobody. I have never seen
nor heard anything. Harm sometimes
comes on a ship, not from inland."
Irus got up and suddenly said:
"You've no helping hand except your children.
Take me! I may be old but I'm faster
than most when I'm tracking down
a lost lamb or a wandering goat.
For someone as homeless as I am,
this cave's a good place: I will serve you."

XXI. The Sirens

Thence he sailed on, sadder.
Standing astern, the old hero stared
at the land of the Cyclopes, brooding.
And then, from one of the mountain tops,
which stood apart from the others,
a thin swirl of smoke rose in the pink sky,

tenue, leggiero, quale esce su l'alba
dal fuoco che al pastore arse la notte.
Ma i remiganti curvi sopra i remi
vedeano, sì, nel violaceo mare
lunghe tremare l'ombre dei Ciclopi
fermi sul lido come ispidi monti.
E il cuore intanto ad Odisseo vegliardo
squittiva dentro, come cane in sogno:
— Il mio sogno non era altro che sogno;
e vento e fumo. Ma sol buono è il vero.-
E gli sovvenne delle due Sirene.
C'era un prato di fiori in mezzo al mare.
Nella gran calma le ascoltò cantare:
— Ferma la nave! Odi le due Sirene
ch'hanno la voce come è dolce il miele;
ché niuno passa su la nave nera
che non si fermi ad ascoltarci appena,
e non ci ascolta, che non goda al canto,
né se ne va senza saper più tanto:
ché noi sappiamo tutto quanto avviene
sopra la terra dove è tanta gente!-
Gli sovveniva, e ripensò che Circe
gl'invidiasse ciò che solo è bello:
saper le cose. E ciò dovea la Maga
dalle molt'erbe, in mezzo alle sue belve.
Ma l'uomo eretto, ch'ha il pensier dal cielo,
dovea fermarsi, udire, anche se l'ossa
aveano poi da biancheggiar nel prato,
e raggrinzarsi intorno lor la pelle.
Passare ei non doveva oltre, se anco
gli si vietava riveder la moglie
e il caro figlio e la sua patria terra.
E ai vecchi curvi il vecchio Eroe parlò:
"Uomini, andiamo a ciò che solo è bene:
a udire il canto delle due Sirene.
Io voglio udirlo, eretto su la nave,
né già legato con le funi ignave:

such as the one that goes up at dawn
from a shepherd's fire, which has burned all night.
But the oarsmen bent over their oars
saw the long shadows of the Cyclopes
trembling on the wine-colored sea,
like bristly hills on the shore.
The old hero's heart yelped
inside him like a dreaming dog.
"What I dreamed was only a dream
of smoke and wind: only the truth is good."
And he remembered the two Sirens.
A meadow bloomed in the middle of the sea.
In that great calm, he heard their song:
"Stop the ship, hear the two Sirens,
whose voices are as sweet as honey!
No man sailing on their black ships
has ever refrained from listening to
and savoring our ancient song,
nor does one leave without gaining knowledge,
for we know all that happens
on earth with its many people!"
He thought of Circe refusing to grant
him the most precious treasure of all,
knowledge, which she guarded well,
the lady of lions and of spells.
But the upright man, whose thirst
for knowledge is divine, must listen,
although his white bones will cover
that meadow, and his skin will shrivel.
He ought not to sail there
if he ever wanted to see his wife
again, his son, and his land.
The hero spoke to his oarsmen:
"Let us find the one true treasure,
the ancient song of the two Sirens.
I want to hear it, upright on the ship,
not tied, as before, with cowardly ropes.

libero! alzando su la ciurma anela
la testa bianca come bianca vela;
e tutto quanto nella terra avviene
saper dal labbro delle due Sirene".
Disse, e ne punse ai remiganti il cuore,
che seduti coi remi battean l'acqua,
saper volendo ciò che avviene in terra:
se avea fruttato la sassosa vigna,
se la vacca avea fatto, se il vicino
aveva d'orzo più raccolto o meno,
e che facea la fida moglie allora,
se andava al fonte, se filava in casa.

XXII. In cammino

Ed ecco giunse all'isola dei loti.
E sedean sulla riva uomini e donne,
sazi di loto, in dolce oblìo composti.
E sorsero, ai canuti remiganti
offrendo pii la floreal vivanda.
"O così vecchi erranti per il mare,
mangiate il miele dell'oblìo ch'è tempo!"
Passò la nave, e lento per il cielo
il sonnolento lor grido vanì.
E quindi venne all'isola dei sassi.
E su le rupi stavano i giganti,
come in vedetta, e su la nave urlando
piovean pietre da carico con alto
fracasso. A stento si salvò la nav
E quindi giunse all'isola dei morti.
E giacean lungo il fiume uomini e donne,
sazi di vita, sotto i salci e i pioppi.
Volsero il capo; e videro quei vecchi;
e alcuno il figlio ravvisò fra loro,
più di lui vecchio, e per pietà di loro
gemean: Venite a riposare: è tempo!
Passò la nave, ed esile sul mare
il loro morto mormorio vanì.

Free, my white head like a white sail
over the heads of my breathless crew.
I will know everything that happens
on this earth from the lips of the Sirens."
He spoke and stung the hearts of his sailors,
who beat the water with their fast oars,
eager to know all that happened on earth:
if their stony vineyards had borne fruit,
or whether their cows had whelped,
if the neighbour's harvest was good,
and what their faithful wives were doing
by the river or spinning at home.

XXII. On the Way

They came to the Lotus Island.
Men and women lay on the shore,
sated with lotus in peaceful oblivion.
They rose and reached the oarsmen
with the flower of bliss in their hands:
"Old pilgrims of the vast sea,
time to taste our honey-sweet sleep!"
But the ship went by, and slowly
their somnolent voices faded.
Then they reached the Island of Rocks.
Giants stood on their cliffs, as though
on watch, howling, and rained heavy stones
on the ship with a sound of thunder.
The ship barely managed to escape,
and so they reached the Island of the Dead,
where people lay by the river,
sated with life under willows and poplars.
They turned their heads and saw those old men,
some of whom were their children,
but as gray and frail as their sires.
They urged them: "It is time to rest!"
The ship went by, and slowly
their spectral murmuring vanished.

E di lì venne all'isola del sole.
E pascean per i prati le giovenche
candide e nere, con le dee custodi.
Essi udiano mugliare nella luce
dorata. A stento lontanò la nave.
E di lì giunse all'isola del vento.
E sopra il muro d'infrangibil bronzo
vide i sei figli e le sei figlie a guardia.
E videro la nave essi, e nel bianco
suo timoniere, parso in prima un cigno
o una cicogna, uno Odisseo conobbe,
che così vecchio anco sfidava i venti;
e con un solo sibilo sul vecchio
scesero insieme di sul liscio masso.
Ed ora l'ira li portò, dei venti,
per giorni e notti, e li sospinse verso
le rupi erranti, ma così veloce,
che a mezzo un cozzo delle rupi dure
come uno strale scivolò la nave.
E allora l'aspra raffica discorde
portava lei contro Cariddi e Scilla.
E già l'Eroe sentì Scilla abbaiare,
come inquïeto cucciolo alla luna,
sentì Cariddi brontolar bollendo,
come il lebete ad una molta fiamma;
e le dodici branche avventò Scilla,
ed assorbì la salsa acqua Cariddi:
invano. Era passata oltre la nave.
E tornarono i venti alla lor casa
cinta di bronzo, mormorando cupi
tra loro, in rissa. E venne un'alta calma
senza il più lieve soffio, e sopra il mare
un dio forse era, che addormentò l'onde.

And thence they reached the Island of the Sun,
where black and white heifers grazed
the fields with their shepherd goddesses.
They bellowed in the golden sunshine,
and the ship slipped away.
They then came to the Island of Winds.
Above a wall of unbreakable bronze,
the wind's sons and daughters stood guard.
They sighted the ship, and in the old captain,
they recognized Odysseus, who had seemed
a swan or a stork from afar, but it was he,
albeit old, who still defied the winds.
They came down on him with one single hiss,
twelve winds on a single man.
Their wrath wheeled the ship around,
carried it for days and nights, and urged it
towards some lonely rocks in the sea,
but so fast that the ship, like an arrow,
slipped through and whooshed away.
Then that harsh discordant hubbub
dragged the ship to Scylla and Charybdis.
Odysseus heard Scylla bark and howl
like a scared pup at the moon
and Charybdis sputter and boil
like a cauldron on a hot flame.
Scylla hurled her twelve sharp claws
as Charybdis sucked in the seawater
but in vain, since the ship made it through.
The winds returned to their fortress
of bronze with a riotous rumble.
A high calm took over the sea,
as smooth as a motionless mirror.
A god unknown was lulling the waves.

XXIII. Il vero

Ed il prato fiorito era nel mare,
nel mare liscio come un cielo; e il canto
non risonava delle due Sirene,
ancora, perché il prato era lontano.
E il vecchio Eroe sentì che una sommessa
forza, corrente sotto il mare calmo,
spingea la nave verso le Sirene;
e disse agli altri d'inalzare i remi:
La nave corre ora da sé, compagni!
Non turbi il rombo del remeggio i canti
delle Sirene. Ormai le udremo. Il canto
placidi udite, il braccio su lo scalmo.
E la corrente tacita e soave
più sempre avanti sospingea la nave.
E il divino Odisseo vide alla punta
dell'isola fiorita le Sirene
stese tra i fiori, con il capo eretto
su gli ozïosi cubiti, guardando
il mare calmo avanti sé, guardando
il roseo sole che sorgea di contro;
guardando immote; e la lor ombra lunga
dietro rigava l'isola dei fiori.
"Dormite? L'alba già passò. Già gli occhi
vi cerca il sole tra le ciglia molli.
Sirene, io sono ancora quel mortale
che v'ascoltò, ma non poté sostare".
E la corrente tacita e soave
più sempre avanti sospingea la nave.
E il vecchio vide che le due Sirene,
le ciglia alzate su le due pupille,
avanti sé miravano, nel sole
fisse, od in lui, nella sua nave nera.
E su la calma immobile del mare,
alta e sicura egli inalzò la voce.
"Son io! Son io, che torno per sapere!
Ché molto io vidi, come voi vedete

XXIII.The Truth

A meadow bloomed in the middle
of a sea as smooth as a cloudless sky.
The Sirens' song was too faint to be heard
from that distant green dot in the sea.
But the old hero felt a secret force
flowing beneath the calm sea,
thrusting the ship towards the Sirens.
He ordered the crew to stop rowing:
"Friends, our ship follows a hidden will.
Let's not cover the Sirens' voices
with the roar of our oars. We'll hear them
soon, quietly, arms on the rowlocks."
That silent force, secret and sweet,
pushed the ship on, ever forward.
And glorious Odysseus saw them
at the furthest tip of the island in bloom,
stretched out among the flowers, their heads
idly upright on their elbows, gazing
out to the motionless sea and facing
the rosy light of the sunrise.
They stood still, and their long shadows
darkened the island of flowers.
"Are you sleeping? The sun has risen
and reaches inside your closed eyelids.
Sirens, I am still that mortal
who heard your song and lived on."
That gentle force, hidden and silent,
pushed the ship onwards, again and again.
The old man saw the Sirens
open up their heavy eyelids
and stare at the new sun
or at him on his black ship.
And on the deadly calm of the sea,
he raised his voice, loud and steady:
"I'm one who returns to know!
I have seen much, as you see me now.

me. Sì; ma tutto ch'io guardai nel mondo,
mi riguardò; mi domandò: Chi sono?"
E la corrente rapida e soave
più sempre avanti sospingea la nave.
E il Vecchio vide un grande mucchio d'ossa
d'uomini, e pelli raggrinzate intorno,
presso le due Sirene, immobilmente
stese sul lido, simili a due scogli.
"Vedo. Sia pure. Questo duro ossame
cresca quel mucchio. Ma, voi due, parlate!
Ma dite un vero, un solo a me, tra il tutto,
prima ch'io muoia, a ciò ch'io sia vissuto!"
E la corrente rapida e soave
più sempre avanti sospingea la nave.
E s'ergean su la nave alte le fronti,
con gli occhi fissi, delle due Sirene.
"Solo mi resta un attimo. Vi prego!
Ditemi almeno chi sono io! chi ero!"
E tra i due scogli si spezzò la nave.

XXIV. Calypso

E il mare azzurro che l'amò, più oltre
spinse Odisseo, per nove giorni e notti,
e lo sospinse all'isola lontana,
alla spelonca, cui fioriva all'orlo
carica d'uve la pampinea vite.
E fosca intorno le crescea la selva
d'ontani e d'odoriferi cipressi;
e falchi e gufi e garrule cornacchie
v'aveano il nido. E non dei vivi alcuno,
nè dio nè uomo, vi poneva il piede.
Or tra le foglie della selva i falchi
battean le rumorose ale, e dai buchi
soffiavano, dei vecchi alberi, i gufi,
e dai rami le garrule cornacchie
garrian di cosa che avvenia nel mare.
Ed ella che tessea dentro cantando,

But everything I looked on in the world
looked back and asked: 'Who am I?'"
That secret force, silent and gentle,
pushed the ship on, ever forward.
The old man saw a great pile of human
bones and wrinkled skins wrapped about
near the two Sirens, their motionless bodies
standing out on the shore like rocks in the sea.
"I see that these old bones of mine
will increase that heap. Yet, speak to me, Sirens!
Tell me one truth, only one truth
before I die, so that I can say I've lived."
But the secret force was inexorably
pushing the ship forward, faster and faster.
Already the high brows of the Sirens
rose over the ship, their gaze fixed.
"I have but one instant! I beg you!
Tell me at least who I am, who I was!"
But the ship broke against the rocks in the sea.

XXIV. Calypso

And the blue sea that loved him
pushed him further, for nine days and nights,
to that far remote island,
to the cave whose entrance blooms
with grapes and twisted vine leaves.
And all around a dense dark wood
of alder trees and cypress trees,
where hawks and owls and crows
nested, and no one else alive —
neither god nor man — had ever set foot.
Sometimes in the thick of leaves
was a frantic flutter of hawk wings.
Owls hooted from the hollow trees.
On the boughs, the chatty crows
talked of what happened on the sea.
In her house, she wove and sang

presso la vampa d'olezzante cedro,
stupì, frastuono udendo nella selva,
e in cuore disse: — Ahimè, ch'udii la voce
delle cornacchie e il rifiatar dei gufi!
E tra le dense foglie aliano i falchi.
Non forse hanno veduto a fior dell'onda
un qualche dio, che come un grande smergo
viene sui gorghi sterili del mare?
O muove già senz'orma come il vento,
sui prati molli di viola e d'appio?
Ma mi sia lungi dall'orecchio il detto!
In odio hanno gli dei la solitaria
Nasconditrice. E ben lo so, da quando
l'uomo che amavo, rimandai sul mare
al suo dolore. O che vedete, o gufi
dagli occhi tondi, e garrule cornacchie?—
Ed ecco usciva con la spola in mano,
d'oro, e guardò. Giaceva in terra, fuori
del mare, al piè della spelonca, un uomo,
sommosso ancor dall'ultima onda: e il bianco
capo accennava di saper quell'antro,
tremando un poco; e sopra l'uomo un tralcio
pendea con lunghi grappoli dell'uve.
Era Odisseo: lo riportava il mare
alla sua dea: lo riportava morto
alla Nasconditrice solitaria,
all'isola deserta che frondeggia
nell'ombelico dell'eterno mare.
Nudo tornava chi rigò di pianto
le vesti eterne che la dea gli dava;
bianco e tremante nella morte ancora,
chi l'immortale gioventù non volle.
Ed ella avvolse l'uomo nella nube
dei suoi capelli; ed ululò sul flutto
sterile, dove non l'udia nessuno:
— Non esser mai! non esser mai! più nulla,
ma meno morte, che non esser più!-

by the cedar-perfumed fire.
A sudden bustle startled her,
and she said to herself: "I hear
the crows talk and the owls hoot
and wings flutter in the leaves.
Have they seen, perhaps, a god
flying like a merganser
over the barren waves of ocean,
leaving no trail, like the wind
on fields of violet and celery?
May their words not reach my ears!
The gods have spurned Calypso —
the lonely Hider — I know that,
since I sent my love back to his sea
and sorrow. What do you see,
round-eyed owls and chatty crows?"
Her golden spool in her hand, she left
her house and looked out. A man lay there
on the sand and near the cave,
still gently rocked by the last wave,
still nodding with his white head,
knowingly. A vine branch hung
on him with its bunch of grapes.
The sea had brought Odysseus
back to her, but as a corpse
in the arms of the lonely Hider
on that remote island greening
in the navel of the eternal sea.
He was naked, he who had refused
the immortal clothes of the goddess:
frail, white, and trembling in death,
he, who had refused eternal youth.
And she wrapped him up in the cloud
of her hair, and she howled at the sea
where nobody could hear her:
"Unborn and immortals live less
but also die less than a life which ends!"

IL POETA DEGLI ILOTI

The Poet of the Helots

Il Poeta degli Iloti

I. Il giorno
Figlio di Dio, molto giocondo in cuore
prendesti terra in Aulide pietrosa!
Tornavi tu dal suolo degli Abanti
ricco di vigne, dalla popolata
di belle donne Calcide; né prima
d'allora avevi traversato il mare.
Ma il largo mare traversasti allora;
ché il re, più re degli uomini mortali,
era là morto, ed una gara indetta
e di lotte e di corse era, e di canto.
E tu nel canto ogni cantor vincesti,
anche il vecchio di Chio cieco e divino,
col tuo ben congegnato inno di guerra.
Ed ora sceso dalla nera nave
movevi ad Ascra, assai giocondo in cuore;
ché per la via ti camminava a paro
un curvo schiavo, che reggea sul dorso
il premio illustre: un tripode di bronzo.

Ché l'orecchiuto tripode di bronzo
gravava in prima al buon Ascreo le spalle;
e prima l'una, e l'altra poi; ché grave
era, di bronzo; e poi l'avea, per l'anse,
sospeso al ramo ch'era suo, d'alloro;
e lo portava: ma venuto a un grande
platano, donde chiara acqua sgorgava,
sostò, già stanco. Ed era quello il fonte
dove il segno gli Achei videro, d'otto
passeri implumi, e nove con la madre.
E di passeri il platano sul fonte
garriva ancora, e il buon Ascreo li udiva,

The Poet of the Helots[1]

I. Day

Son of God,[2] it is with a glad heart
you settled in stony Aulis,
having returned from Abae,
land of vines, from Chalcis,
land of beauties, and you had never
crossed the sea before.
But you crossed the sea,
as the king, higher than all mortals,
had died, and they held a contest,
of strength and speed and song.
And in song you beat every singer,
even the old man of Chios,[3] blind and god-like,
with your clever war-song.
As you got off the black ship,
you moved back to Ascra with a glad heart,
accompanied along the way
by a slave bent under the weight
of your glorious prize: a bronze tripod.

The bronze-eared tripod had been heavy
on the shoulders of the man from Ascra:
first on one and then on the other, heavy,
made of bronze. He had hung it
by the handles to his laurel branch
and carried it, but when he came to a
tall tree by a clear river,
he stopped and rested, tired. That was the river
where the Achaeans saw the sign
of eight fledglings plus their mother.[4]
And the tree still echoed with the song
of birds, and the man of Ascra heard them

1.   See introduction, p. xi.
2.   This epithet refers to Hesiod, as according to *Works and Days,* he was descended from a god. He was a native of Ascra in Boeotia.
3.   Homer.
4.   The seer Calchas, the priest in Agamemnon's army, interpreted this sign as the length of the Trojan War: nine years.

pensando in cuore un nuovo inno di guerra.
E riprendeva già la via, col caro
tripode, in dosso, che brillava al sole,
quando sorvenne un viator che bevve;
e seguitò. Ma poco dopo "O vecchio,"
disse, "ch'io porti il tuo laveggio: è peso".

E tolse prima il tripode, che l'altro
gli rispondesse: dopo, gli rispose:
"Grave era, è grave. Ed anche tu sei vecchio".
"Ma sono schiavo" gli rispose il vecchio:
"schiavo; e dal monte Citerone io venni
menando al mare, ad una curva nave,
due bei vitelli, nati schiavi anch'essi.
Torno al padrone. Ma tu dove, o babbo?"
"Ad Ascra: ad Ascra, misero villaggio,
tristo al freddo, aspro al caldo, e non mai buono".
E non addimandato altro gli disse:
"Venni per mare, ad Aulide: ho passato
l'Euripo. Indetta a Calcide una gara
e di lotte e di corse era, e di canto.
Vinsi codesto tripode di bronzo
cantando gesta degli eroi..." "Sei dunque
rapsodo errante, e sai le false cose
far come vere, ma non dir le vere".

Non rispondeva il vecchio Ascreo, ché tutto
era in pensar le mille navi in porto,
mentre sul curvo lido la procella
scotea le chiome degli Achei chiomanti.
E il sole era già caldo, e la campagna
fervea di mugli. Ché la pioggia a lungo
nei dì passati avea temprato il suolo,
e i contadini aravano le salde,
ed era tempo d'affidar le fave
ai solchi neri, e la lenticchia ai rossi.
E nudo un uomo traea giù da un carro,
presso la strada, con un suo ronciglio,

and thought of a new war-song.
While he was on his way
with his tripod shining in the sun,
there came a passer-by, who drank
and went on, but then he said:
"Old man, let me carry your heavy vase."

He took the tripod before the other could answer,
who then answered "It is heavy, and you are old."
"But I'm a slave," said the old man,
"and I came from Mount Cithaeron
bringing two young slave calves
to a curved ship by the sea.
I return to my master. But where are you going, father?"
"To Ascra, Ascra, a poor village,
sad in the winter, hard in the summer, and never good."
And without being asked, he added:
"I came to Aulis by sea. I crossed the strait.
In Chalcis they held a contest,
of strength and speed and song.
I won this bronze tripod
by singing songs of heroes." "Then
you are a wandering poet, and you turn
falsehood into truth, but you can't sing the truth."

The old man from Ascra did not answer
as he was thinking of the many ships at port
with the stormy wind blowing through
the long hair of the long-haired Achaeans.
The sun was hot and the country echoed
with lowing herds. The rain had long
tried the soil in the past few days,
and the farmers were ploughing the fields,
and it was time to give beans to the black clumps
and lentils to the red ones.
And a naked man with a pointy hook
unloaded the fat manure from his cart.

il pingue concio. E il buon Ascreo ne torse
il volto offeso. Ma lo schiavo curvo
sotto il ben fatto tripode di bronzo,
disse gioia a quel nudo uomo, e quel concio
lodò, maturo. E brontolò stradando:
"Ben fa, chi fa. Sol chi non fa, fa male".

Ed era presso mezzodì, né casa
ora appariva, a cui cercare un dono
piccolo e caro. Ché tra rupi e cespi
di stipe in fiore essi ripìano, muti.
Taceva anche la lodola dal ciuffo;
anche il cantore. Egli tacea per l'astio
ch'altri tacesse. Ma lo schiavo andando
volgea lo sguardo alle inamene roccie.
E disse alfine: "Ecco!" E mostrò la roccia
verde, in un punto, per nascente ontano.
"C'è tutto, al mondo, ma nascosto è tutto.
Prima, cercare, e poi convien raspare".
Egli depose il tripode di bronzo,
raspò, rinvenne un sottil filo d'acqua.
Poi dal laveggio che brillava al sole
un pane trasse, che v'avea deposto,
e lo partì col buon Ascreo, dicendo:
"So ch'è più grande la metà che il tutto".

Finito, prima che la fame, il cibo,
mossero ancora per la via rupestre
che già scendeva. Ed ecco che lo schiavo
guardando attorno vide una bolgetta
in un cespuglio. E presala, vi scòrse
splendere dentro due talenti d'oro.
E guardò giù per il sentiero, e scòrse
lontan lontano cavalcare un uomo.
E disse: "Padre, per un po' sul dorso
reggimi il grave tripode di bronzo,
ché n'avrei briga nel veloce corso".
E corse, e giunse al cavalier, cui rese,

The Ascrean turned his face away from it, but the slave,
bent under the weight of the bronze tripod,
greeted the man and praised
the fat manure, then muttered:
"Those who do, they do good. Do nothing, and you do evil."

    It was midday, and not a house
in sight where they could find
a small precious gift. Among rocks and bushes,
the two men climbed silently from stone to flower.
Even the feathered nightingale was quiet,
and so was the singer, because he hated
the other man's silence. But the slave
kept staring at the naked rocks.
And then, "Look," he said, showing a rock
greening with a young alder tree.
"Everything is there, but everything is hidden.
You must search first and then dig."
He put down the bronze tripod,
dug, and found a rivulet.
And from the shiny vase he carried,
he took a loaf of bread, which he'd put in,
and shared it with the Ascrean man, saying,
"Half is bigger than a whole."

    The food went sooner than their hunger,
and they went down their rocky path.
Then the slave saw a bag
hidden in a bush and took it
and saw two golden talents shining there.
And down the way he saw a man,
riding a horse in the distance,
and said: "Father, hold your tripod,
which would burden me in my run."
He ran down to the knight, who swore

poi ch'egli suo glielo giurò, quell'oro.
Poi, trafelato, il buon Ascreo sorvenne.
"Facile t'era aver per te quell'oro!"
disse allo schiavo. E mormorò lo schiavo:
"Facile, sì: c'è poca strada al male.
Il male, o padre, è nostro casigliano".

Così parlando andavano, e la strada
era già piana, e si vedean tuguri
di contadini ed ammuffiti borghi.
E lor giungea da tempo uno schiamazzo
di voci, come un abbaiar di cani
lontani. E sempre lor venìa più presso.
Erano gente che in un trivio aperto
rissavano con voci aspre di cani.
E alcun di loro già brandìa la zappa,
poi che l'irosa voce era già rauca;
quando lo schiavo nel buon punto accorse,
deposto in terra il tripode di bronzo;
e tenne l'uno e sgridò l'altro, e disse:
"Pace! È la pace che ralleva i bimbi.
Sono i pesci dell'acque, e son le fiere
dei boschi, e sono gli avvoltoi dell'aria,
ch'hanno per legge di mangiar l'un l'altro.
Gli uomini, no, ché la lor legge è il bene".

E quelli ognun tornava all'intermessa
opera, in pace. E i bovi sotto il giogo
rivedeano il lor uomo con un muglio,
compiendo il solco al suon della sua voce
ch'era arrochita: e le ricurve zappe
sfacean le zolle seppellendo il seme.
E lo schiavo riprese sopra il dorso
l'aspro di segni tripode di bronzo,
e riprendendo la sua via diceva
ad un rubesto giovane: "Lavora,
o gran fanciullo, se la terra e il cielo
t'amino, amando essi chi lor somiglia!

the gold was his, and gave it to him.
The Ascrean man came panting:
"It would have been a lucky find,"
said he, and the slave murmured, "Yes,
the road to evil is short.
Evil, father, lives within us."

And on they went, as the road was plain,
and one could see the farmers' shacks
in their decrepit villages.
They heard a squall of voices,
like barking dogs in the distance
getting nearer and nearer.
It was some people at a crossroad,
fighting and rioting with harsh voices,
and some of them wielding a hoe,
as their voice swelled with anger.
The slave ran to them,
putting down the bronze tripod.
He held one and reproached the other,
and said, "Peace will raise the children!
Fish and wild animals and vultures,
they eat each other, and that's their law,
but that is not the law of humans."

And everyone peacefully returned
to their work. The oxen under the yoke
saluted their masters with a bellow
as they ploughed the land
at the sound of their harsh voices, and their curved hoes
broke clumps and buried the seed.
The slave took back the carved tripod,
and went on his way. He told
a ruddy youngster: "Work,
big boy, so that heaven and earth may love you
as they love those who resemble them!

Ché la nube carreggia, con un cupo
brontolìo, l'acqua; e da lontano, ansando,
il vento viene; e infaticato il sole
torna ogni giorno. Ma la terra è tarda,
madre che fece tanti figli, e tutti
li ebbe alla poppa. O dàlle ora una mano!"

E lo schiavo stradò col suo cantore
a paro a paro. E già scendea la sera,
e velava una dolce ombra le strade.
Né più borghi muffiti erano intorno,
né casolari. Erano intorno macchie
folte di lauro che odorava al cielo.
E videro ambedue ch'era smarrita
ormai la strada. Ed il cantore stanco
disse allo schiavo: "Mal tu m'hai condotto".
E gli rispose il paziente schiavo:
"In te fidavo: Ché del buon cammino
chi c'è, se non il buon cantor, maestro?"

II. La notte
E sul lor capo era l'opaca notte
piena di stelle. E risplendea nel cielo
l'Orsa minore, che accennò qual fosse
la vera strada, né però dall'alto
la rischiarava, colaggiù, nell'ombra.
E l'uomo allora e presso lui lo schiavo
sostarono nel bosco ove in un giogo
s'allargava assai piana una radura,
donde era meglio preveder le fiere,
se alcuna v'era che traesse al fiuto.
E poi lo schiavo conficcò nel suolo
il suo bastone, e presso quello il ramo
di sacro lauro, del cantore, e sopra
la sua schiavina sciorinò, che fosse
schermo dal lato onde veniva il freddo.
E disse: "O padre, bene io so le notti
gelide, e il sonno sotto la rugiada.
Ma è ben tardi perché tu l'impari".

The cloud carries the water, thundering,
the wind comes panting from afar,
the sun returns tirelessly each day.
But the earth is slow, having mothered
many children and nursed them. Help her then!"

    And the slave went along with the singer,
and the evening fell
covering the road with its sweet shade.
The decrepit villages were gone,
and the shacks too. Only thick bushes around them
and the sweet scent of laurel leaves in the air.
They both saw they had lost their way.
The weary poet said, "I followed you!"
And patiently the slave answered,
"But I trusted you, as who's a better guide
than a great poet?"

II. Night

    Above their heads the obscure night
was full of stars. The Bear glittered,
brightly hinting at the right way to go
but without shedding light from up in the sky
on their path through the shadows down below.
Then the man rested, the slave beside him,
in a forest in a mountain valley,
near where a level plain stretched out —
a good place, that, to see wolves coming
if one of them had caught your scent.
The slave stuck his walking-stick into the ground
and nearby, the poet's staff of sacred laurel,
and he stretched out his cloak there, a screen from the wind.
"Father," he said, "Well I know these cold nights.
I know well how to sleep and wake up fresh with dew.
To learn it at your age is a hard thing to do."

Ma allo schiavo il pio cantor rispose:
"Ospite caro, basta ch'io ricordi.
Ero fanciullo ed imparai le notti
gelide e il sonno sotto la rugiada.
Ché da fanciullo pascolai la greggia,
reggendo in mano la ricurva verga
del pecoraio, non lo scettro, ramo
di sacro alloro che, senz'altro squillo
d'arguta cetra, colma a me di canto,
come alle genti di silenzio, il cuore.
Mio padre ad Ascra dall'eolia Cyme
venne, fuggendo, non la copia e gli agi,
sì la cattiva povertà; che venne,
tanto l'amava, su la nave anch'ella,
né più si stolse e poi restò col figlio.
E io badai le pecore sui greppi
dell'Elicone, il grande monte e bello,
e le notti passai su la montagna.

E in una notte come questa… il sonno
non mi voleva. Ché splendean le stelle
tutte nel cielo, e fresche del lavacro
veniano su le Pleiadi che al campo
lascian l'aratro e trovano la falce.
E insonne udivo uno stormir di selve,
un correr d'acque, un mormorio di fonti.
E s'esalava un infinito odore
dai molli prati, e tutto era silenzio,
e tutto voce; ed era tutto un canto.
Ed ecco tutto io mi sentii dischiuso
all'universo, che d'un tratto invase
l'essere mio; né così lieve un sogno
entra nell'occhio nostro benché chiuso.
E tutto allora in me trovai, che prima
fuori appariva, e in me trovai quel canto,
che si frangea nell'anima serena
piena, nell'alta opacità, di stelle.

To the slave, the reverent poet replied:
"All I have to do, my friend, is think back
to when I was a boy, and I learned those things too —
how to sleep the cold nights through and wake fresh with dew.
As a boy, I pastured my flocks round here,
holding in my hand the curved staff
of a shepherd — not a sceptre, but a branch of sacred
laurel — enough on its own for me
to fill my heart with reverent silence
and with song, without any jangling lyre.
My father came from Aeolian Cyme
all the way to Ascra, running away
not from luxury or plenty, but from poverty.
It sailed here with him — it loved him so —
and it's never shifted, and it stayed with his son.
I looked after the sheep on Mount Helicon —
this grand and beautiful, this holy mountain —
and I passed the nights up here alone.

And on a night like this one…sleep wouldn't have me.
The stars all shining in the mud-black sky.…
The Pleiades had washed their faces in the sea
and were trading the plough in for a brilliant scythe.
Wide awake, I heard the rustle of woods,
the running of waters, the murmur of streams.
A fragrance wafted high from the meadows,
infinitely rich. Everything was silent,
but everything had voice: it sang a song.
I was opened right up to the universe,
which entered into me wholly, right then and there,
as gently as a dream can enter
through the eyes of a dreamer, shut though they are.
I found it was all inside of me,
what had always seemed outside of me.
It broke open in my quiet mind,
grand and dark and full of stars.

E quel canto parlava della Terra
dall'ampio petto, che, infelice madre,
nell'evo primo non facea che mostri,
orrendi enormi, e li tenea nascosti
in sé, perché non li vedesse il Cielo.
E lei guardava coi mille occhi il Cielo,
molto in sospetto, ché l'udia sovente
gemere e la vedea scotersi tutta
per la strettura; e venir fumo fuori
nel giorno, e fiamme nella nera notte.
Al fin la Terra spinse fuor d'un tratto
la grande prole; e con un grande sbalzo
sorsero i monti dalle cento teste,
e d'ogni testa usciva il fumo e il fuoco,
che tolse il giorno e insanguinò la notte.
E non era che notte, risonante
di strida, rugghi, sibili, latrati,
e già non altro si vedea, che i mostri
lambersi il fuoco con le lingue nere.

E i mostri urlando massi ardenti al Cielo
avventarono; e il Cielo, arso dall'ira,
spezzò le stelle e ne scagliò le scheggie
contro la Terra, e in una notte d'anni
tra Cielo e Terra risonò la rissa.
Qua mille braccia si tendean nell'ombra
coi massi accesi, e mille urli ad un tempo
uscìan con essi; ma dall'alto gli astri
pioveano muti con un guizzo d'oro.
E il masso a volte si spezzò nell'astro.
E sfavillante un polverìo si sparse
nel nero spazio, come la corolla
d'un fior di luce, che per un momento
illuminò gli attoniti giganti,

And it sang of ample-bosomed Earth,[5]
unhappy mother, who in those early days
couldn't bear anything but monsters,
horrifying and huge, and she kept them hid
in her ample bosom so the Sky would not see them.
The Sky watched her with his thousand eyes,
full of suspicion, and he'd hear her groan,
see shakes pass through her entire body,
see smoke stream out of her during the day,
and flames flash out when the sun went down.
At last, suddenly, Earth gave birth
to her great offspring, and with a huge shudder,
mountains rose up with their hundred heads,
and from every head rose smoke and fire,
which pulled a shroud over the day
and spattered blood on the holy night.
There was nothing but night, alive with roars,
and cries and howls and barks and growls;
and nothing was seen, except for the monsters,
the flames licking their blackened maws.

The monsters set to hurling flaming
masses of rock right up at the Sky.
And the Sky, with brilliant anger flaming,
smashed the stars and flung their fragments
down at the Earth. And the din of their fight
crushed a thousand years into a single night.
Here a hundred arms drew back in the night
holding boiling stones, and with them went
a hundred shouts, a crowded cry,
but silent stars rained down from on high,
silently, trailing their flairs of gold.
And stones crashed against stars.
And a glittering powder drifted down
through the black darkness like the golden crown
of a flower made of light, which shone
on the giants, visibly astonished.

5.   These lines summarize Hesiod's description of the origins of the Greek
gods in his *Theogony.*

e il mare immenso che ondeggiava al buio,
e in terra e in aria rettili deformi,
nottole enormi; e qualche viso irsuto
di scimmia intento ad esplorar da un antro.
E poi fu pace. Ed ecco uscì dall'antro
il bruto simo, e nella gran maceria,
dove sono i rottami anche del Cielo,
frugò raspò scavò, come fa il cane
senza padrone, ove si spense un rogo.
E fruga ancora e raspa ancora e scava
ancora. Ma dal Cielo ora alla Terra
sorride il sole e piange pia la nube.
È pace. Pur la Terra anco ricorda
l'antica lotta, e gitta fuoco, e trema.
E al Cielo torna l'ira antica, e scaglia
folgori a lei con subito rimbombo.
È pace sì, ma l'infelice Terra
è sol felice, quando ignara dorme;
e il Cielo azzurro sopra lei si stende
con le sue luci, e vuol destarla e svuole,
e l'accarezza col guizzar di qualche
stella cadente, che però non cade.

    Come ora. E sol com'ora anco è felice
l'uomo infelice; s'egli dorme, o guarda:
quando guarda e non vede altro che stelle,
quando ascolta e non ode altro che un canto".
Così parlava, e dolce sorse un canto:
sul rumor delle foglie e delle fonti,
un dolce canto pieno di querele
e di domande, un nuvolo di strilli
cadente in un singulto grave, un grave
gemere che finiva in un tripudio.
E il buon Ascreo diceva: "Ecco, fu tolto
il sonno, tutto al querulo usignolo
che così piange per la notte intiera,
né sotto l'ala mai nasconde il capo;

The sea was seen on its way through the dark.
Reptiles and owls crowded earth and air.
And a hairy-faced monkey came out of a cave.
Then there was peace. And out of the cave
came the hideous ape, and it began to root
and rummage and dig down in the rubble underfoot
among fragments of the Sky
like a dog will do when it loses its master
and the embers have gone cold on his fiery grave.
So he rummages in the rubble, and he digs and roots.
But now, in the space between Earth and Sky,
the buoyant sun smiles and the pious cloud cries.
There is peace. And yet, the Earth still remembers
yesterday's battle, and every now and then
she shakes and she rumbles or throws up fire.
And to the Sky, too, every now and then,
the old anger returns, and he casts in fire
bronze thunderbolts, sudden flashes of ire.
There is peace, but the unhappy Earth
only feels happy when she sleeps unknowing.
And the blue Sky broods over her with his million lamps,
and he wants to wake her, but instead he's content
to burn, every now and then, the odd falling star,
which he'll never let fall on his dreaming darling.

  Like right now. And it's only in moments like these
that the unhappy man is happy: when he sleeps
or watches and looks up and sees nothing but stars,
when he listens and there comes to him nothing but songs."
So he spoke, and slowly, a sweet song rose up
from the rustling of leaves and the trickling of streams,
a sweet song made up out of bitter complaints
and questionings, a cloud of screams
falling into a deep and bottomless plaint,
a groan that ended like a joyful triumph.
And the good poet said, "Use your ears and eyes.
The sleepless nightingale cries the whole night through,
never burying her sleeping head away,

ma solo mezzo, a quella cui la sera
gemere ascolta e riascolta l'alba.
Miseri! e un solo è il lor dolore, e forse
l'uno non ode mai dell'altro il pianto!"

    E lo schiavo diceva: "Oh! non è pianto
questo né l'altro. Ma la casereccia
rondine ha molti i figli e le faccende,
e sa che l'alba è un terzo di giornata;
e dolce a quegli che operò nel giorno,
viene la sera, e lieto suona il canto
dopo il lavoro. E l'usignol gorgheggia
tutta la notte né vuol prender sonno…
ch'egli non vuole seppellir nel sonno,
avere in vano dentro sé non vuole
un solo trillo di quel suo dolce inno!"
Così parlava. E sorse aurea la luna
dalla montagna, ed insegnò la strada
al buon Ascreo, che mosse con lo schiavo.
A mano a mano lo accoglieva il canto
degli usignoli, fin che su l'aurora
gli annunziò ch'era vicino un tetto,
una garrula rondine in faccende.

    E poi giunsero al monte alto e divino,
a un tempio ermo tra i boschi. E il pio cantore
disse allo schiavo: "Ospite amico, è questo
il luogo dove pasturai fanciullo
il gregge, e dove appresi il canto, e dove
cantai la rissa tra la Terra e il Cielo.
Ma poi mi piacque, non cantare il vero,
sì la menzogna che somiglia al vero.
Ora il lavoro canterò, né curo
ch'io sembri ai re l'Aedo degli schiavi".

    Disse: e nel tempio solitario appese
il bello ansato tripode di bronzo.

and the swallow sings as the evening's blue
turns gold and listens to the break of day.
Poor things! Their suffering is one and the same,
but they'll never hear each other's cries."

    The slave replied, "No! Neither one nor the other
is crying really. The homely swallow
has children to care for and things to do
and knows that the early bird gets the worm.
And she knows how sweetly the evening comes
to those who have given their day to labor,
how nice a song sounds when the work is done.
The nightingale warbles through to tomorrow
because she refuses to bury in slumber and
to leave imprisoned in her delicate form
a single trill of her glorious song."
So he spoke, and a crescent moon rose, golden,
showing the way to the good Ascraean
and to the slave. And all around them,
the song of the nightingale accompanied them
until dawn when the signal that a house was nearby
was given by a swallow who had things to do.

    They came at last to the holy mountain,
to a temple hidden deep in the woods.
And the poet said to the slave, "My friend,
this is the place where once I stood,
a mere lad of sixteen, shepherding my flock.
This is the place where I learned to sing,
and where I first sang of the clash and shock
when the Earth and the Sky made war on each other.
Back then it pleased me not to sing the truth,
but to sing the untruth that looks like the truth.
I will sing about work from now on.
I don't worry too much if, to the kings of this Earth,
I seem nothing more than a poet for slaves."

    He spoke and hung up in the solitary temple
the shining tripod with its cast-bronze handles.

POEMI DI ATE

Poems of Ate

I. Ate

O quale uscì dalla città sonante
di colombelle Mecisteo di Gorgo,
fuggendo ai campi glauchi d'orzo, ai grandi
olmi cui già mordea qualche cicala
con la stridula sega. E tu fuggivi,
figlio di Gorgo, dall'erbosa Messe,
dove un tumulto, pari a fuoco, ardeva
sotto un bianco svolìo di colombelle.
Presto e campi di glauco orzo e canori
olmi lasciava, e nella folta macchia,
nido di gazze, s'immergea correndo,
pallido ansante, e gli vuotava il cuore
la fuga, e gli scavava il gorgozzule,
e dentro dentro gli pungea l'orecchia.
Poi che tumulto non udì nè grida
più d'inseguenti, egli sostò. La sete
gli ardea le vene, ed ei bramava ancora
tuffare in una viva acqua corrente
la mano impura di purpureo sangue.

Una rana cantava non lontana,
che lo guidó. Qua qua, cantava, è l'acqua:
bruna acqua, acqua che fiori apre di gialle
rose palustri e candide ninfee.
Ora egli udì la rauca cantatrice
della fontana, Mecisteo di Gorgo,
e seguì l'orma querula e si vide
a un verde stagno che fiorìa di gialle
rose palustri e candide ninfee.
Come egli giunse, la canora rana
tacque, e lo stagno gorgoglió d'un tonfo.
Or egli prima nello stagno immerse
le mani e a lungo stropicciò la rea
con la non rea: di tutte e due già monde

I. Ate

Oh, how he ran from the city
of doves, Mecisteus of Gorgo,
to pale green fields of barley
and to tall alder trees pierced
by the shrill sound of cicadas.
He fled from Messe, green city,
which burnt in uproar beneath
a snow-white flock of doves.
He left the fields and the trees,
entered a wood, which was full of magpies,
with a heavy heart, his chest empty,
a lump in his throat, and his ears ringing.
But with his chasers gone, he stopped,
his veins ablaze with thirst,
yearning to dip his blood-stained hands
into a stream of cold water.

A battalion of croaking frogs
sang of water in the wood:
cloudy water, spotted with yellow
roses and white water lilies.
Mecisteus heard the song
lustily sung by those raucous singers
and followed their grouchy sound
to a swamp, which bloomed with yellow
roses and white water lilies.
As he came, the croaking ceased.
He heard the water splash and gurgle.
He dipped his hands in the swamp
and rinsed both his bloodied hands,
and when he had washed both his hands,

del pari, fece una rotonda coppa,
e la soppose al pìspino. Nè bevve.
L'acqua era nera come morte, e rossi
come saette uscite dalla piaga
erano i giunchi, e livide, di tabe,
le rose accanto alle ninfee di sangue.

E Mecisteo fuggì dal nero gorgo
chiazzato dalle rose ampie del sangue;
fuggì lontano. Or quando già l'ardente
foga dei piedi temperava, un tratto
sentì da tergo un calpestìo discorde:
due passi, uno era forte, uno non era
che dell'altro la sùbita eco breve:
onde il suo capo inorridì di punte
e il cuore gli si profondò, pensando
che già non fosse il disugual cadere
di goccie rosse dentro l'acque nere,
nè la lontana torbida querela
di quella rana, ma pensando in cuore
ch'era Ate, Ate la vecchia, Ate la zoppa,
che dietro le fiutate orme veniva.
Né riguardò, ma più veloce i passi
stese, e gli orecchi inebrïò di vento.

Ma trito e secco gli venìa da tergo
sempre lo stesso calpestìo discorde,
misto a uno scabro anelito; nè forse
egli pensò che fosse il picchiar duro
del taglialegna in echeggiante forra,
misto alla rauca ruggine del fiato:
era Ate, Ate la zoppa, Ate la vecchia,
che lo inseguiva con stridente lena,
veloce, infaticabile. E già fuori
correa del bosco, sopra acute roccie;
e d'una in altra egli balzava, pari
allo stambecco, e a ogni lancio udiva
l'urlo e lo sforzo d'un simile lancio,
poi dietro sé picchierellare il passo

he cupped them, filled them
with dripping water, and drank:
death-black water, reeds like
red streams of blood from a wound,
swollen dark roses and lilies.

Mecisteus left the swamp
with its blood-stained roses.
He went away from that place,
and as he slowed his pace, he noticed
someone walking behind him.
One step was fast and then the next
a briefest echo of the first,
and he shivered in horror, his heart
shuddered at the thought that this
was not the uneven dripping
of blood into blackened waters
nor the croaking of the frogs. No,
he knew it was Ate, the old
Ate, Ate the cripple,
who followed his every step.
He didn't look back, he ran,
his ears filled with whistling wind.

The footsteps came clip-clopping,
the same uneven footsteps
mixed with raucous panting,
not like the sound of a man
chopping wood on a cliff
among rough howling winds.
Ate the old, the cripple,
followed him on his track, fast, inexorable.
Out of the wood, he ran across the rocks,
jumping from stone to stone
like a stag. And after each jump,
he heard himself shout. Clip
clop, that uneven step

eterno con la sùbita eco breve.
Fin che giunse al burrone, alto, infinito,
tale che all'orlo non giungea lo stroscio
d'una fiumana che muggiva al fondo.
Allor si volse per lottar con Ate,
il buono al pugno Mecisteo di Gorgo;
volsesi e scricchiolar fece le braccia
protese, l'aria flagellando, e il destro
piede più dietro ritraeva… e cadde.
Cadde, e, precipitando, Ate vide egli
che all'orlo estremo di tra i caprifichi
mostrò le rughe della fronte, e rise.

II. L'etèra

O quale, un'alba, Myrrhine si spense,
la molto cara, quando ancor si spense
stanca l'insonne lampada lasciva,
conscia di tutto. Ma v'infuse Evèno
ancor rugiada di perenne ulivo;
e su la via dei campi in un tempietto,
chiuso, di marmo, appese la lucerna
che rischiarasse a Myrrhine le notti;
in vano; ch'ella alfin dormiva, e sola.
Ma lievemente a quel chiarore, ardente
nel gran silenzio opaco della strada,
volò, con lo stridìo d'una falena,
l'anima d'essa: ché vagava in cerca
del corpo amato, per vederlo ancora,
bianco, perfetto, il suo bel fior di carne,
fiore che apriva tutta la corolla
tutta la notte, e si chiudea su l'alba
avido ed aspro, senza più profumo.
Or la falena stridula cercava
quel morto fiore, e battè l'ali al lume
della lucerna, che sapea gli amori;
ma il corpo amato ella non vide, chiuso,
coi molti arcani balsami, nell'arca.

still there, always that echo,
until he reached the highest cliff
from which you could hear the river
bellow deep inside the valley.
Mecisteus then turned around
to fight like a boxer, his fists clenched.
He punched the air, jabbed, backed away,
and fell headlong off the cliff.
And as he fell, he saw her, Ate,
still standing there on the edge of the cliff,
her head among the flowers, her face
creased, creased with ecstatic laughter.

II. The Courtesan

And Myrrhine[1] passed, beloved,
when her lamplight dimmed at dawn
after a sleepless night spent watching
her lovers. But Evenus filled it
with the dew of an olive tree
and hung the lamp in a marble
temple on the way to the fields
to shed light on Myrrhine's way.
At last, she slept alone.
But as the dim lamplight pierced
the great dark silence of the road,
her soul flew out like a butterfly
to see her white body once more,
a spotless flower of flesh
whose petals spread through the night,
to close, but only at sunrise,
eager, fruitless, and scentless.
It was that dead flower she sought,
the fluttering moth at the lamplight,
which had watched so many lovers.
But the body was locked in a tomb
with the scent of secret balms.

1.   The names in this poem are quite common in Greek and Roman comedies
and are not intended to refer to any particular character or individual.

Né volle andare al suo cammino ancora
come le aeree anime, cui tarda
prendere il volo, simili all'incenso
il cui destino è d'olezzar vanendo.
E per l'opaca strada ecco sorvenne
un coro allegro, con le faci spente,
da un giovenile florido banchetto.
E Moscho a quella lampada solinga
la teda accese, e lesse nella stele:
MYRRHINE AL LUME DELLA SUA LUCERNA
DORME. È LA PRIMA VOLTA ORA, E PER SEMPRE.
E disse: "Amici, buona a noi la sorte!
Myrrhine dorme le sue notti, e sola!
Io ben pregava Amore iddio, che al fine
m'addormentasse Myrrhine nel cuore:
pregai l'Amore e m'ascoltò la Morte".
E Callia disse: "Ell'era un'ape, e il miele
stillava, ma pungea col pungiglione.
E disse Agathia: Ella mesceva ai bocci
d'amor le spine, ai dolci fichi i funghi".
E Phaedro il vecchio: Pace ai detti amari!
ella, buona, cambiava oro con rame.
E stettero, ebbri di vin dolce, un poco
lì nel silenzio opaco della strada.
E la lucerna lor blandia sul capo,
tremula, il serto marcido di rose,
e forse tratta da quel morto olezzo
ronzava un'invisibile falena.
Ma poi la face alla lucerna tutti,
l'un dopo l'altro, accesero. Poi voci
alte destò l'auletride col flauto
doppio, di busso, e tra faville il coro
con un sonoro trepestìo si mosse.

L'anima, no. Rimase ancora, e vide
le luci e il canto dileguar lontano.
Era sfuggita al demone che insegna
le vie muffite all'anime dei morti;

She did not want to leave,
unlike all ethereal souls,
eager to fly and vanish
like a cloud of incense smoke.
And down the black road they came,
a merry bunch from a banquet hall,
walking and singing in the night's dark.
When they reached the tomb, Moscho
lit up his torch and read:
"Myrrhine sleeps by the lamplight,
alone, at last, and forever.
Friends, the gods are good!
Myrrhine sleeps alone!
I prayed and prayed for Eros
to numb my heart from desire,
but it seems that Death replied."
And Callia: "A bee she was,
with a sting exuding honey."
Agathias: "She mixed flowers
and thorns, honey and weeds."
And Phaedros the Old: "Enough!
She gave us gold for copper."
They lingered, drunk with sweet wine,
enclosed in the great dark silence,
as the lantern shed its light
on their rotten garlands of roses.
That putrid smell aroused
her, the invisible moth.
But the torches were lit, and one
played the flute as the men
moved away with swift footsteps.

But she lingered there and saw
the lights and the voices fade.
She had missed the demon[2] that leads
the dead on their rotten ways.

2.   A possible reference to Socrates' description of the road to Hades (Plato,
Phaedo 107, d-e).

gli era sfuggita: or non sapea, da sola,
trovar la strada: e stette ancora ai piedi
del suo sepolcro, al lume vacillante
della sua conscia lampada. E la notte
era al suo colmo, piena d'auree stelle;
quando sentì venire un passo, un pianto
venire acuto, e riconobbe Evèno.
Ché avea perduto il dolce sonno Evèno
da molti giorni, ed or sapea che chiuso
era nell'arca, con la morta etèra.
E singultendo disserrò la porta
del bel tempietto, e presa la lucerna,
entrò. Poi destro, con l'acuta spada,
tentò dell'arca il solido coperchio
e lo mosse, e con ambedue le mani,
puntellando i ginocchi, l'alzò. C'era
con lui, non vista, alle sue spalle, e il lieve
stridìo vaniva nell'anelito aspro
d'Evèno, un'ombra che volea vedere
Myrrhine morta. E questa apparve; e quegli
lasciò d'un urlo ripiombare il marmo
sopra il suo sonno e l'amor suo, per sempre.

E fuggì, fuggì via l'anima, e un gallo
rosso cantò con l'aspro inno la vita:
la vita; ed ella si trovò tra i morti.
Nè una a tutti era la via di morte,
ma tante e tante, e si perdean raggiando
nell'infinita opacità del vuoto.
Ed era ignota a lei la sua. Ma molte
ombre nell'ombra ella vedea passare
e dileguare: alcune col lor mite
demone andare per la via serene,
ed altre, in vano, ricusar la mano
del lor destino. Ma sfuggita ell'era
da tanti giorni al demone; ed ignota
l'era la via. Dunque si volse ad una
anima dolce e vergine, che andando

She had missed him and lost her way.
She stood a while by her temple,
uncertain, by the flickering light
of her knowing lamp. The night
was deep and dotted with stars.
She heard fast steps approaching
and the sound of tears: Evenus.
He had not slept in days,
leaving his sleep with the sleeping
woman dead in her tomb.
He opened the door of the temple,
in tears, and took the lamp.
He entered. Then with his sword,
he forced the heavy stone coffin,
lifted the lid with both hands,
bending his knees. Behind him
a shadow, whose flapping wings
beat with the man's heavy panting,
a shadow who wanted to see her.
He saw her, shouted, the coffin
closed down on his love, forever.

Away fled the soul, a rooster
announced the beginning of life!
She was among the dead,
and the path was not one, but many,
departing into the void.
Her way was unknown, but many
a shadow was crossing the shadows
and fading, led by the demon,
some of them willing, some not.
She'd lost the demon and her way,
so she asked a sweet young soul,

si rivolgeva al dolce mondo ancora;
e chiese a quella la sua via. Ma quella,
l'anima pura, ecco che tremò tutta
come l'ombra di un nuovo esile pioppo:
"Non la so!" disse, e nel pallor del Tutto
vanì. L'etèra si rivolse ad una
anima santa e flebile, seduta
con tra le mani il dolce viso in pianto.
Era una madre che pensava ancora
ai dolci figli; ed anche lei rispose:
"Non la so!"; quindi nel dolor del Tutto
sparì. L'etèra errò tra i morti a lungo
miseramente come già tra i vivi;
ma ora in vano; e molto era il ribrezzo
di là, per l'inquïeta anima nuda
che in faccia a tutti sorgea su nei trivi.
E alfine insonne l'anima d'Evèno
passò veloce, che correva al fiume
arsa di sete, dell'oblìo. Nè l'una
l'altra conobbe. Non l'avea mai vista.
Myrrhine corse su dal trivio, e chiese,
a quell'incognita anima veloce,
la strada. Evèno le rispose: "Ho fretta".

    E più veloce l'anima d'Evèno
corse, in orrore, e la seguì la trista
anima ignuda. Ma la prima sparve
in lontananza, nella eterna nebbia;
e l'altra, ansante, a un nuovo trivio incerto
sostò, l'etèra. E intese là bisbigli,
ma così tenui, come di pulcini
gementi nella cavità dell'uovo.
Era un bisbiglio, quale già l'etèra
s'era ascoltata, con orror, dal fianco
venir su pio, sommessamente… quando
avea, di là, quel suo bel fior di carne,
senza una piega i petali. Ma ora
trasse al sussurro, Myrrhine l'etèra.

one still longing for life,
but the chaste little soul
shook like the tip of a tree.
She was lost as well, she said,
and vanished. Myrrhine asked
a pious one who sat with
her hands on her teary face:
a mother, thinking still
of her babes, but her answer was no,
and she vanished in the sorrowful void.
Myrrhine wandered long,
as unhappy in death as in life,
but the dead abhorred
her poor restless soul, naked,
standing at every junction.
Evenus' sleepless soul
passed her by, at last,
eager to go into oblivion.
But neither recognized each other.
At the crossroad, Myrrhine asked
that stranger soul in a hurry:
"No," he said and vanished.

    Evenus shrank from her
in horror. The poor naked soul
pursued him, but soon he faded
away in the eternal mist.
She paused, again, breathless,
hearing a distant whisper:
soft and faint, like chicks
chirping inside an egg.
She had heard that sound before,
with horror, inside her womb:
a feeble sound from within
her white flower of flesh,
her spotless flower of flesh.

Cauta pestava l'erbe alte del prato
l'anima ignuda, e riguardava in terra,
tra gl'infecondi caprifichi, e vide.
Vide lì, tra gli asfòdeli e i narcissi,
starsene, informi tra la vita e il nulla,
ombre ancor più dell'ombra esili, i figli
suoi, che non volle. E nelle mani esangui
aveano i fiori delle ree cicute,
avean dell'empia segala le spighe,
per lor trastullo. E tra la morte ancora
erano e il nulla, presso il limitare.
E venne a loro Myrrhine; e gl'infanti
lattei, rugosi, lei vedendo, un grido
diedero, smorto e gracile, e gettando
i tristi fiori, corsero coi guizzi,
via, delle gambe e delle lunghe braccia,
pendule e flosce; come nella strada
molle di pioggia, al risonar d'un passo,
fuggono ranchi ranchi i piccolini
di qualche bodda: tali i figli morti
avanti ancor di nascere, i cacciati
prima d'uscire a domandar pietà!

    Ma la soglia di bronzo era lì presso,
della gran casa. E l'atrio ululò tetro
per le vigili cagne di sotterra.
Pur vi guizzò, la turba infante, dentro,
rabbrividendo, e dietro lor la madre
nell'infinita oscurità s'immerse.

III. La madre

O quale Glauco, ebbro d'oblìo, percosse
la santa madre. E non poté la madre
che pur voleva, sostener nel cuore
quella percossa al volto umile e mesto;
ché da tanti dolori liso il cuore,

She moved closer, cautiously
placing her feet on the grass,
poor naked soul looking down
on the barren white flowers.
And there, in a bed of lilies,
shapeless between life and death,
thinner than a thin shadow,
she saw her unborn children,
their bloodless hands filled
with poisonous hemlock flowers
and spikes of evil barley.
They played with them at the edge
of death and the great wide void.
Myrrhine reached for her babies,
pale wrinkly creatures who faintly
cooed at the sight of her, dropping
their flowers. They
sprang up on their flabby legs
and long arms, like an army of frogs
limp on a muddy road
at the sound of a footstep approaching.
So they left, those children dead
before life, before
they could come and beg for mercy!

But the burnished threshold of Hades
was there with the gloomy growl
of the underworld dogs in its hall.
The children flocked inside
shivering while behind them, their mother
plunged into endless darkness.

III. Mother

Glaucos,[3] drunk with oblivion, slapped
his saintly mother, and she could not bear it,
much as she tried. Her heart could not bear
that slap on her meek and mournful face.
Her heart, so consumed by so many sorrows,

3.   The name does not refer to any particular individual or character. The poem
narrates another episode of violence: a son causing the death of his mother.

ecco, si ruppe; e ne dové morire.
E subito il buon demone sorvenne,
e più veloce d'un pensier di madre
ultimo, la soave anima prese,
la sollevò, la portò via lontano,
e due tre volte la tuffò nel Lete.
E le dicea: "Dimentica per sempre,
anima buona; ché sofferto hai troppo!"
E pose lei nel sommo della terra,
dove è più luce, più beltà; più Dio:
nel calmo Elisio, donde mai non torna
l'anima al basso, a dolorar la vita.

    Ma nel profondo della terra il figlio
precipitò, nel baratro sotterra,
tanto sotterra alla sua tomba, quanto
erano su la tomba alte le stelle.
E là fu, nella oscurità, travolto
dalla massa d'eterna acqua, che sciacqua
pendula in mezzo all'infinito abisso;
che, mentre oscilla il globo della terra
là dentro fiotta, e urta le pareti
solide, e con cupo impeto rimbomba.
E l'anima di Glauco era travolta
nell'acqua eterna, e or lanciata contro
le roccie liscie, or tratta dal risucchio
giù. Né un raggio di luce, ma una romba
senza pensiero, e senza tempo il tempo.
Quando, un flutto sboccò con un singulto
in un crepaccio, e Glauco sgorgò dentro
l'antro sonante, e si trovò su l'onda
d'un nero fiume che correa sotterra
rapacemente. Ed era tutto un pianto,
un pianto occulto, il pianto dopo morte,
oh! così vano, le cui solitarie
lacrime lecca il labile lombrico.
E il fiume cieco del dolor sepolto

broke. And thus, she had to die.
Fast and sudden the good demon came,
more solicitous than a mother's last thought.
He took away her sweet, blessed soul,
lifted it up, stole it away, and dipped it
three times into the River Lethe,
whispering softly: "Forget, forget,
my good soul! Your pain was too great, too great!"
And he made her ascend to the top of the world —
a place of more light, more beauty, more God! —
into the peace of the heavens, wherefrom
no soul ever returns to the sorrowful earth.

But her son fell headlong down and deep
into a dark abyss underground,
his grave cast as deep inside the earth
as the sky, which shone on it, was high.
He was in the darkness, carried around
by a large and turbulent mass of water
hanging inside the infinite void;
and when the earth swung from side to side,
that great river surged, slapping the walls
of the earth with a crashing sound of thunder.
Glaucos' soul drowned in the water,
dragged and hauled to and fro
against the earth's walls or sucked down
into absolute darkness at the sound of a reckless
rumble in a long and ageless time.
Once a wave surged and threw him
into a crevice, it stranded him
inside a cave by the roaring shore
of a dark ravenous river flowing
in the abyss. There was crying everywhere,
a gloomy cry, the cry of the dead:
tears shed in vain, tears of the lonely
licked away by the earth's sickly worms.
The blackened river of forgotten sorrow

portò Glauco vicino alla palude
Acherusìade, ove tra terra e acqua
errano l'ombre a cui la morte insegna,
e che verranno ad altra vita ancora,
quando il destino li rivoglia in terra.

E vide le aspettanti anime Glauco
sul denso limo, a cui l'urtava il flutto,
e gridò Glauco, alto, e chiamò la madre:
"Madre che offesi… madre che percossi…
madre che feci piangere… Ma vengo
sul fiume eterno, o mamma, a te, del pianto!
O mamma che… feci morire! E morto
ti sono anch'io; nato da te! più morto!
Sì: t'ho percossa. Ma non sai con quanta
forza alle scabre roccie mi percuota
l'acqua laggiù, nel baratro; e che buio
laggiù! che grida! Oh! mai non fossi nato!
Mamma… pietà! perdonami! Se lasci
ch'io salga; e basta che tu voglia, io salgo;
oh! sarò buono! buono, ora per sempre!
non ti batterò più!… Mamma, già l'onda
mi porta via… perdona dunque! Io torno
laggiù… fa presto. Un tempo eri più buona,
o mamma!… O madre, ti mutò la morte!"

Così pregava, il figlio. Ecco, e l'ondata
dal molle limo lo staccò, lo volle
con sé, lo stese, lo portò nel fiume
del pianto vano. E singultendo, il fiume
lo versò nell'abisso; e nell'abisso
se lo riprese il vortice segreto.
E l'anima dell'empio era travolta
dall'acqua eterna, e tratta dal risucchio
giù, poi, nel buio, qua e là percossa.
Ed ella su, nel sommo della terra,
dove è più luce, più beltà, più Dio,

carried Glaucos to the Acheron swamp,
a dark limbo between land and water
of wandering souls cleansed by death,
who will one day return to a body,
when Fate will summon them back to the earth.

Glaucos saw the souls there waiting
on the thick mud of the thunderous shore.
With a shout, he called his mother:
"Mother, I hurt you! Mother, I slapped you!
Mother, I made you cry, but I come
to you now by the river of eternal tears.
Mother, I killed you! But I am dead
too, your child, deader than you!
Yes, I hit you, but look how hard
this water hits me and throws me
against the hard rocks in the darkness below,
and how dark, how shrill, how filled this place
is with tears! I now regret being born!
Mother, have mercy. Mother, forgive me!
Let me come up, just say the word.
I will be good, I promise, now and forever!
I will not hurt you again! Look,
the waves come to take me. Forgive me, quick!
You were good to me once, mother of mine,
but I see that death has changed you now!"

So he begged her, her son. The wave
caught him, stole him away, claimed him,
and lay him down flat upon the shore of
the river of tears, which gurgled in vain
and poured him into the void. And there
it sucked him into its secret vortex.
Glaucos' unholy soul was caught
inside the ageless waters, swallowed
and beaten down in the darkness below.
But she, holy, was seated in heaven —
where there's more light, more beauty, more God —

sedea serena; e con la guancia offesa
sopra la palma, si facea cullare
dal grande mare d'etere, dal breve,
lassù, mollissimo, oscillìo del mondo.
Ecco, levò dalla tranquilla palma
la guancia offesa, e riguardava intorno,
inorecchita. E il buon demone accorse
e le diceva: "Vieni al dolce Lete,
a bere ancora: non assai bevesti!"
Ed ella bevve. Ma via via dagli occhi
le usciva il pianto e le cadea nell'onda.
E le premeva il demone, soave-
mente, la nuca, e le diceva: "Ancora!
Ancora! Bevi! Non assai bevesti!"
E docile beveva ella, e nel Lete
le cadea sempre più dirotto il pianto.
Oh! non beveva che l'oblìo del male,
la santa madre, e si levò piangendo,
e disse: "Io sento che il mio figlio piange.
Portami a lui!" Né il demone s'oppose;
ché cuor di madre è d'ogni Dio più forte.
E con lei scese, ed ella andò sotterra
sempre piangendo e giunse alla palude
Acherusìade. Ed ella errò tra l'alga
deforme, ed ella s'aggirò tra il fango,
sempre accorrendo ad ogni sbocco, appena
sentia mugghiare una marea sotterra,
e il pianto vano venir su, dei morti,
sui neri fiumi, di su i rossi fiumi.

Ed un flutto, laggiù, con un singulto
gittò Glauco in un antro, e poi su l'onde
del nero fiume che correa sotterra,
del pianto occulto, pianto dopo morte;
e lo portò vicino alla palude:
e gridò Glauco, alto, e chiamò la madre:
"Madre, eri buona, e ti mutò la morte!
mamma, io ti feci piangere; mammina,

serene, her doleful cheek still resting
in her hand and lulled eternally, gently,
by the great ether sea, by the far and almost
inaudible rocking of the worlds below.
Then she removed her hand from her cheek
and listened. The good demon came to her:
"Drink," he said "from the River Lethe,
drink some more, since you had not had enough."
She meekly drank, her abundant tears
falling down from her eyes to the waves.
While the demon held her head down,
gently, he whispered: "More! Drink more,
more, since you have not had enough."
She meekly drank, her abundant tears
falling like rainfall into the Lethe.
But all that water just wiped the memory
of any evil done to her, and she rose:
"I hear my son cry," she said in tears,
"Take me to him." The demon consented,
for a mother's heart is stronger than any god.
He accompanied her to the world below,
to the Acheron swamp down below.
She walked around on a bed of seaweed,
she walked around on the thick, muddy shore,
jumping at every wave that rolled ashore,
listening to the roaring of tides
and the desperate cry of the dead souls
from all the red and black rivers.

    Finally, Glaucos landed by a cave,
washed ashore by a sobbing wave,
after sailing down on a river
made of black waters, down underground.
It carried him up to the Acheron swamp
where he shouted loud and called his mother:
"Mother, good mother, whom death has now changed,
mother, I hurt you, mother of mine!

io sì ti feci, io figlio tuo, morire…"
Ma ella, prima anche di lui, gridava
dal triste limo, tra il fragor dei flutti:
"Mia creatura, non lo feci apposta
io, a morir così d'un subito, io
io, a non dirti che non era nulla,
ch'era per gioco… Vieni su: perdona!"

E Glauco ascese. E poi la madre e il figlio
vennero ancor dalla palude in terra,
l'una a soffrire, e l'altro a far soffrire.

Mother, I killed you, I, your son...."
But her cry came before his, ringing louder
from the muddy shore and over the waves:
"Dear son, my creature, it was not my will
to die, so sudden, so soon. I should
have forgiven you sooner. It was nothing.
Only a joke. Return to me. Forgive!"

    And Glaucos returned to the earth, mother
and son returned to the living earth.
She to bleed, he to wound.

SILENO

SILENUS

SILENO

    — Figlio di Pan, figlio del dio silvestre
che nei canneti sibila e frascheggia,
là, dell'Asopo, e frange a questa rupe
il lungo soffio della sua zampogna;
tornar nell'ombra io volli a te, Sileno,
ora che tace la diurna rissa
del maglio e della roccia, or che non odo
più lime invide, più trapani ingordi;
or che gli schiavi qua e là sdraiati
sognano fiumi barbari; e la luna
prendendo il monte, il monte di Marpessa,
piove un pallore in cui tremola il sonno.
Sono un fanciullo, sono anch'io di Paro;
Scopas il nome; palestrita: ed oggi,
coronato di smilace e di pioppo,
correvo a gara con un mio compagno:
e giunsi qui dove gl'ignudi schiavi
Paflàgoni con cupi ululi in alto
tender vedevo intorno ad una rupe
le irsute braccia ed abbassar di schianto.
Ecco, il compagno rimandai soletto
al grammatista e al garrulo flagello;
ma io rimasi ad ammirar gl'ignudi
schiavi intorno la rupe alta ululanti.
Su sfavillìo di cunei l'arguto
maglio cadeva; e io seguia con gli occhi
l'opera grande della breve bietta,
ch'entra sottile come la parola,
poi sforza il masso, come quella il cuore;
quando, con uno scroscio ultimo, il blocco
s'aprì, mostrando, come in ossea noce
bianco gariglio, te di Pan bicorne
figlio, o Sileno: e tu ridevi al sole
riscintillante sopra l'ulivete;
e tu puntavi con l'orecchie aguzze

Silenus

"Son of Pan, of the sylvan god
who whistles and howls through the reeds
past the river and plays his pipe
like a gust of wind against rocks:
I returned to you, Silenus,
when the daily riot of
hammer and stone had ended.
No more eager files or drills when
slaves sleep and dream of faraway
rivers: I went up to the mountain
of Paros, as the moon dripped down
its paleness, where dreams tremble.
I am young, a Parian lad.
Scopas's my name, an athlete too.
Today I raced with a friend
crowned in smylax and poplar.
I came here, where naked slaves
from Asia lift big stones,
howling grimly, their hairy arms
dropping and moving rocks.
I sent my friend back to our town,
to our school teacher and his whip.
I stayed and stared at the slaves
howling and lifting big rocks:
their noisy hammers beat on
shiny wedges. I followed
the cunning work of their chocks,
thin like words as they enter
the rock, but forceful, like words are
to hearts. Then, with a big crash,
the block split open like a walnut shell
showing its kernel: you, the son
of the horned god Pan, Silenus,
laughing, bright among the trees,
with your pointy ears pointing like arrows

l'aereo mareggiar delle cicale.
Ma che mai cela questa rupe? Io venni
a domandarti perché mai sorridi
solo, costì, col tuo marmoreo volto,
e come tendi le puntute orecchie
al sibìlio de' fragili canneti.
Od altro ascolti e vedi altro, Sileno?-

Scopas, alunno dell'alpestre Paro,
così parlava al candido Sileno
figlio improvviso della roccia, nato
sotto martelli immemori di schiavi.
Il giovinetto gli sedea di contro
sopra un macigno, con al vento i bruni
riccioli, in mezzo a molti blocchi sparsi,
come il pastore tra l'inerte gregge.
E gli rispose il candido Sileno,
o parve, a un tratto con un volger d'occhi
simile a lampo che vaporò bianco
e scavò col fugace alito il monte.
Ed a quel lampo il giovinetto vide
ciò che non più gli tramontò dagli occhi.

Vide, sotto la scorza aspra del monte,
vide il tuo regno, o bevitor di gioia,
vecchio Sileno: una palestra: in essa
sorprese il breve anelito del lampo
in un bianco lor moto i palestriti:
l'ombra seguace irrigidì quel moto
per sempre; e stette nelle braccia tese
degli oculati pugili già pronto
lo scatto di fischiante arco di tasso,
ed alla mano al lanciator ricurvo
restò sospeso impazïente il disco
in cui pulsava il vortice di ruota,
ed alla pianta alta de' corridori

at the clouds of cicadas in the sky.
What hides in the rocks of this mountain,
and why do you smile to yourself
with your face of white marble?
And, when your pointy ears move
to the frail hissing of reeds,
what else do you see and hear?"

The son of mountainous Paros,
Scopas, thus spoke to Silenus,
son of the rocks, who emerged one day
under the indifferent hammers of slaves.
The lad sat by him with his long
black curls among marble blocks
like a shepherd among his flock,
and the white Silenus answered,
or so it seemed, as his eyes turned
and flashed like white lightning
piercing the rock.
And in that flash, the lad could see
something his eyes would never forget.

Under the crust of the mountain,
he saw your realm, Silenus,
drinker of joy: a gymnasium[1]
where the flash of light revealed
hundreds of athletes in slow motion
and captured them forever:
the shadow cast them in stone.
And in the boxers' arms, outstretched,
he could see the ready tension
of a well-drawn wooden bow.
In the hands of discus-throwers,
the discus hung suspended,
restless, pulsing and swirling,
and a sudden gust of wind blew
on the runners' feet as they ran.

1.   The images that Scopas sees through the Silenus foreshadow what the
artists will later sculpt: athletes such as the Discobolus of Myron, the birth of
Aphrodite, and a group of young girls ascending to the temple of Athena.

l'impeto rapido oscillò del vento:
gli efebi intenti a contemplar la gara
ressero sul perfetto omero l'asta.
In tanto a luminosi propilei,
con sul capo le braccia arrotondate,
vedeva lente vergini salire:
la pompa che albeggiò per un momento,
eternamente camminò nell'ombra.

Vide, sotto la scorza aspra del monte,
emersa dalle grandi acque Afrodite
vergine, al breve anelito del lampo
che la scopriva, con le pure braccia
velar le sacre fonti della vita:
l'ombra seguace conservò per sempre
la dolce vita ch'esita nascendo.
E vide anche la morte, anche il dolore:
vide fanciulli e vergini cadere
sotto gli strali di adirati numi,
e tutti gli occhi volgere agl'ingiusti
sibili: tutti; ma non già la madre:
la madre, al cielo; e proteggea di tutta
sé la più spaurita ultima figlia.
In tanto le Nereidi dal mare
volsero il collo, con la nivea spinta
del piede su le nuove onde sospesa;
mentre al bosco fuggivano le ninfe
inseguite da satiri correnti
con lor solidi zoccoli di becco;
e un baccanale dileguò sul monte.

Il giovinetto udì strepere trombe,
gemere conche, ed ascoltò soavi,
tra l'immensa manìa bronzosonante,
squillare i doppi flauti di loto.
Ed ecco il monte ritornò com'era,
tacito immoto, se non se nel fosco
gomito d'una forra anche appariva

And the young cadets who looked on
held their spears on perfect shoulders.
He saw the girls climbing slowly,
their rounded arms above their heads,
to the temple drowned in sunlight.
They flashed into sight just for a moment
and walked on through the darkness forever.

    Under the crust of the mountain,
he saw Aphrodite, rising pure
from the great sea. The lightning
showed her shielding
her growing womb with her arms,
and the shadow cast in stone
the frail birth of all lives.
He saw death, and he saw sorrow,
he saw girls and lads all fall
for the wrath of envious gods,
and all eyes turned away from injustice,
except Niobe's, a young mother
who faced the sky as she shielded
the frailest of her many children.
And he saw Nereids[2] swim away
with foamy feet paddling up
on the waves of the new sea.
And the nymphs ran to the woods,
fleeing lewd and bawdy satyrs
with their sturdy equine hooves.
And a bacchanal was there.

    With the blare of trumpets
and the dark echo of gongs and
in the midst of that bronze clangor,
the shrill voice of double flutes.
Then the mountain fell silent
again, except for

2.   There is no reference to a single work of art by Scopas (or a copy of it) but
several references to various works by him.

l'ultimo bianco di lucenti groppe
di centauri precipiti, e sonava
un quadruplice tonfo di galoppo,
che poi vanì. Ma quando tacque tutto,
oh! come sotto il velo di grandi acque,
s'udiva ancora eco di cembali, eco
di timpani, eco di piovosi sistri;
ed euhoè ed euhoè gridare
come in un sogno, come nel gran sogno
di quelle rupi candide di marmo
dormenti nella sacra ombra notturna.
E con quel grido si mescea nell'eco
il lungo soffio della tua zampogna,
o Pan silvano; e percotea la fronte
del sorridente bevitor di gioia,
e del fanciullo che sedea tra i blocchi,
quale un pastore tra l'inerte gregge.

a last white spot of horsebacks
of fleeing centaurs flashing
in the dark curve of a gorge
and the thud of galloping
horses, which vanished. Then,
like under a shroud of water,
the faint echo of cymbals,
of drums and rain-like rattles,
cries of euoi euoi,[3]
dream-like, like in the dream
of snow-white cliffs of marble,
quiet in the holy night.
Pan, the blowing of your pipe
intermingled with those cries,
hitting on your smiling forehead,
drinker of joy, Silenus,
and the lad among white blocks
like a shepherd among his flock.

3.   The ritual shout of joy at the festivals of Dionysus.

POEMI DI PSYCHE

POEMS OF PSYCHE

POEMI DI PSYCHE

I. Psyche

O Psyche, tenue più del tenue fumo
ch'esce alla casa, che se più non esce,
la gente dice che la casa è vuota;
più lieve della lieve ombra che il fumo
disegna in terra nel vanire in cielo:
sei prigioniera nella bella casa
d'argilla, o Psyche, e vi sfaccendi dentro,
pur lieve sì che non se n'ode un suono;
ma pur vi sei, nella ben fatta casa,
chè se n'alza il celeste alito al cielo.
E vi sfaccendi dentro e vi sospiri
sempre soletta, ché non hai compagne
altre che voci di cui tu sei l'eco;
ignude voci che con un sussulto
sorgere ammiri su da te, d'un tratto;
voci segrete a cui tu servi, o Psyche.

Intorno alla tua casa, o prigioniera,
pasce le greggi un Essere selvaggio,
bicorne, irsuto; e sui due piè di capro
sempre impennato, come a mezzo un salto.
E tu ne temi, ch'egli là minaccia
impazïente, e sempre ulula e corre;
e spesso guazza nel profondo fiume,
come la pioggia, e spesso crolla il bosco,
al par del vento; e non è mai l'istante
che tu non l'oda o non lo veda, o Psyche,
Pan multiforme. Eppur talvolta ei soffia
dolce così nelle palustri canne,
che tu l'ascolti, o Psyche, con un pianto
sì, ma che è dolce, perché fu già pianto
e perse il tristo nel passar dagli occhi

I. Psyche[1]

Psyche, thinner than the strand of smoke
that streams from the house, which, when it ceases,
makes people think that the house is empty.
Lighter even than the shadow that the smoke
traces on the earth as it vanishes in the sky.
You're a prisoner in the lovely house
of clay, O Psyche, where you work,
light as you are, not making a sound.
Yet there you are, still, in that well-made house,
its thread of gray breath floating up to the sky.
And you work, and you sigh,
always alone, with no companions
other than the voices of which you are the echo:
naked voices which you're startled to see
rising above you suddenly.
Secret voices you serve, O Psyche.

Around your house, dear prisoner,
a savage creature pastures his sheep,
hairy and horned with two goat-feet
that seem always primed for a sudden leap.
And you live in fear, in fear of his threat,
his urging impatience, his howl and pursuit.
And sometimes he's pouring into the river,
like the rain. At others, he's thrashing the woods
like the wind. And there's never a single moment
that you're not seeing or hearing, O Psyche,
that shapeshifter Pan. And sometimes he sighs
so softly through the reeds in the river-bed
that you listen to him, dear Psyche, in tears —
but tears that are sweet since they've already been shed,
and they lost their sadness when they left your eyes

---

1.   Pascoli's poem uses Psyche to represent the individual soul that returns to
nature after its death and Pan as the god of nature to which the soul eventually
returns.

la prima volta. E tu ripensi a quando
vergine fosti ad un'ignota belva
data per moglie, crudel mostro ignoto.
E sempre al buio tu con lui giacesti
rabbrividendo docile, ed alfine,
vigile nel suo sonno alto di fiera,
accesa la tua piccola lucerna,
guardasti; e quella belva era l'Amore.

   E lo sapesti solo allor che sparve,
l'Amore alato. E ne sospiri e l'ami.
E nella casa di ben fatta argilla,
dove sei schiava delle voci ignude,
sempre l'aspetti, che ritorni, e dorma
con te. Tu piangi, quando Pan, la notte,
fa dolcemente sufolar le canne;
piangi d'amore, o solitaria Psyche,
nella tua casa, dove più non tieni
posto, che l'ombra, e non fai più rumore,
che l'alito; e le voci odi che fanno
all'improvviso a te cader dal ciglio
la stilla che non ti volea cadere.

   Però che sono e sùbite e severe
le più; ma più di tutte una che sempre
contende e grida, ad ogni tuo sospiro
verso l'alata libertà: "Non devi!"
Quella non t'ama, credi tu; ma un'altra
è, sì, che t'ama, e ti favella a parte
e ti consola, e teco piange, e parla
così sommessa che tu credi a volte
che sia meschina prigioniera anch'ella.

   E tu devi, d'un mucchio alto di semi,
far tanti mucchi, e sceverare i grani
d'orzo, i chicchi di miglio, le rotonde
veccie, i bislunghi pippoli di vena.
E come fine polvere di ferro
sparsa per tutto il mucchio è la semenza

the first time. And you think back to when you were just
a girl, given in marriage to an unknown
beast, unknown and cruel and brutish.
And you'd lie beside him as the sun went down,
trembling softly, till finally,
awake beside the slumbering monster,
you held your little lamp above
and looked at him; saw that beast was Love.

But you recognized him only as he disappeared,
winged Love. And you mourn him and love him.
And in the house of close-packed clay,
where you are slave to the eerie voices,
you constantly await the day
of his return. You cry when Pan,
all through the night, makes the reeds whisper.
You cry out of love, dear lonely Psyche,
in your house, a home for you no longer,
where you see only shadows and don't make a sound
except for your breath, and you hear the voices,
which against your will, all of a sudden,
make teardrops rain on the stony ground.

But the voices are the more sudden and severe:
and the harshest of all is the one that you hear
shouting or screaming every time you sigh
for winged freedom. "You mustn't do it!"
That one doesn't love you, but there's another
who hears and nurtures you like a mother
and cries with you and speaks to you
so mutedly that you would wager
that she's a wretched prisoner too.

And you're given this task: to sort the grains
from a towering silo top-full of grains —
the grains of millet from the granules of wheat,
of rice or buckwheat or split-faced barley,
and lastly, like a fine dusting of iron,
scattered through the silo, the poppy

dei papaveri. E tu, Psyche, tu gemi
trepida, inerte; e poi con le tue dita
d'aria ti provi, e scegli a lungo i semi
del papavero immemore, e in un giorno
tanti ne cogli, quanti appena udresti
cantare nella secca urna d'un fiore.
E piangi, ed ecco vengono le figlie
dell'alma Terra, frugole e succinte,
dalla pineta dove a Pan selvaggio
frangean tra gli aghi dei pinastri il suolo.
Non so chi disse alle operaie nere
di Pan la cosa. Ma si fa d'un tratto
un brulichìo per l'odorata selva;
e sgorgano esse a frotte dai minuti
lor collicelli, mentre Pan nell'ombra
s'addorme al canto delle sue cicale.
E salgono alla casa, onda su onda,
fila incessanti di formiche, ed opre
vengono a te; ma prima i grani d'orzo,
pesi, e i bislunghi pippoli di vena
portano, due di loro uno di quelli;
fanno le veccie di tra il biondo miglio,
poi fanno il miglio minimo, poi vanno.
E resta a te la polvere di semi,
di cui ciascuno dal suo nulla esprima
un lungo stelo e il molle fior del sonno.

    E il molle sonno tu lo chiami, o Psyche,
dacché di quelle voci una, la voce
che non t'ama e ti sgrida aspra, ti disse:
"Vil fanticella, prendi questa brocca
e va per acqua al nero fonte; al fonte
di cui sgorga l'oscura onda, sotterra,
al fiume morto. Esci per poco, e torna".
E tuo mal grado, o schiavolina, andasti
con la tua brocca di cristallo al fonte;
e là vedesti, su la grotta, il drago,
l'insonne drago, sempre aperti gli occhi;

seeds. And you, Psyche, you sigh,
tremulous, lethargic, and then you try
with your light fingers. You begin to pick out
at length the forgetful poppy seeds,
and in a day you'd picked out more
than you'd ever heard clatter in the urn of a flower.
And you cry, but look! Here come the daughters
of the nourishing Earth. Thin-waisted, they toil
in the grove where for Pan they plow the soil
beneath needles dropped by the conifers.
Who knows who told the black workers
of Pan about this? Then suddenly
there's a stirring all through the fragrant trees,
and they climb out in droves from their tiny hillocks
as Pan, in the shade, falls slowly to sleep,
lulled by the lilting song of the crickets.
And they march to your house, wave after wave,
an endless column of ants, to save
you labor. First off, they separate
the barley from the tawny wheat,
then carry off the buckwheat, grain by grain,
two ants for every boulder of grain.
Then they cart off the rice and the heavy millet.
And they leave to you a dusting of seeds,
each one of which contains within it
a languid stem and the petals of sleep.

    And you now call for that flower of sleep,
since the voice that always made you shiver
took you aside one day and whispered to you:
"Silly little girl, go get that pitcher
and fetch some water from the black fountain
whose dark water spurts from the dead river.
Do it quickly, and then come home again."
And in spite of yourself, good little servant,
you went to the fountain with your crystal pitcher,
and there in the grotto you saw the dragon
that never sleeps, his eyes always open.

e tu chiudesti, o Psyche, i tuoi, da lungi
rabbrividendo; ed ecco, non veduto,
uno ti prese l'anfora di mano,
che piena in mano dopo un po' ti rese,
e dileguò. Tu lentamente a casa
tornavi smorta, e con un gran sospiro
apristi gli occhi, e nel cristallo puro
tu guardasti l'oscura acqua di morte,
e vi vedesti il vortice del nulla.
E ne tremasti. E Pan allora un dolce
canto soffiò nelle palustri canne,
che tu piangesti a quel pensier di morte
come piangevi per desìo d'amore:
lo stesso pianto, così dolce, o Psyche!

  Ma pur ne tremi, o Psyche, ancora, e mesta
invochi il sonno, perché a te nasconda
quell'altro sonno, che non vuoi, più grande!
Ma delle voci di cui tu sei schiava,
quella che t'ama e ti consola a parte,
ecco che ti favella e ti consola:
"Povera Psyche, io so dov'è l'Amore.
Oh! l'Amore t'aspetta oltre la morte.
Di là, t'aspetta. Se tu passi il nero
fiume sotterra, troverai l'Amore.
Tremi? C'è un vecchio, vecchio come il tempo,
che tutti imbarca, e non fa male a Psyche!
E c'è un cane, oltre il fiume, che divora
ciò ch'è di troppo, e non fa male a Psyche!
Pallida Psyche, prendi tra le labbra
che sembrano due petali appassiti
di morta rosa, un obolo, e leggiero
tienlo, così, che te lo prenda il vecchio,
né tu lo senta; e chiudi gli occhi, e dormi.
E prendi una focaccia, anche, col miele
e col mite papavero, e leggiera
tienla, così, che te la prenda il cane,
né tu lo senta; e chiudi gli occhi, e dormi.
Appena desta, rivedrai l'Amore".

But you closed yours for a good long moment
and shuddered. It was then that someone unseen
took the jug from your hand, and after a moment,
gave it back to you, full, and slipped away.
Slowly you returned the way you had come,
and with an enormous sigh, pale as death,
you opened your eyes, and in the spotless pitcher,
you saw the pitch-black water of death.
Nothingness swirled, and it made you tremble.
So Pan breathed a tune through the swamp's tall reeds
since you were crying at the thought of death
the way you used to cry for love —
the same cry, Psyche — and how sweet it was!

    And yet you tremble still, my Psyche,
and call for sleep, because it hides
that vaster sleep you can't abide.
But suddenly that voice is there,
the one that loves and nurtures you:
"I know where Love is, wretched Psyche –
he waits for you beyond the grave!
That's where he waits, and if you cross
those pitch-dark waters, you'll find Love there.
There is a man as old as time,
who ferries souls and won't harm you, Psyche.
And there's a hound that devours excess —
whatever's too much — but won't harm you, Psyche.
Pale Psyche, take between your lips
two desiccated petals of a long-dead rose.
Take an obol and hold it tightly like this,
so the old man can take it — you won't feel a thing —
then close your eyes, my dear, and sleep.
And take a bit of bread and honey
and poppy, and hold it lightly like this,
so the dog can take it — you won't feel a thing —
then close your eyes, my dear, and sleep.
As soon as you wake, you'll see Love again."

Tu la focaccia prendi su, col miele,
tu chiudi nelle labbra scolorite
l'obolo; e non so quale alito lieve
ti porta via. Per dove passi, un'ombra
passa, non più che d'ali di farfalla.
Ma tu non dormi; e lievemente il vecchio
ti prende il piccolo obolo di bocca;
ma tu lo senti, e senti anche la rauca
lena del vecchio rematore, come
se alcuno seghi il duro legno, e come
se alcuno picchi su la putre terra;
anche senti un latrato, solitario;
e tremi tanto, che di man ti sfugge
ah! la focaccia, e fa un tonfo nell'acqua
morta del fiume. Ed anche tu vi cadi,
cadi nel queto vortice del nulla.

Ma Pan il gregge pasce là su l'orlo
del morto fiume. Non udivi il suono,
là, della vita? Tremuli belati
e cupi mugli, il gorgheggiar d'uccelli
tra foglie verdi, e sotto gravi mandre
lo scroscio vasto delle foglie secche.
E ti cullava nella vecchia barca
un canto lungo, che da te più sempre
s'allontanava sino a dileguare
nella dimenticata fanciullezza.
Pan! era Pan! Egli ti porge un braccio
ispido, e su ti leva intirizzita,
gelida, o Psyche; immemore; e ti corca
nuda così, lieve così, nel vello
del suo gran petto, e in sé ti cela a tutti.

Quali alte grida là dal mondo! Quali
tristi lamenti intorno alla tua casa,
d'argilla, o Psyche, donde più non esce
il tenue fumo, alla tua casa vuota
di cui sparve il celeste alito in cielo!

You get a bit of bread and honey,
you press between your pallid lips
an obol, and a breath of air
carries you off. And you pass where nothing
passes but the shadow of a butterfly's wing.
But you're not asleep as the old man lightly
fishes the obol out of your mouth.
You feel it all, just as you feel
the force of the old man's vigorous strokes —
as if someone were sawing a log of oak
or shovelling into the putrid earth,
and you hear a single, lonely bark,
and you're trembling so badly that from your hand
the bread has slipped and made a splash
in the dead water! And you fall in too,
into the silence and the dark.

But Pan is pasturing his flocks
on the banks of the river. Didn't you hear
the sounds of life? Tremulous bleating,
resonant lowing, the twittering
of birds among green growth, and underneath
the constant crunching of desiccated leaves.
And a song rocked you like a wave from beneath,
an old song for an old boat
that slowly but surely made you float
into your forgotten childhood.
Pan stretches out his hairy arm
and lifts you up all numb with cold,
remembering nothing, — poor Psyche — and he folds
you into the cave of his arms
and there conceals you from everyone.

What loud cries back on earth! What sad
laments around your house of clay,
O Psyche, where tenuous smoke no longer
leaves the chimney, an empty house
which gives up its gray-green breath to the sky.

Ti cercano le genti, o fuggitiva.
O Psyche! o Psyche! dove sei? Ti cerca
nel morto fiume il vecchio che tragitta
tutti di là. Ti cerca, acre fiutando,
dall'altra riva il cane che divora
ciò ch'è di troppo. Tutti, o Psyche, invano!
O Psyche! o Psyche! dove sei? Ma forse
nelle cannucce. Ma chi sa? Tra il gregge.
O nel vento che passa o nella selva
che cresce. O sei nel bozzolo d'un verme
forse racchiusa, o forse ardi nel sole.

 Ché Pan l'eterno t'ha ripresa, o Psyche.

II. La civetta

 "O tristi capi! O solo voci! O schiene
vaie così come la biscia d'acqua!
Via di costì!" gridava agro il custode
della prigione. Era selvaggio il luogo,
deserto, in mezzo della sacra Atene,
con sue deformi catapecchie al piede
di bigie roccie dalle strie giallastre,
piene di buchi, verdeggianti appena
qua e là di partenio e di serpillo.
Il sole era sui monti, e nell'azzurro
passava fosco a ora a ora un volo
d'aspri rondoni che girava attorno,
sopra la rocca, alla gran Dea di bronzo,
forte strillando. Ed anche in terra un gruppo
di su di giù correva, di fanciulli;

And people are looking for a fugitive.
O Psyche, Psyche! Where can you be?
The old man who ferries all who've lived
across the lifeless river is looking
for you. On the opposite bank, the mad
dog, who devours excess, is looking
for you. And all in vain, O Psyche!
But where, O Psyche, where can you be?
Perhaps among the reeds or flocks,
or in the west wind as it blows,
or in the forest as it grows.
Or crawling as a lowly worm,
or maybe in the sun's gold burn.

    Eternal Pan has taken you back.

II. The Owl[2]

"You grim skulls, nothing but voices,
your backs mottled as a water-snake's —
get outta here!" the prison guard roared.
It was a rough place, semi-deserted,
though in the middle of holy Athens
with its ramshackle shacks crowding the bottom
of the gray cliffs, stippled with amber
and brushed with green, here and there,
where thyme flourished or feverfew.
The sun shone over the blue mountains,
darkened every now and again
by a crowd of swifts that circled the Rock,
circled the powerful goddess of bronze,[3]
making a racket. And down on the ground,
another crowd was running about,
a crowd of kids, and they were making

2.   "The Owl" narrates the day of Socrates' death in Athens, drawing inspiration from Plato's *Phaedo*, but presenting the events from the point of view of some children, whose names are mostly taken from Herondas' *Mimiamboi* (third century before Christ). Here, the owl is not only Athena's sacred bird, but also the symbol of Socrates' immortal soul leaving his body.
3.   A reference to the statue of the goddess Athena on the Acropolis.

strillando anch'essi. Ed ecco s'aprì l'uscio
della casa degli Undici, e il custode
alzò dal tetro limitar la voce.

  Egli diceva: "È per voi scianto ancora?
Ieri da Delo ritornò la nave
sacra, e le feste sono ormai finite.
Non è più tempo di legar col refe
gli scarabei! Non più, di fare a mosca
di bronzo!" Un poco più lontano il branco
trasse, in silenzio. Poi gridarono: "Ohe?
che parli tu di scarabei, di mosche?
È una civetta". In vero una civetta
tutta arruffata era nel pugno a Gryllo
figlio di Gryllo facitor di scudi,
ch'era il più grande. Ma l'avea pocanzi
in un crepaccio Hyllo predata, il figlio
d'Hyllo vasaio, ch'era il più piccino.
In un crepaccio della bigia rupe,
sotto un cespuglio di parïetaria,
vide due rilucenti Hyllo stateri
d'oro, nell'ombra, e s'appressò; ma l'oro
non c'era più: poi li rivide i due
fissi e tondi nell'ombra occhi d'uccello.
Una civetta della Dea di Atene
immobilmente riguardava il figlio
d'Hyllo vasaio; che con le due mani
all'improvviso l'abbrancò su l'ali,
e la portava. E Coccalo sorvenne
che gliela prese; a Coccalo la prese
Cottalo; e Gryllo a lui la vinse: allora
Cottalo pianse, Coccalo sorrise,
e il piccolino frignò dietro il grande.

a racket too. But then a door
opened to the House of the Eleven,[4] and the guard
began to speak from the dark threshold.

    "You guys still on holiday, are you?
The sacred ship got back from Delos
yesterday, and the festival
is finished. The time for catching beetles
in a net or playing hide and seek
is over!" A short way off, the crowd
of kids dragged their feet, silent.
Then they shouted, "Hey! What
do you mean 'beetles,' 'flies'? It's an owl!"
It was in fact a tousled owl
that the biggest boy had on his fist —
young Gryllus, son of the shield-maker.
But it was actually the smallest boy —
Hyllus, the son of the vase-maker —
who'd caught the owl a short time before
in a crevice in the blue mountains.
In a crevice in a grey cliff,
underneath a clinging bush,
Hyllus saw two round gold coins
that then disappeared; then he saw them again,
two bird's eyes gleaming in the shadows.
An owl of the goddess of Athens
was staring fixedly at little Hyllus,
who suddenly reached out his little hands
and grabbed the bird by its wings and held it.
Then Coccalus came along and stole it,
and Cottalus took it from Coccalus,
then Gryllus won it off Cottalus.
Cottalus cried, Coccalus smiled,
and little Hyllus went around whimpering
following Gryllus, the biggest boy.

4.   The Athenian magistrates in charge of death sentences.

Ma Gryllo avvinse con un laccio un piede
della civetta, e la facea sbalzare
e svolazzare al caldo sole estivo.
E dai tuguri altri fanciulli, figli
d'arcieri sciti, figli di metèci,
trassero. E in mezzo a tutti la civetta
chiudeva apriva trasognata gli occhi
rotondi, fatti per la sacra notte.
E il coro "Balla" cantò forte "o muori!"

E nel carcere in tanto era un camuso
Pan boschereccio, un placido Sileno
col viso arguto e grossi occhi di toro.
Dolce parlava. E gli sedeva ai piedi
un giovanetto dalla lunga chioma,
bellissimo. E molti altri erano intorno,
uomini, muti. Ed a ciascuno in cuore
era un fanciullo che temeva il buio;
e il buon Sileno gli facea l'incanto.
"Voi non vedete ciò ch'io sono. Io sono"
egli diceva "ciò che di me sfugge
agli occhi umani: l'invisibile. Ora
s'ei guarda, come fosse ebbro, vacilla;
ma non è lui, non è quest'io, che trema:
trema ciò ch'egli guarda, che si vede,
che mai non dura uguale a sé, che muore.
Io, di me, sono l'anima, che vive
più, quanto più vive con sé, lontana
dal mondo, nella sacra ombra dei sensi.
E s'ella parta libera per sempre,
nella notte immortale, ove si trovi
ella con tutto che non mai vacilla,
ella morrà? non vedrà più?" Qualcuno
"Vedrà" rispose; "Non morrà" rispose.

Poi fu silenzio. Il musico vegliardo
Pan era solo, accanto al suo pensiero
invisibile. Il bello adolescente,

    So there he was with the owl on a string,
hopping and hovering in the summer sun.
Out of the slums more children came:
the children of immigrants or Scythian archers.
In the midst of it all, the captive owl
drowsily blinked its big round eyes,
eyes designed for the sacred night.
The children shouted, "Dance or die!"

    Meanwhile in the prison, there was
a snub-nosed rustic Pan, an even-
tempered Silenus, with a wily mug
and eyes as big and wide as a bull's.
He was speaking softly, and at his feet
was a beautiful young lad with flowing locks,
and others too, all listening.
Each one of them, deep inside,
was a little boy afraid of the dark,
so the goodly Silenus was telling them a story.
"You can't see what I am," he was saying.
"I'm the part of me that can't be seen,
the invisible part. The body may falter
as if I was drunk, but that's not me.
The part you can look at, that can be seen,
is what falters. The part that never stays
the same, that dies. What I really am
is a soul that will live on of its own power
far from the world in the sacred dark
of the senses. And if it gets free forever
in the undying night, where it finds itself
with everything else that never falters,
will it ever die? Or will its eyes be opened?"
"Its eyes will be opened," someone said.
And he replied, "It will not die."

    Then there was silence. Snub-nosed Pan
was like an old musician, alone with his thoughts,
invisible. The beautiful youth

supino il capo, con la lunga chioma
spiovente, lungi dalla nuca, all'aria,
beveva l'eco delle sue parole.
Ed ecco entrò dall'abbaino un canto
d'acute voci: "Balla, dunque, o muori!"

E il custode dal tetro uscio i fanciulli
striduli fece lontanar nel sole,
fuor dell'ombra dei tetti e della roccia.
Ma là, nel sole, molleggiò più goffa
sul pugno a Gryllo, s'arruffò, chiudendo
aprendo gli occhi, la civetta, e i bimbi
ridean più forte. Onde il custode: "O Gryllo
figlio di Gryllo, tu che sei più savio,
dà retta. Sai: codesto uccello è sacro
alla Dea nostra, a cui tu canti l'inno
movendo nudo coi compagni nudi
per la città. La nostra Dea sa tutto,
ché gli occhi ha grigi, di civetta, e vede
con essi per l'oscurità del cielo".
"No, che non vede" disse Hyllo "né vuole
vedere, e chiude gli occhi tondi al sole".
"Passero, taci. Tu, Gryllo" il custode
riprese, "grande già mi sei. Conosco
tuo padre, il buono artefice di scudi.
Tu gli somigli come fico a fico.
Fa chetare le tortore ciarliere.
C'è dentro la mia casa uno che muore!"
"Chi? Questa sera?" "Al tramontar del sole!"
"Perché?" "La nave ritornò da Delo.
Ed egli vide un sogno: una vestita
di bianche vesti, che gli disse: O uomo,
il terzo giorno toccherai la terra!

was lying with his head back, with his long hair
pouring down through the air away from his neck.
He was drinking in the sound of his master's words.
Then the shrill sound of voices came in through the window:
"Dance or die! Dance or die!"

The guard shooed them away, made the noisy
kids scatter into the sunshine
out of the shadow of the holy rock.
But that only made the owl light up
on Gryllus' wrist, made him ruffle his feathers,
blink his big eyes open and closed —
and the boys all laughed, louder than ever.
So the guard called out, "Gryllus, Gryllus,
son, you're the oldest: lead by example.
You know that bird is sacred to Our Lady,
to whom you sing the hymn, in procession pure,
naked alongside your naked peers
through our holy city. There is nothing Our Lady
does not see, for her eyes are gray,
so she sees through the darkness of the night."
"But she's not seeing anything," Hyllus butted in.
"She's shut her eyes tight to the blazing sun!"
"Enough from you, cuckoo. But Gryllus, you're
not just a kid now. I know your father:
a good shield-maker and a good man.
The apple doesn't fall far from the tree.
See if you can quieten these twittering swallows.
There's a man in here who's about to die!"
"Who is it? This evening?" "When the sun goes down."
"But why?" "The ship is coming back from Delos.[5]
He had a dream of a woman in white
who told him, man, on the third day,
you'll go down below the earth.[6]

5.   Socrates' execution had to be postponed until the sacred ship Paralos
returned from Delos, where the annual celebration of Athens' liberation from
Crete was held. During that time, no death sentences could be carried out.
6.   A reference to Plato's *Crito*, where Socrates recounts a dream he had before
his death.

E la cicuta, sì, berrà dentr'oggi.
Tra poco, o Gryllo. Che in silenzio ei muoia!"

Tacquero allora i giovanetti a lungo
pensando all'uomo che così, per mare,
tornava in patria. E Gryllo disse: "È l'uomo
che andava scalzo e passeggiava in aria,
e diceva che il sole era una pietra,
e sapeva che terra era la luna..."
Ed in silenzio trassero alla roccia
tutti, e stettero presso la prigione,
come aspettando. E la civetta, al lento
filo costretta, si posò sul ramo
d'un oleastro che sporgea dal masso
sopra i ricciuti capi dei fanciulli.
Si chinò, s'arruffò, molleggiò, cieca
per la gran luce rosea del tramonto.
E dai tegoli un passero la vide
e garrì contro la non mai veduta,
e vennero altri passeri al garrito;
e il frastuono eccitò le rondinelle,
e fuori ognuna si versò dal nido;
e da un tacito ombroso bosco sacro
venne la capinera e l'usignuolo.
E grande era lo strepito e il bisbiglio,
pur non udito dai fanciulli, attenti
ad una voce che venìa di dentro,
di chi tornava alla sua patria terra
invisibile, e placido parlava
a un'altra barca che incrociò sul mare.

E poi cessato il favellìo di dentro,
un dei fanciulli disse: "Hyllo, tu monta
su le mie spalle, e narra quel che vedi".

He'll drink hemlock by the end of the night.
In a little while. Let him die in peace."

    The kids went quiet then for a long time,
thinking of the man who would be, in that way,
returning to his homeland. And Gryllus said,
"He's the man who went around
without any shoes on, who walked on air,
who said the sun was made of rock
and knew the moon was a kind of earth...."
And in silence they dragged themselves to the Rock,
all of them, and stood near the prison,
as if waiting for something. And the owl,
still tied to the slack string,
settled on a branch of oleaster,
which stretched out from the mass of rock
above the children's curly heads.
He stooped, ruffled his feathers, hopped
about, blinded as he was
by the grand pink glare of the sunset.
And from the tiles a swift saw him
and chirped, surprised at the unknown bird.
Other swifts came to the chirruping.
The racket excited the swallows,
and they all rushed out of their nests,
and from a sacred silent shadowy wood
came nightingales and blackcaps,
and great was the hubbub and hullabaloo
though the boys didn't hear it, attentive as they were
to a voice that came from the inside
of a man who was returning to his homeland,
invisible, and was placidly speaking
to another ship that was crossing the sea.

    But once the murmuring inside
had stopped, one of the lads piped up,
"Hey, Hyllus, climb up on my shoulders
and say what you can see inside!"

Hyllo montò sul dorso a quel fanciullo,
e sogguardò per l'abbaino: "Io vedo".
"Hyllo, che vedi?" "Un buon Sileno vecchio".
"Che dice?" "Dice che andrà via, che il morto
non sarà lui: seppelliranno un altro".
Il sole in tanto ritraeva i raggi
dai bianchi templi della sacra Atene.
Sola splendea la cuspide dell'asta
che aveva in mano la gran Dea di bronzo.
Brillò d'un tratto e poi si spense; e il sole
calò raggiando dietro il Citerone.
"Hyllo, che vedi?" "Beve". "La cicuta!"
"Piangono, gli altri; uno si copre il capo
con la veste, uno grida". "Esso, che dice?"
"Dice di far silenzio, come quando
si sparge l'orzo, presso l'ara, e il sale".

Ed era alto silenzio, che s'udiva
il passo scalzo su e giù dell'uomo,
e poi nemmeno si sentì quel passo..
"Hyllo, che vedi?" "È sul lettuccio; un altro
gli preme un piede. S'è coperto. Muore…"
"Dunque non esce?" "Ora si scopre. Dice:
Un gallo al Dio che ci guarisce i mali!"
"Che? La cicuta è un farmaco salubre?"
"Uno gli chiude ora la bocca e gli occhi".
Dunque non parte? è sempre lì? Sì, morto.

E bisbigliando stavano i fanciulli
lungo la roccia, al buio. Ecco e la porta
s'aprì. N'usciva con singhiozzi e pianti
un vecchio, un giovinetto, altri poi molti
tristi gemendo. E dall'inconscie dita

So Hyllus climbed up on his shoulders
and peered into the prison. "I see...."
"What can you see?" "A nice old Pan."
"What's he saying?" "That he'll get away.
That the dead person won't be him.
That they'll be burying someone else."
Meanwhile the sun was withdrawing its rays
from the white temples of holy Athens.
Only the tip of the spear still shone
that the great bronze Athena held in her hand.
It shone for a moment and then went out.
And the sun went down behind the mountain.
"Hey Hyllus, what can you see?"
"He's drinking...." "The hemlock!" "The others are crying.
One of them's covering his head with his tunic.
Another one's wailing." "And what's he saying?"
"He's saying to keep silent, like in front of an altar
when they scatter barley seed or salt."

   And then, deep silence, in which you heard
him pacing back and forth. And then,
even the pacing came to an end.
"Hyllus, what can you see?" "He's on
the bed. Somebody's holding his feet...
they're covering him with a sheet. He's dying."
"So he's not coming out?" "He's uncovered his face!
He's saying: 'A cock to the god of healing!'"
"What? Is hemlock a medicine?"
"Someone's closing his eyes and mouth."
"So he's not leaving — he's still inside."
"Yes, he's still inside. He's dead."

   The young lads went on whispering
in the shadow of the Rock, in the blinding darkness.
The door opened. An old man came out
whimpering, and then a younger man,
and many others besides, all of them crying.
With a sudden tug, the cord slid

il filo uscì con un lieve urto a Gryllo:
e il sacro uccello della notte in alto
si sollevò con muto volo d'ombra.
E i compagni del morto ed i fanciulli
scosse un subito fremito, uno strillo
di sopra il tetto, Kikkabau… dall'alto,
Kikkabau… di più alto, Kikkabau…
dal cielo azzurro dove ardean le stelle.
E disse alcuno, udendo il fausto grido
della civetta: "Con fortuna buona!"

through Gryllus' fingers as he stood there wondering,
and the sacred guardian of the night
lifted itself silently through the dark.
The friends of the one who had passed away,
the little kids standing there marvelling –
they all heard its sudden cry,
a hoot from above the roof, *kikkabau!*[7]
From over the holy rock, *kikkabau!*
From higher and higher and higher still,
where the stars burn bright in the heavenly blue.
Then someone said, in answer to
the owl, "Go well, my friend. Go well."

7.   Onomatopoeic sound of owls according to Aristophanes' *The Birds.*

I GEMELLI

THE TWINS

I GEMELLI

Che sente il fiore cui la molle forza
di vita svolge i petali del boccio?
Quel che sentiva allora la fanciulla,
che si svolgea dal calice più bianca
e più sottile, il collo così lasso,
che lo piegava l'occhio di sua madre.
La neve già struggeva, ma non tutta:
se ne vedeva qua e là sui monti.
Spuntava l'erba, verdicava il salcio,
e ravvenate ora mescean le polle.
Era sui monti, era a bacìo la neve
ancora: ella si fece anche più bianca
e più sottile: un pianto nella casa
sonò: poi, la fanciulla era sparita.

E il suo gemello la richiese al padre
meditabondo. Egli accennò lontano.
E la richiese alla soletta madre,
che gli sorrise, e lacrimò più tanto.
"Sappi: è nel prato asfòdelo… C'è bello…
Lieta, sebbene senza il suo gemello…
No, non è sola, ma tra un fitto sciame…
Un fiore hanno alla sete ed alla fame…
Sì: tu ci andrai… Sì: la vedrai… tra giorni…
Resta con me! S'ora ci vai, non torni!"
Ma il giovinetto andò per prati e boschi,
sempre cercando. Un giorno seguì l'api
a un prato, le ronzanti api ad un fonte.
Nel fonte ritrovò la sua sorella.

Il giovinetto si chinò sul fonte,
e la fanciulla apparve su dal fonte.

The Twins[1]

What does a flower feel when
a feeble life unfolds its petals?
It feels what the girl felt then,
a thin white flower blossoming
slowly, her neck so weak
her mother's look could bend it.
The snows were almost gone,
dotting the mountains in patches,
grass and willows greening,
rivers brimmed with water,
the northern hill still white.
But she was whiter still,
and thinner: a faint echo
of tears, and she was gone.

Her twin asked his pensive father,
who went quiet and looked away.
Her twin then asked his lonely mother,
who smiled to him and cried some more.
"Your sister walks on fields of flowers,
merry, though without her twin.
She is not alone but in a buzzing swarm
of blessed souls who feed on flowers,
and you will join them too one day.
But stay now, for if you go, you're gone."
The boy did go through woods and meadows,
followed the bees, and the buzzing bees
led him straight up to the riverbank.
In the river, he found his sister.

As he looked into the water below,
the water showed his sister's face.

---

1.   Pascoli presents Pausanias' (*Description of Greece* 9. 31.8) version of the
Narcissus myth in which Narcissus fell in love with his face in the water since
his reflection reminded him of his dead twin sister. Pascoli associates the twins
with two flowers of the same family, the snowdrop and the spring snowflake,
both of which bloom in early spring.

Egli era mesto, ed era, anch'ella, mesta.
Ma le sorrise, ed ella gli sorrise.
Aprì la bocca per chiamarla a nome;
subito anch'ella aprì la bocca a un nome.
Ed egli chiese, chi l'avea rapita,
se lieta le era la solinga vita;
ed ella presto rispondea, ma troppo,
ch'ella parlava mentre egli parlava.
Ed egli tacque, ed ella tacque: allora
egli riprese, ma riprese anch'ella.
E il giovinetto non intese, e pianse.
E la fanciulla si confuse, e pianse.

Ora una voce chiamò lui: la voce
della sua madre che l'avea smarrito.
"Ci chiama. Vieni con il tuo gemello
dalla tua madre. C'è, con lei, più bello!"
Ella rispose; ma fondea nell'ansia
le sue parole con le sue parole.
"Qui non c'è fiori per il tuo digiuno!
Tu sei nel prato ove non è nessuno!"
La madre ancora lo chiamò. Le labbra
chinò... che freddo in quelle dolci labbra!
Le diede un bacio sussurrando, Addio!
ed un gorgoglio udì nell'acqua: Addio!
E il giovinetto s'alzò su dal fonte,
e la fanciulla sparve giù nel fonte.

"O madre! O madre! È dove tu m'hai detto!
Ma ella è sola, nel fonte soletto.
Non ho veduto altro che il suo, di capi.
Non ho sentito altro ronzio, che d'api.
Non ha vicine altre compagne care!
Non ha quei fiori per il suo mangiare!
Vieni tu, madre; ella ritornerà!"
"O figlio! O figlio! T'ha deluso un Dio!
Il fior che dissi è il fiore dell'oblio.
E tu non vieni dal fiorito prato
ch'è più lontano del cielo stellato!

As he was sad, she, too, was sad,
but when he smiled, she smiled.
He opened his mouth to call her name.
Her lips did too, to call that name.
"And who took you away?
And are you happy where you are?"
But her reply then came too fast,
her lips moved as his moved too.
He stopped talking, she stopped too.
He started again, but so did she.
And both misread, and thus they cried.

    He heard his mother call him home,
call the boy she thought was lost.
"Sister, come!" he said to her.
"Hurry, come, you'll like it there!"
She did reply but her anxious face
mixed her words with what he'd said.
"Where's the flower they say you eat?
The grass around you is empty."
His mother called again, and his lips —
cold and sweet — then touched the water.
"Good-bye," he whispered in a kiss.
"Good-bye," the water gurgled.
The boy then left the riverbank,
and the girl vanished.

    "Mother, she is where you said,
but she is lonely in lonely waters!
I saw no face but her lonely one.
I saw no swarm around her head
except the one of the buzzing bees.
No dear friends are there with her,
no flowers either for her meal.
Come, oh come, and bring her home!"
"Son, dear son, a god deceived you.
She feeds on flowers but in heaven,
and you're on earth, and heaven's far.

A chi ci va, gli è presso, come l'orto;
ma chi ne torna, anche se arriva smorto
a dove dormì, è tuttavia di là!"

Ma il giovinetto le afferrò la mano,
e disse: "O Vieni, se non è lontano!"
E, giunti al prato, si chinò sul fonte,
e la sorella venne su dal fonte.
Ah! ma nel fonte presso il suo sorriso
c'era la madre col suo mesto viso!
"O madre! O madre! Ecco che lei s'attrista
dacché nel grave tuo dolor t'ha vista!"
"O figlio! O figlio! Io sono lì pur quella!
Non hai due madri! E non hai più sorella!"
E turbò l'acqua. E madre e figlia sparve
oscuramente, qua e là, nel gorgo;
fin che ondeggiando, tremuli, a fior d'acqua
vennero ancora figlio e madre in pianto.

Ed egli allora oh! sì, capì. Ma venne
per molti giorni al tralucente lago,
a rivedere in sé la sua sorella
che in lui viveva; ed esso in lei moriva.
Ed era il tempo che il nostro dolore
cadea qual seme, e ne nasceva un fiore:
un fior dal sangue delle nostre vene,
un fior dal pianto delle nostre pene.
Ed egli fu il leucoio, ella il galantho,
il fior campanellino e il bucaneve.
E questo avea tre petali soltanto;
e quello, sei, coi sommoli un po' verdi.
Candidi entrambi, a capo chino entrambi.

Spuntava il croco, il morto per amore
bel giovinetto. E non fu lor compagno.
E non l'AI AI videro del giacinto

It is hard to return once you go there,
but it is easy enough to reach,
no further than our garden wall."

     And the boy grabbed her hand, in awe:
"Let us go, if it is not far!"
He then bent down towards the river,
and up again his sister came
with her mother's mournful face beside hers.
"Mother, look how sad she is
to see the sadness in your face!"
"Son, dear son, that is my face,
in the water, and the other is yours."
A touch to crease the water, and girl
and mother vanished in the gurgle.
Then boy and mother came again,
shaking, in tears, onto the water.

     He understood. But many times
he went again to that clear river
to see his sister's face in his,
living in him, who wasted away.
It was the time when human sorrows
fell like seeds and turned to blossom:
a bud from the blood in our crimson veins,
a gem from the tears of our endless pain,
and he was a snowflake, and she a snowdrop:
a snow flower and a milk flower.
She had then three petals only
and he had six with greenish tips.
Both had white recumbent heads.

     The crocus bloomed just when he died,
another youth then turned to flower.[2]
He died too soon to see Hyacinthus

2.   A reference to Ovid's *Metamorphoses* 4.283: a young man fell in love with
the nymph Smylax but his love was unrequited. The gods turned him into a
crocus.

dal vento ucciso. Non fioriva ancora.
Erano soli soli; ché la neve
era sui monti, era a bacìo, tuttora.
E qualche alato, ch'ebbe vita umana
già, come loro, già piangea, ma seco,
sommessamente: o dentro sé pensava
quel pianto amaro ch'è poi dolce canto.
I due puri gemelli esili fiori,
fu breve la lor vita anche di fiori.
Amor fu quello prima dell'amore.
Non, forse, amore, ma dolor, sì, era.

Sparvero prima della primavera.

taken away by frozen winds.[3]
The twins had bloomed alone, early,
with snows still on the northern hill
and a few birds — once humans too —
crying, yes, but to themselves
sweetly, softly, thinking how
tuneful is the song born out of tears.
The twins turned to thin flowers, but
brief were their lives even as flowers.
Theirs was a love before the season
of love, or maybe it was pain that took them

before spring.

3.   Another reference to Ovid's *Metamorphoses* (X, 162-219). The god Apollo fell in love with Hyacinthus, but Zephyr, the divine personification of the homonymous wind, was jealous and engineered the death of the young man, so that Apollo would not have him. Apollo then turned the blood of Hyacinthus into the flower that now bears this name.

I vecchi di Ceo

THE OLD MEN OF KEA

I VECCHI DI CEO

I. I due atleti

Nella rocciosa Euxantide, sul monte
tra la splendida Iulide e l'antica
sacra Carthaia, cauto errava in cerca
non so se d'erbe contro un male insonne
o di fiori per florido banchetto,
Panthide atleta: atleta già, ma ora
medico, di salubri erbe ministro.
E coglieva, più certo, erbe salubri,
ché il capo bianco non chiedea più fiori.
Partito già da Iulide pietrosa
era su l'alba. Or l'affocava il sole;
sì che saliva al vertice del monte
folto di quercie cui nel mezzo è l'ara
del Dio che manda all'arsa Ceo le pioggie
tra un bombir lieto. E giunse tra le quercie
sul ventilato vertice. E gli occorse
uno ascendente per la balza opposta.
E riconobbe un vecchio ospite, atleta
anch'esso: Lachon, che vedeasi in casa
molte corone, il secco appio dell'Istmo,
il Nemèo verde, non ormai già verde,
e l'alloro e l'olivo: altri germogli
no; non di cari figli altra corona.
Ché solo egli era. E per la via selvaggia
coglieva anch'esso erbe salubri o fiori,
per morbo insonne o florido convito:
ma, più certo, salubri erbe, ché un cespo
svelgendo allora da un sassoso poggio,
le vecchie rughe egli facea più tante.

The Old Men of Kea[1]

I. Two Athletes

In rocky Kea, up on the mountain
between shining Ioulis and ancient Karthaia,
Panthis the fêted athlete
wandered, looking for herbs to allay
some tireless malady or maybe— who knows? —
for flowers for a festive banquet,
Panthis the athlete, now also a healer,
master of the herbs that soothe.
More likely, then, it was herbs he was gathering –
flowery garlands don't go with white hair.
He'd already set out from stony Ioulis
when dawn came on. Now the sun shone,
and now he was nearly at the top of the mountain,
which was covered with oaks, with an altar in the middle,
to the god who sends rain to parching Kea
with some playful thunder.[2] Now he was there
on the windy peak, where he suddenly noticed
somebody coming up the other side.
He recognized him — an old guest-friend,
a fellow athlete — Lachon, who had
so many garlands hung up in his hall:
from Isthmia and Nemea, of laurel and olive,
green when he'd won them, green no more.
But his life had not been crowned with children.
He lived alone and went along
the untended ways, gathering herbs,
or flowers maybe for some happy feast
or to allay some stubborn illness.
Herbs, more likely. Drawing up a bucket
from an old stone well on his own each day
had lined his ageing face with wrinkles.

1.   Pascoli's poems has two protagonists: the old athletes Panthis and Lachon,
celebrated for having won several times at the Panellenic Games in Isthmia and
Nemaea. They are about to commit suicide according to the law of Kea, which
prescribes a dignified exit for elderly people. They meet and they reminisce
about their life, discussing the differences in their chosen paths.
2.   A reference to Zeus.

Ora gli stette agli omeri Panthide,
non anco visto, immobile, col fascio
dei lunghi steli dietro il dorso; e l'altro
sentì che un'ombra gli pungea la nuca;
e si voltò celando la mannella
della sua messe. Ma con un sorriso
a lui mostrò la sua Panthide, e disse:
"Oh!" disse "vedo. Non è crespo aneto,
Lachon, per un convito; non è mirto;
né cumino né molle appio palustre…"
Erano cauli con, nel gambo, rosse
chiazze e con bianchi fiorellini, in cima.
E Lachon interruppe: "Ospite, il Tempo,
che viene scalzo, all'uno e all'altro è giunto,
della cicuta; come è patria legge:
-CHI NON PUÒ BENE, MALE IN CEO NON VIVA".
Disse Panthide: "Ricordiamo il detto
dell'usignolo che di miele ha il canto,
dell'isolana ape canora: Il cielo
alto non si corrompe, non marcisce
l'acqua del mare… L'uomo oltre passare
non può vecchiezza e ritrovare il fiore
di gioventù". "Noi ritroviamo il fiore
della cicuta!" con un riso amaro
Lachon riprese, e poi soggiunse: "Un fascio
coglierne, tutto in un sol dì, per vecchi,
ospite, è grave. Oh! non ha senno l'uomo!
Sin dalla lieta gioventù va colto,
un gambo al giorno, il fiore della morte!"

II. L'inno eterno

E sederono all'ombra d'una quercia
l'un presso l'altro. Sotto la lor vista
tra bei colli vitati era una valle
già bionda di maturo orzo; e le donne
mietean cantando, e risonava al canto

And now Panthis was standing behind him.
He still hadn't noticed him behind his back
with a big bundle of twigs in his hands.
Lachon felt his shadow on his neck like an itch
and turned around, hiding his bundle behind him.
Panthis smiled and held out his own.
"Oh, I see. It isn't dill
for a picnic, nor cumin, nor myrtle, nor is it
celery...." What it was was a bunch of reddish
stems with a spray of bright white flowers
at the top. Then Lachon said, "Dear friend,
the time has now crept upon us
for hemlock. It's ancestral law:
those who can't live happily
in Kea, shouldn't live in pain."
Panthis nodded. "Let's recall
the message of the nightingale,
whose song is flowing and sweet as honey:
The lofty heavens can't be sullied,
the limpid ocean can't rot,
and old men can't pass through old age
to pluck the flower of youth again."
"Well, then, let's find the flower of hemlock,"
Lachon said, with a smile, and added,
"Gathering a whole bunch in a single day
is no laughing matter for men of our age.
But really, being human doesn't make much sense.
From innocent childhood, every day,
all we're really gathering are the flowers of death."

II.The Eternal Song

They sat down in the shade of a spreading oak-tree,
one next to the other. Out in the distance
between hilly vineyards was a fertile valley
already blond with ripening barley.
Women were bringing in the harvest,
singing as they worked, and their song

l'aspro citareggiar delle cicale
su per le vigne solatìe dei colli.
E nella pura cavità del cielo,
di qua di là si rispondean due voci
parlando di lor genti che lontane
tenea Corinto dove è un tempio dove
sono fanciulle ch'hanno ospiti tanti…
E nel mezzo alla valle era Carthaia
simile a bianco gregge addormentato
da quell'uguale canto di cicale.
Il mare in fondo, qualche vela in mare,
come in un campo cerulo di lino
un portentoso biancheggiar di gigli.
Tra mare e cielo, sopra un'erta roccia,
la Scuola era del coro; era, di marmo
candido, la ronzante arnia degl'inni.
Ivi le frigie tibie, ivi le cetre
doriche insieme confondean la voce
simile ad un gorgheggio alto d'uccelli
tra l'infinito murmure del bosco.
Ivi sonava, dolce al cuor, la lode
del giovinetto corridore e il vanto
del lottatore; e per sue cento strade
l'inno cercava le memorie antiche,
volava in cielo, si tuffava in mare,
incontrava sotterra ombre di morti,
tornando, ebbro di gioia ebbro di pianto,
con due fogliuzze a coronar l'atleta.

    Era lontano, e non vedean che il bianco
dei marmi al sole, i due pensosi vecchi.
Eppur di là l'alterna eco d'un inno
giungeva al cuore, o forse era nel cuore.
Da destra il giorno si movea col sole,
portando il canto e l'opere di vita,

was echoed by the clacking chatter
of the crickets all through the sun-drenched vines.
In the perfect absence called the sky,
there was another echo — two old men talking
about Corinth, where there's apparently a temple
with young priestesses who're very kind to guests....[3]
Down in the valley they could see Karthaia,
a white flock of sheep that'd been lulled to sleep
by the crickets' familiar lullaby.
The sea was behind it, with here and there
a sail or two, like a field of blue linen
with sunspots of snowy miraculous lilies.
Between the sea and the sky, half-way up a cliff,
there was a chorus of singers, a buzzing crowd
nested in a hive of marble.[4]
Phrygian pipes and Dorian lyres
sounded together in a hubbub that was like
the hullabaloo of birds on high
or the endless thrashing of the canopy.
They were singing an inspiring song
in praise of a runner, a champion.
The song went down a hundred alleys
searching for the past, digging out old memories,
then flew up to the sky, dove down in the sea,
met the souls of the dead in the underworld,
and then it came back, drunk with joy.
Drunk with tears, it came back again
to crown the champion with a garland of leaves.

    The two old men were far away —
all they could see was the glare of the marble.
But the sound of the singing still reached them there —
it reached their hearts or had been there all along.
The sun was bringing in the day from the East
with songs and all the notes of life,

3.   A reference to the sacred prostitution in the Temple of Aphrodite in
Corinth.
4.   The Choregeion, a school for singers.

verso sinistra, al mesto occaso, donde
co' suoi pianeti si volgea la notte
tornando all'alba e conducendo i sogni,
echi e fantasmi d'opere canore.
Fluiva il giorno, rifluìa la notte.
Sotto il giorno e la notte, e la vicenda
di luce e d'ombra, di speranza e sogno,
stava la terra immobile. Ma il coro
era più rapido. Arrivava un'onda
dal mare, un'altra ritornava al mare.
Era la vita. Dopo il moto alterno
d'un'onda sola che salìa cantando
scendea scrosciando, mormorava il mare
immobilmente. E molte vite in fila
salìan dal mare riscendean nel mare:
quindi l'eterno. E dall'eterno altre onde:
i figli. Altre onde dall'eterno: i figli
dei figli. E onde e onde, e onde e onde...

III. Efimeri

Disse Panthide: "Ospite, ho cinque figli
molto lodati, come sai: Zelòto
il primo: Argeo, buono alla lotta, eppure
fiorito appena di peluria il labbro,
l'ultimo: è questi ora su l'Istmo, ai giochi.
Lachon, ascolta. Ieri udii, su l'alba,
un grido in casa, un fievole vagito
che mi chiamava al talamo del figlio
più grande. Andai. Vidi una luce: un uomo
novo fiammante! E con le sue manine
egli annaspava come a dire — O vedi
ch'io l'ho pur qui la lampada di vita
accesa a quella ch'alla tua s'accese!
Più non è danno se la tua si spenge:

bringing it over to its grave decline
when Night comes on in his cloak of planets,
bringing dreams and echoes, echoes of songs.
So daylight ebbed, and dark flowed in.
And beneath night and daylight, sun and shadow,
hope and dream, the earth remained.
But the chorus moved to a quicker tempo.
For every wave that crashed on the shore,
another was there to take its place.
It was death and life – an individual wave,
rising and shining, then crashing down
in an ocean that moaned without measure or end.
Life after life, rising and falling
in the endless sea, an eternal song,
and out of eternity came other waves,
like progeny, which then gave birth
to further waves, more progeny,
and waves and waves and waves and waves.

III. The Ephemeral Ones

Panthis said, "My friend, as you know,
I have five sons, all renowned.
Zelotus is the eldest; young Argeus —
who's good at fighting, even though
the hair is only now blossoming at his lip —
strong Argeus is the youngest,
and he's the one at Isthmia now,
competing in the famous games.
Listen, Lachon. Yesterday I heard
a cry in the house at the break of day,
a muffled sobbing, which called me to the bedroom
of my eldest son. I went in and saw
a light — a brand-new, shining little man
clutching up at me with his hands
as if to say, 'Here is a torch
lit from a torch that you once lit.
There's no harm, now, if yours goes out.

Son io Panthide. Puoi partire, o nonno!-
Parlato ch'ebbe, egli movea le labbra
come assetato… E io dovrei tutt'ora
tener le labbra al pispino del fonte,
vietando io vecchio al mio novello il bere?
gli dovrei forse intorbidar la polla?
Io parto. E, come io sono lui, non muoio".
E Lachon disse: "Oh! io vorrei che un poco
la piccoletta fiaccola negli occhi
miei balenasse! Oh! io vorrei per poco
con la mia mano ripararle il vento!
vorrei, seduto per qualche anno al fonte
di vita, senza berne più che un sorso,
vorrei vedere quella rosea bocca
arrotondarsi sul bocciuol materno!
Ospite, io credo, più di me tu muori".

   Tacquero intenti a udirsi, dentro, l'inno
del lor respiro, onda che viene e onda
che va, seguite da un pensiero immoto.
Le mietitrici avean ripreso il canto
tra l'orzo biondo, e risonava al canto
l'aspro citareggiar delle cicale.
E disse Lachon: "Troppo bella, o sacra
isola Ceo! Chi nacque in te, che volle
morire altrove? Ma sei poca a tanti!"
A cui Panthide: "Poca sì… ma Delo
appena morti i figli suoi bandisce.
Partono i morti dalla sacra Delo
sopra la nave nera, esuli, e vanno
mirabilmente pallidi, sul mare,
alla Rhenèa dove non son che morti;
e sole capre e pecore selvaggie
belano errando sopra il lor sepolcro".
Lachon pensava e su la palma il capo

I'm the new Panthis. You can go, granddad!'
When he'd spoken his mind, he smacked his lips,
obviously thirsty.… So should I keep
my lips to the fountain, old as I am,
stopping my grandson from getting a drink?
Should I be slobbering in his water?
I'm off! But not dying, because I'm him."
Lachon replied, "I would love
for a tiny light to dance in my eyes!
I wouldn't mind shielding someone else
from the winter winds. I'd be happy to sit
for a little while longer by the fountain of life —
not to take a sip myself,
but to look on as a little guy
puckered up to his mother's breast.
I think you're dying more than me."

   They fell silent, content to listen
to the internal song, the song of the breath,
a wave that comes along, then goes.
The harvesters were singing again
in the blond barley, and their song
was echoed by the clacking chatter
of the crickets. Then Lachon said,
"Holy Kea, splendid island,
why would anyone born on you
ever want to die elsewhere?
A tiny place but loved by many."
Panthis replied, "Tiny is right.
But tiny Delos exiles its children
as soon as they're dead. The dead depart
from the holy island on a black ship:
exiles, marvellously pale,
they travel over the sounding sea
to Rhenea, then lie down and sleep
while solitary goats and sheep
wander, bleating over their graves."
Lachon was thinking, his face leant
pensively on his open palm.

reggea dubbioso. "Io mi ricordo" ei disse
"un inno udito, ora è molt'anni, in Delfi,
lungo l'Alfeo: Siamo d'un dì! Che, uno?
che, niuno? Sogno d'ombra, l'uomo!"
L'ombra di lui teneva su la palma il capo:
pensava, a piè dell'albero; e vicine
stridere udiva l'ombre delle foglie.

IV. L'inno antico

Poi raccolti i lor fasci di cicute
sorsero entrambi, e dissero: "Va sano!..."
"Va sano!..." E ritornavano cogliendo
ancor pei greppi i fiori della morte.
Esalava il canùciolo e il serpillo
odor di cera e dolce odor di miele.
Ronzavano api e scarabei de' fiori.
E Lachon giunse al prònao d'Apollo,
alla Scuola del coro. Era già sera,
una sera odorosa; ed il suo nome
udì gridare a voci di fanciulli.
Eran fanciulli che, in lor giochi, un inno
volean cantare a mo' dei grandi, un inno
vecchio, che ognuno aveva, in Ceo, nel cuore.
Presto un impube corifeo la schiera
ebbe ordinata, e già da destra il coro
movea cantando per la via del sole,
verso la sera, con gridìo d'uccelli.

Pubertà,
fonte segreto che spiccia
senza un tremito e un gorgoglio,
ma che di tenero musco
veste insensibilmente lo scoglio:
a te dia Lachon l'erba del leone,
l'appio verde del bosco Nemèo.

Conobbe l'inno, il primo inno cantato
a lui quand'era il suo destino in boccia
tuttora, quanti anni passati? Tanti!

"I can remember a song," he said,
"from years ago in holy Delphi,
by the banks of the Alpheus. *We last but one day.*
One, or none? Man is the dream
of a shadow, no more. His shadow leant
his head on his hand: a man was thinking
underneath a tree, alone, with the sound
of shadows rustling where there had been leaves.

IV. The Ancient Song

The old men gathered their bundles of twigs
and got up to go. They said to each other,
"Go well, my friend," then headed home,
picking the fatal flowers on the way.
The smell of herbs was in the air,
the tang of thyme and the sweetness of honey.
Lachon came to the sanctuary of Apollo,
to the choral school. It was already evening.
He heard some children calling his name —
children at play, but who wanted to sing
the ancient song the grown-ups sang,
that everyone on Kea held in their hearts.
Soon a hip-high chorus leader
had his singers in a line,
and the chorus was moving like the sun
towards the sunset as the gulls cawed.

> *Coming of age –*
> *the secret energy that quickens*
> *   without any tremor or murmur*
> *and that surreptitiously covers over*
> *   each dead stone with a green moss,*
> *let Lachon consecrate to you*
> *the green celery from wooded Nemea.*

He knew the song, a song they'd sung
back in the days his fate was unwritten.
How many years had passed since then?

E da sinistra volsero i fanciulli,
come i notturni aurei pianeti, a destra.

   Nulla sta!
   Tutto nel mondo si muove,
            corre, o giovinetto atleta,
   come nell'inclito stadio
            tu col piede di vento alla meta:
   di che la prima delle tue corone
   tu riporti all'Euxantide Ceo.

   I fanciulli si volsero con gli occhi
al cielo e al mare, fermi su la terra
sacra, alzando le acute esili voci.

   Ora è ora d'amare.
            L'appio verde vuoi sol tu?
   Corrano, un tempo, le gare,
            dove Lachon non sia più,
   giovani ch'ansino e rapidi sbuffino l'anima
   tua, la tua, lungo l'Alfeo!

   E nel cospetto dei fanciulli apparve
Lachon il vecchio con le sue cicute,
e intorno al vecchio corsero i fanciulli
gridando: "A noi, perché ci sia ghirlanda!
l'appio a noi! l'appio verde! l'appio verde!"

   V. L'inno nuovo

   E Panthide a quell'ora era pur giunto
sotto l'aerea Iulide natale.
E vide in mare una bireme, e vide
che ammainando entrava già nel porto.
E dall'aerea Iulide e dal grande
leon di pietra accovacciato in vetta,
il popolo scendea lungo l'Elixo,
scendea dall'alto in lunga fila al mare.

Now they were swinging back from the West
towards the East like the planets at night.

> *But nothing stays —*
> *there isn't anything that's stable.*
> *It runs, my young champion runner,*
> *the way you run through the stadium,*
> *quick as the wind with your fleet foot,*
> *and so you brought your trophy home,*
> *the green celery to windy Kea.*

The boys turned back the other way,
their eyes fixed on where sky meets sea,
their feet planted on the holy island
as they lifted their boyish voices in song.

> *Now, though, is the time for love.*
> *Is the green celery all that you want?*
> *One day other young men will run*
> *the races that Lachon can run no longer,*
> *young men breathing the same spirit –*
> *his, yours, along the Alpheus river.*

The boys looked up, and there was Lachon,
old Lachon with his celery crown.
They ran up to him and swarmed around him
shouting, "Give me the crown! I want a crown!"

V. The New Song

Panthis had now arrived beneath
high-up Ioulis where he was born.
Out at sea, he saw a ship
drawing near, dropping sail,
making its way into the harbour.
From high-up Ioulis, the people came down,
past the stone lion crouched on the slope,
along the river, and down to the sea.

Veniano primi i giovinetti a corsa,
dando alla brezza i riccioli del capo;
poi le donne altocinte, ultimi i vecchi,
spartendo tra due passi una parola.
Poi che giungea dall'Istmo, la bireme,
portando alfine i buoni atleti a casa,
e quante niuno ancor sapea, ghirlande.
E trasse al lido anche Panthide, in seno
celando il fascio delle sue cicute.
Stava in disparte. Ed ecco dalla nave
scese una schiera di settanta capi
bruni, tutti fioriti di corimbi,
e su la spiaggia stettero. Un chiomato
citaredo sedé sopra un pilastro,
e presso lui gli auleti con le lunghe
tibie alla bocca. E il mare eterno, il mare
alterno, a spiaggia sospingea l'ondate,
le ricogliea, così tra il canto e il pianto.

    Stridè la tibia, tintinnì la cetra,
e il coro alzò tra il sussurrìo del mare
un inno di Bacchylide. In disparte
era Panthide, e il vecchio cuor batteva
contro la manna delle sue cicute.
L'onda ascendeva, discendeva l'onda;
e il coro andò, poi ritornò sul lido.

    O sacra Ceo!
mosse ver te la fulgida
Fama che in alto spazia,
a te recando un messo
        pieno di grazia,
che nella lotta il pregio
        fu del valido Argeo;

    e noi la grande
gloria, sull'istmio vertice,
venuti dall'Euxanti-
d'isola dia, facemmo
        chiara coi canti

The boys were first, running ahead,
their curly hair flowing in the breeze,
next came the women, high-bosomed,
then finally the old, limping down,
sharing some gossip along the way.
The ship from Isthmia had come,
bringing the athletes back home,
and an unknown number of victory garlands.
Panthis came down to the shore as well,
holding his bundle of twigs to his breast.
He stood to one side, and now from the ship
a whole row of youths descended,
their dark hair blossoming with flowers,
and lined up along the sounding beach.
One of them sat on a toppled column
and played a lyre, while all around him,
others brought long flutes to their lips.
And the eternal sea alternately
swelled the waves and let them crash,
up and down, a sigh and a song.

    The flutes sounded, the lyre rang out,
and the chorus sang Bacchylides
with the sea sighing behind them.
Panthis stood there, a little to one side,
his bundle shaking to the beat of his heart.
Waves rose and waves fell.
The chorus formed a circle on the sounding shore.

> *Holy Kea!*
> *Now glorious fame approaches you*
> *with a messenger rich in grace.*
> *In the famous foot-race,*
> *Argeus took the prize,*
>
> *and we re-echo the praise*
> *he won on Isthmia's land,*
> *we lads of Kea, loved by the gods,*

nostri, noi coro adorno
        di settanta ghirlande:

ed or la musa indigena
suscita il dolce strepito
        di tibie lyde
per onorar d'un inno
        il tuo figlio, o Panthide!

    Udì Panthide, e il cuor batté più forte
contro la manna delle sue cicute.
Ora poteva sciogliere la vita
felicemente, come alcuno un fascio
d'erbe e di fiori che nel giorno colse,
sfa, su la sera, che ne fa ghirlanda,
tornato a casa. Ché dei cinque figli
niuno lasciava senza lode in terra.
Gli avea ben fatto il Sole, e dalle Grazie
avea sortito ciò che all'uomo è meglio.
Ammirato dagli uomini mortali
tornava a casa, per pestare, il saggio
medico, l'erbe nel mortaio di bronzo.
E la notte era dolce, aurea; tranquillo
era il suo cuore. Ché il Panthide nuovo
s'era acquetato sul materno petto,
e il forte Argeo, stanco di mare e gioia,
dormiva, già sognando altre corone.
Buona, la sorte! buona! Ché concesso
non gli era mica di salire al cielo!

we, adorned with flowery garlands
seventy odd.

And now the glorious song
our native muse composed
sounds from the flute and lyre
so we can honour with an ode
Argeus the victor, Panthis his sire.

Panthis listened, and his heart beat wildly,
rattling the twigs he held to his chest.
Now he could let go of life
contentedly, the way a man
might gather a bundle of herbs all day
and then unbundle it at home
at night to make himself a garland.
Not one of his five sons would leave
the earth without some athlete's glory.
The sun had blessed him. Fate had granted
what's best for a man. Highly esteemed
among mortal men he went back home
to grind his herbs, the skilled healer,
in a bronze mortar. The night was sweet,
the night was golden, and his heart was at peace.
Little Panthis had settled down
at his mother's breast, and strong Argeus,
all tired out with happiness
and the long trip home, was already dreaming
of other crowns. How kind fate was!
The only thing it had ever denied him
was to climb up into the realms of the gods.

ALEXANDROS

ALEXANDROS

I

— Giungemmo: è il Fine. O sacro Araldo, squilla!
Non altra terra se non là, nell'aria,
quella che in mezzo del brocchier vi brilla,

o Pezetèri: errante e solitaria
terra, inaccessa. Dall'ultima sponda
vedete là, mistofori di Caria,

l'ultimo fiume Oceano senz'onda.
O venuti dall'Haemo e dal Carmelo,
ecco, la terra sfuma e si profonda

dentro la notte fulgida del cielo.

II

Fiumane che passai! voi la foresta
immota nella chiara acqua portate,
portate il cupo mormorìo, che resta.

Montagne che varcai! dopo varcate,
sì grande spazio di su voi non pare,
che maggior prima non lo invidïate.

Azzurri, come il cielo, come il mare,
o monti! o fiumi! era miglior pensiero
ristare, non guardare oltre, sognare:

il sogno è l'infinita ombra del Vero.

III

Oh! più felice, quanto più cammino
m'era d'innanzi; quanto più cimenti,
quanto più dubbi, quanto più destino!

Ad Isso, quando divampava ai vènti
notturno il campo, con le mille schiere,
e i carri oscuri e gl'infiniti armenti.

Alexandros[1]

I

We have arrived. The end. Herald, proclaim it!
No further earth but that up in the heavens,
that crescent that now shines down on your shields,

my soldiers! A wandering earth, forsaken,
unreachable. And from this final shingle
you see it there, my mercenaries and pikemen,

that final stream that runs without a wrinkle.
O, you who've come from Haemon and Carmelus,
look how this earth dissolves and starts to mingle

with the midnight sky, with its shining darkness.

II

Streams that I forded! With you, you will carry
as in clear waters the forests' secret calm,
with you the rivers' murmuring you will carry.

Mountains that I climbed, and after you climbed them,
the world you looked down on seemed less unbounded
than it had seemed when it was hid behind them.

Blue like the sky, blue like the sea — O mountains!
O rivers! Perhaps it would have been better
to have your dreams and not to look beyond them.

A dream is an endless shadow on what's there.

III

And I happiest the longer the journey,
the greater the doubts, the greater the hazards,
the greater the fortune that lay before me!

At Issus! When the winds stirred up the banners
in the dead of night — and the soldiers waiting,
their chariots dark, and their infinite herds.

1.   Pascoli uses the Greek spelling of the name Alexander.

A Pella! quando nelle lunghe sere
inseguivamo, o mio Capo di toro,
il sole; il sole che tra selve nere,

sempre più lungi, ardea come un tesoro.

IV

Figlio d'Amynta! io non sapea di meta
allor che mossi. Un nomo di tra le are
intonava Timotheo, l'auleta:

soffio possente d'un fatale andare,
oltre la morte; e m'è nel cuor, presente
come in conchiglia murmure di mare.

O squillo acuto, o spirito possente,
che passi in alto e gridi, che ti segua!
ma questo è il Fine, è l'Oceano, il Niente…

e il canto passa ed oltre noi dilegua. —

V

E così, piange, poi che giunse anelo:
piange dall'occhio nero come morte;
piange dall'occhio azzurro come cielo.

Ché si fa sempre (tale è la sua sorte)
nell'occhio nero lo sperar, più vano;
nell'occhio azzurro il desiar, più forte.

Egli ode belve fremere lontano,
egli ode forze incognite, incessanti,
passargli a fronte nell'immenso piano,

come trotto di mandre d'elefanti.

VI

In tanto nell'Epiro aspra e montana
filano le sue vergini sorelle
pel dolce Assente la milesia lana.

At Pella! When, through never-ending evenings
we followed — O my old bull-headed stallion![2] —
the sun, which with the forests' shadows growing

longer and longer, would burn like a treasure.

IV

Philip, my sire! Of ends I had no inkling
back then when I began, but I remember
altars, a hymn, Timotheus intoning —

it's with me still, a captivating whisper —
to journey beyond death! My heart preserves it
the way a seashell holds the ocean's murmur.

O piercing sound, O captivating spirit
that stays with us and bids us seize the challenge!
But this is the End, the Ocean, the Limit —

the song has passed on over us and vanished.

V

And now, arrived at the end, he weeps, breathless.
He cries from the one eye as black as Hades
and from the other as blue as the sky is.

Thus is it always — for so it is fated —
in the black eye dwells hope, always the weaker;
in the blue eye, desire, still undefeated.

He hears the dumb beasts lowing in the distance.
He hears vague forces — unknown, unabating —
passing by him across the enormous lowland

like a vast herd of elephants migrating.

VI

Meanwhile in Epirus, up in the mountains,
his maiden sisters are twirling their spindles,
they are spinning wool for their distant kinsman.

2.   Alexander's horse was called Bucephalus, literally "ox-headed."

A tarda notte, tra le industri ancelle,
torcono il fuso con le ceree dita;
e il vento passa e passano le stelle.

Olympiàs in un sogno smarrita
ascolta il lungo favellìo d'un fonte,
ascolta nella cava ombra infinita

le grandi quercie bisbigliar sul monte

Late every night, they are twisting their spindles
with the other women, with waxen fingers.
Outside the wind blows and the starlight twinkles.

His mother Olympias, lost in slumber,
listens to the chattering of the fountain,
listens, in the limitless hollow shadows,

to the oak trees whispering on the mountain.

Tiberio

TIBERIUS

TIBERIO

I

Discende a notte Claudïo dal monte
Borèo: col vento dalle nubi fuori
rompe la luna e gli balena in fronte,

fuggendo. Egli rimira, a quei bagliori,
Livia e l'infante: intorno vanno frotte
silenziose di gladïatori.

S'ode tra lunghe raffiche interrotte
l'Eurota in fondo mormorar sonoro;
s'ode un vagito. E nella dubbia notte

le nere selve parlano tra loro.

II

Rabbrividendo parlano le selve
di quel vagito tremulo, che a scosse
va tra quel cauto calpestìo di belve.

Sommessamente parlano, commosse
ancor dal vento, che vanì; dal vento
Borea, che le aspreggiò, che le percosse.

Dal ciel lontano a quel vagito lento
egli era accorso; ma nell'infinito
ansar di tutto, dopo lo spavento,

risuona ancora quel lento vagito.

III

Chi vagisce, è Tiberio. E il vento accorre
dal ciel profondo tuttavia; spaura
le nubi in fuga, e sbocca dalle forre.

Le selve il mormorìo della congiura
mutano in urlo, e gli alberi giganti
muovono orridi in una mischia oscura.

TIBERIUS[1]

I

That night, Claudius comes down from the mountain.
The wind shifts the clouds and down spills the moonlight.
It pours down onto him like a fountain

as he flees. So he looks behind him, now that there's light,
at Livia and the child, while all around,
armies travel through the night.

You can hear, between the gusts of wind,
the river in flood murmuring.
You can hear a child whimpering

and invisible treetops whispering.

II

The trees are talking with a shiver up their spine
about that childish whimper, among muffled
running of beasts all the way down the line.

They talk under their breath, stirred and shaken
by the northerlies, which have left them alone,
but which stirred them up and left them shaken.

From a far-off sky, the wind had blown
on that slow whimper, but in
the outbreath, when the thrill had gone,

the child's cry is there again.

III

The crying child is Tiberius.
The wind still flows down from the depths of the sky.
It drives the clouds from the mountain tops.

Now the trees' whispering turns into a cry,
and the looming treetops come to blows,
crashing together violently.

1.   Pascoli here elaborates on a passage in Suetonius' *The Lives of the Twelve Caesars*, 3.

Lottano i pini coi disvincolanti
frassini, e l'elci su la stessa roccia
coi faggi urtano i vecchi tronchi infranti.

E il fiore della fiamma apresi e sboccia.

IV

Sboccia la fiamma, e il vento la saetta,
come una frusta lucida e sonante,
via per ogni pendìo, per ogni vetta.

Il vento con la frusta fiammeggiante,
col mugghio d'una mandrïa di tori,
cerca il vagito del fatale infante.

Ardono i monti; ma ne' suoi due cuori
Livia tranquilla, indomita, ribelle,
tra i rossi òmeri de' gladïatori,

nutre Tiberio con le sue mammelle.

The pines are at war with the towering oaks.
The elms stand proud like a row of towers,
while the firs hurl themselves forward in rows.

And fire blooms like a million flowers.

IV

Fire blossoms, and the wind drives it on
like a charioteer's whip that flashes and sings.
It races into every crevice of the mountain.

The wind, its flaming whip lashing,
groaning like a herd of bulls,
gropes for the destined infant's mewling.

Livia, while the mountain burns,
quietly and undistressed
between her guards' brawny shoulders,

suckles Tiberius at her breast.

Gog e Magog

Gog and Magog

Gog e Magog

I

A mandre, come gli asini selvaggi,
in vano andava e ritornava in vano
Gog e Magog coi neri carriaggi;

e la montagna li vedea nel piano
errare, udiva di tra le tormente
di quelle fruste lo schioccar lontano;

ed un bramir giungeva, della gente
di Mong, come umile abbaiar di iene,
all'inconcussa Porta d'occidente.

II

Ché tra due monti grande era, di rosso
bronzo una porta; grande sì, che l'ombra
ne trascorreva all'ora del tramonto

mezza la valle. Il figlio dell'Ammone
la incardinò per chiudere gl'immondi
popoli, e i neri branchi di bisonti:

la sprangò, chiuse. Ma ristette al sommo
dei monti: un chiaro strepere di trombe
giungea dalle Mammelle d'Aquilone.

III

V'era il Bicorne... E gli ultimi che, infanti,
aveano udito il gran maglio cadere
su le chiavarde, erano grigi vecchi;

e non partiva... E i figli lor, giganti
dagli occhi fiammei, dalle lingue nere,
o nani irsuti dai mobili orecchi,

erano morti; e d'ognun d'essi, i mille
erano nati, quante le faville
da un tizzo: ma il Bicorne era lassù.

Gog and Magog

I

To and fro, like wild herds,
riding down on their black carts,
Gog and Magog passed in vain

from the mountain to the plain,
to and fro, their whips lashing
in the stormy clouds flashing.

Like hyenas sadly barking,
the Mongol tribe came and roared
at the closed western door.

II

A door between two mountains stood,
made of bronze and red like blood,
casting shadows on the plain.

Alexander locked that door.
He locked out the filthy tribes
and the black herds of wild boars.

There he stood once, looking west
from the top of the North's Breasts,
his clear trumpets sounding bright.

III

The two-horned king[1] stood guard
still, and the children, who had heard
the door lock first, were old,

and their offspring had then died:
fire-eyed, black-tongued giants
or grim dwarves with mobile ears.

They burst out like sparks
from a firebrand in the dark,
but the high king of kings

---

1. Alexander the Great.

IV

In alto in alto, a guardia dell'Erguene-
cun; e lo squillo delle sue diane
movea valanghe e rifrangea morene.

S'empiva, ogni alba, il cielo di poiane;
e l'Orda a valle, come nubi al suono
del nembo, nera s'addossava al Kane:

carri che rotolavano dal cono
delle montagne; un subito barrito
d'elefanti; una voce come tuono…

V

Ma meno udian di giorno quel tumulto
lassù; di giorno anche le genti chiuse
ruggìano, e il cibo dividean con l'unghie.

Vaniva il grido di lassù nell'urlo
della lor fame. Era, di giorno, tutto
al sangue, Alan, Aneg, Ageg, Assur,

Thubal, Cephar. Più, nelle notti lunghe,
s'udiva, quando concepìan, nel Yurte,
le loro donne i figli di Mong-U.

VI

La luna andava su per orli gialli
di nubi, in fuga: per l'intatta neve
stavano in cerchio mandre di cavalli:

le teste in dentro, immobili, tra il bianco,
stavano: a ora a ora un nitrir breve,
un improvviso scalpitìo del branco.

Ché tutta la montagna solitaria
muggìa. Temeva anche la luna, e lieve
balzava su, da nube a nube, in aria.

IV

on the Ergenekon remained.
He caused floods and moved moraines
with his trumpets sounding high.

Eagles filled the sky at dawn
as the horde came near their khan,
as when clouds gather, storms thunder.

And down the slope, their chariots rolled:
a sudden voice like a thunderbolt,
or elephants trumpeting....

V

Through the years that turmoil vanished,
and the tribes roared on, when, famished,
they fought for food with their sharp nails.

And their war-cry died in the wail
of their hunger, which prevailed:
Alan, Aneg, Ageg, Assur, Thubal, Cephar.[2]

In the long nights filled with stars,
the Mong women in their yurt
shouted loud when giving birth.

VI

The moon fled from cloud to cloud.
On the purest snow, there stood
herds of horses in a circle

on the white, so still were they,
a brief neighing here and there,
a quick pawing on the ground.

And the lonely mountain had a sound
of bellowing: the moon was scared
and from the clouds it jumped in the air,

2.   Names of barbaric tribes which Pascoli found in Arturo Graf's *Rome in the Memory and Imagination of the Middle Ages* (1872), p. 532.

VII

O risplendea sul murmure infinito,
pendula. Cinto d'edere e d'acanti
l'Eroe, tolte le faci del convito,

scorreva in festa i gioghi lustreggianti,
e laggiù, dalle tonde ombre dei pini,
l'Orda ascoltava lunghi aerei canti;

udiva lunghi gemiti marini
di conche, e, tra il tintinno della cetra,
timpani cupi, cimbali argentini.

VIII

Gog e Magog tremava; e le sue donne
dissero: "Non ha madre Egli, cui dolce
gli sia tornare, pieno d'ambra e d'oro?

non figli, greggi? non fiorenti mogli
presso cui, sazio di narrar, si corchi?
Forse hanno a sdegno lui così bicorne!

Dunque e perché non scende Egli dal monte
né prendesi una dalle nostre torme,
che gli sia bestia, tra Gog e Magog?"

IX

Gog e Magog tremava… Uno dei nani
cauto trovò gli stolidi giganti.
"Noi moriamo, o giganti, ed Egli no.

Io che muovo gli orecchi come i cani,
intesi cose. Non c'è sempre avanti
Zul-Karnein. A volte a Rum andò.

Parte col sole. A un fonte va, di stelle
liquide, azzurro. Con le due giumelle
v'attinge vita. Ogni cent'anni un po'".

VII

or it shone on the sea, suspended,
on the banquet almost ended
by the hero[3] crowned with leaves,

festive, riding on green meadows
while the horde, among pine shadows,
listened to long eerie songs:

the echoing sounds of marine gongs,
the conch-shell's otherworldly keen,
and the silvery rattle of tambourines.

VIII

The tribes trembled with great wonder:
"Doesn't he have a sweet mother
to return to, rich with amber?

Not a flock, a child, a lover,
to lie with when the day is over?
Or do his horns provoke their hate?

Why doesn't he then come and mate
with a woman from our kin
whom he can subdue and win?"

IX

The tribes trembled. One dwarf said
to the giants, "We'll be dead
but the king will never die.

With my dog-ears, once I heard
that the king does not stand guard
always. Westwards sometimes he sails

with the sun, towards a well,
blue with life, with swimming stars.
He drinks from it every hundred years."

---

3.   Alexander the Great.

X

Ora Egli un giorno (la Montagna tetra
parea più presso e, come scheletrita,
mostrava il bianco ossame suo di pietra)

per l'ombra, dove non sapea che dita
reggeano erranti lampade d'argento,
per l'ombra andava al fonte della vita.

E non più squilli di tra i gioghi, e il vento
soffiava in vano. La gran Porta un poco
brandiva, a tratti, con émpito lento.

XI

Gog e Magog tre dì, vigile, attese;
tre notti attese; e non udì, che a sera
la Porta a quando a quando brandir lenta.

Non c'era più sui monti… E l'Orda prese
la via dei monti. Andava l'Orda nera
formicolando sotto la tormenta.

All'alba mugliò lugubre un bisonte,
nitrì un cavallo, si spezzò la schiera…
Uno squillo correa da monte a monte.

XII

E dissero le donne: "Uomo da nulla
Zul-Karnein! Tornasti in fretta! O forse
non c'era al fonte sola una fanciulla?

non una tua sorella, che la secchia
abbandonò vuota sul fonte, e corse
ansando in casa alla tua madre vecchia?

Or fa, divino ariete, sonare
le trombe! Al suono delle tue fanfare
l'uom ci si desta, e poi… non dorme più".

X

And the dark mountain seemed nearer
and revealed its barest bone,
its skeleton all made of stone.

The hero went to that pure river
through the shade where eerie fingers
held mysterious lamps of silver.

No more jingles on the slopes,
and the wind there blew in vain,
and the great door's breath was faint.

XI

Gog and Magog waited three days
and three nights, and all they heard
was the faint creaking of the door.

He wasn't there. The mountain ways
were flushed with the swell of the horde
like ants swarming before the storm.

A bison lowed at the break of day.
A horse neighed, their ranks shattered.
And somewhere in the valley, a trumpet brayed.

XII

And the women said, "O Zul-Karnein!
You've come home so quickly! What kind
of man can't find a single maiden?

Not even a sister, who at the sight of her brother
might let the bucket fall from her hands
and rush inside for your ageing mother?

But now, O ram, have your trumpets blare!
At the sounding of your fanfare,
warriors rise and sleep no more!"

XIII

E gli uomini ululàrono: "Ha bevuto
in Rum al fonte delle stelle azzurro!
Zul-Karnein è sempre ciò che fu".

E lor fu in odio ogni altra vita, e il frutto
d'ogni altro ventre; e il rosso sangue munto
bevvero alle bisonti, alle zebù.

Né più sonava per la valle un muglio.
Non sonò più, Gog e Magog, che l'urlo
interminato delle tue tribù.

XIV

Ma sì, partì Zul-Karnein, nel fuoco
d'un vespro: per il monte erano stese
porpore cupe a margini di croco.

Nel cocchio d'oro folgorando ascese
l'Eroe; nell'ombra lontanò tra un gaio
ridere di berilli e di turchese,

Un balenìo di cuspidi d'acciaio,
un'eco d'inni che tremola ed erra
qua e là... Tacque infine irto il ghiacciaio.

XV

Tre anni attese il Tartaro, tre anni
spiò l'arrivo degli stessi draghi
dagli occhi d'oro sopra la montagna

tacita e sola. Il Tartaro guardava,
né già temeva, e più sentìa la fame
e l'ira, e con man d'orso per la valle

svellea betulle, sradicava ontani.
Ma vide gli occhi degli stessi draghi
la terza volta, e venne alla montagna.

XIII

And the men cried, "He has sampled
in the West from that well that is blue with life!
What he was, he will be forevermore."

Every other life they encountered
they hated, and they nurtured their life
with blood from the bison and the boar.

And the valleys and hills no longer resounded.
There was no sound at all, of alarm or strife,
only the tribes' interminable murmur.

XIV

But Zul-Karnein did leave in the glow
of a sunset: above the mountain were stretched
sheets of purple shot with yellow.

The hero ascended in a golden cart
and vanished over the distant hills
with a twinkle of emerald and a sparkle of sapphire.

The flash of a hundred points of steel,
an echo of hymns that warble, wander
here and there…and the glacier was still.

XV

The Tartars waited for three years,
watched the arrival of the same stars
with golden eyes above the mountains.

The Tartars watched the stars above them
and felt less fear than mortal hunger,
and with hands like claws and savage anger,

uprooted birches, took out alders and firs.
Then they saw the golden eyes of the same stars
the third time and came to the mountain.

XVI

A piè delle Mammelle d'Aquilone
giunsero cauti. E il vecchio nano astuto
con mani e piedi rampicò sui tufi.

E vide in cima un grande padiglione
come di tromba, e vi scivolò muto:
v'udì soffi, vi scorse occhi di gufi.

Un nido immondo riempiva il vuoto
di quella tromba. Un grande gufo immoto
v'era, due ciuffi in capo irti, da re.

XVII

Prese due penne il vecchio nano, e stette
sopra una roccia, ed agitò le penne,
e chiamò l'Orda, che attendeva: "A me,

Gog e Magog! A me, Tartari! O gente
di Mong, Mosach, Thubal, Aneg, Ageg,
Assum, Pothim, Cephar, Alan, a me!

A Rum fuggì Zul-Karnein, le ferree
trombe lasciando qui su le Mammelle
tonde del Nord. Gog e Magog, a me!"

XVIII

O stolti! Quelle trombe erano terra
concava, donde il vento occidentale
traeva, ansando, strepiti di guerra.

Rupperle disdegnando col puntale
de' lor pungetti, e dalle trombe rotte
gufi uscivan con muto batter d'ale.

Risero accorti, e sparsi per le grotte
bevvero sangue. Sopra loro un volo
muto, di sogni, e i gridi della notte.

XVI

To the bottom of the North's Breasts they stole
carefully. And the old halfling
climbed onto the tuff with his hands and feet.

At the top, he saw a giant sink-hole
like the mouth of a trumpet. He entered dumbly,
heard hoots, saw a pair of enormous eyes.

A filthy nest plugged that sink-hole.
At its centre sat a big still owl
like a scruffy king with a crown of tufts.

XVII

The old dwarf took two feathers,
stood on a rock, and shook them,
and called to the attendant horde: "Come!

Gog and Magog, Tartars, people of Aneg,
of Mong, Mosach, Thubal, Ageg,
Assur, Pothim, Cephar, Alan, come!

Zul-Karnein has fled to the West
and left his trumpets on the Breasts
of the North. Gog and Magog, come!"

XVIII

Fools! Those trumpets were hollowed earth
from which the western wind, panting,
had dragged its false alarms of war!

Disgusted, the Tartars broke them, piercing
them with their spears —a flight of owls
arose, their wings mutely beating.

They laughed. At last, they saw things right!
They sat and drank blood. Above them, a mute
flight of dreams and the cries of the night.

XIX

Alla gran Porta si fermò lo stuolo:
sorgeva il bronzo tra l'occaso e loro.
Gog e Magog l'urtò d'un urto solo.

La spranga si piegò dopo un martoro
lungo: la Porta a lungo stridé dura-
mente, e s'aprì con chiaro clangor d'oro.

S'affacciò l'Orda, e vide la pianura,
le città bianche presso le fiumane,
e bionde messi e bovi alla pastura.

Sboccò bramendo, e il mondo le fu pane.

XIX

The horde stopped at the door. Above
them the impenetrable bronze rose high.
The Tartars shook it with a single shove.

Once the bolt gave in to their industry,
the great door creaked open, pain-
fully, with a clear and golden cry.

The horde looked out and saw the plains,
the white cities along the rivers,
and the fields and pastures green with rain.

And they poured out screaming, and the world was theirs.

La buona novella

THE GOOD TIDINGS

LA BUONA NOVELLA

I. In oriente

I

Si vegliava sui monti. Erano pochi
pastori che vegliavano sui monti
di Giuda. Quasi spenti erano i fuochi.

Altri alle tombe mute, altri alle fonti
garrule, presso. Il plenilunio bianco
battea dai cieli sopra le lor fronti.

Ognun guardava ai cieli, come stanco,
stanco nel cuore; ognuno avea vicino
il dolce uguale ruminar del branco.

Sostava sino all'alba del mattino
il cuor del gregge, sazio di mentastri;
ma il cuore de' pastori era in cammino

sempre; ch'erano erranti come gli astri,
essi: avean la bisaccia irta di peli
al collo, e tra i ginocchi i lor vincastri,

e cinti i lombi, e nella mano steli
d'issopo. E alcuno, come è lor costume,
cantava, fiso, come stanco, ai cieli.

E il canto, sotto i cieli arsi dal lume,
a piè dell'universo, era sommesso,
era non più che un pigolìo d'implume

caduto, sotto il suo grande cipresso.

II

Maath cantava: — O tu che mai non poni
il tuo vincastro, e che pari nell'alto
le taciturne costellazïoni,

The Good Tidings

I. In the East

I

They kept vigil on the hills
of Judaea, a few shepherds
around dying bonfires.

Others were by silent tombs
or garrulous springs. The moon
shone white on their foreheads.

Each stared at the sky, weary,
with a heavy heart, while the flock
pastured in peace

and slept through the night,
filled with green grass.
But as for the shepherds,

their hearts wandered far,
like stars that ever wander,
with their rough goatskin sacks
and their shepherds' staves,

short tunics, and hyssop stalks.
And some sang a song
to the far sky, as is their custom:

a song under the burning moonlight,
feeble, at the universe's feet, like
the chirp of a hatchling

fallen under a great tree.

II

Maath[1] sang: "Shepherd God,
eternally, tirelessly herding
your flock of taciturn stars,

1. Luke 3.26.

*Dio! che la nostra vita cader d'alto
fai, come pietra, dalla tua gran fionda…
la pietra cade sopra il Mar d'asfalto.*

*Pietra ch'è nel Mar morto e non affonda,
la vita! Cosa grave che galleggia,
e va e va dove la porta l'onda!*

*O Dio, noi siamo come questa greggia
che va e va, né posso dir che arrivi,
nemmen se giunga al pozzo della reggia! —*

*Addì cantava: — Tu, sola tu, vivi,
o greggia, che non mai dalle tue strade
vedi la Morte ferma là nei trivi.*

*Vedo qualche smarrito astro che cade:
muore anche l'astro. Ma tu, pago il cuore,
stai ruminando sotto le rugiade.*

*O greggia, solo chi non sa, non muore!
Tu non odi l'abisso che rimbomba
presso il tuo dente, e strappi lieta il fiore*

del loto eterno ai sassi della tomba-

III

*E un canto invase allora i cieli: pace
sopra la terra! E i fuochi quasi spenti
arsero, e desta scintillò la brace,*

*come per improvvisa ala di venti
silenzïosi, e si sentì nei cieli
come il soffio di due grandi battenti.*

*Erano in alto nubi, pari a steli
di giglio, sopra Betlehem; già pronti
erano, in piedi, attoniti ed aneli,*

you throw our life from above
like a stone from your great slingshot....
It falls onto the stony sea,

the dead sea that cannot sink it:
a heavy thing that floats,
carried around by every wave!

God, we are like this flock,
going ever and never reaching
home, even in the halls of kings!"

Ahdid[2] sang: "No one truly lives
but this flock that can't see
that Death awaits at the crossroad.

I see a falling star, lost in the sky.
It, too, dies! But the flock
knows it not and feeds on fresh dew.

O flock, unaware and immortal,
ignoring the roaring of hell,
happily chewing the evergreen

flower that grows by your tomb!"

III

A chant filled the heavens: "Peace
on Earth!" And the bonfires
blazed, and a fire was kindled

by the sudden wing of silent
winds, and a soft gust
opened two great curtains

in the sky where clouds bloomed
like lilies over Bethlehem.
Astonished, amazed, in awe,

2.   Luke 3.28.

i pastori guardando di sui monti,
e chi presso le tombe, onde una voce
uscìa di culla, e chi presso le fonti,

onde un tumulto scaturìa di foce:
e un angelo era, con le braccia stese,
tra loro, come un'alta esile croce,

bianca; e diceva: "Gioia con voi! Scese
Dio sulla terra". Ed a ciascuno il cuore
sobbalzò verso il bianco angelo, e prese

via per vedere il Grande che non muore,
come l'agnello che pur va carponi;
il Dio che vive tutto in sè, pastore

di taciturne costellazïoni.

IV

Mossero: e Betlehem, sotto l'osanna
de' cieli ed il fiorir dell'infinito,
dormiva. E videro, ecco, una capanna.

Ed ai pastori l'accennò col dito
un angelo: una stalla umile e nera,
donde gemeva un filo di vagito.

E d'un figlio dell'uomo era, ma era
quale d'agnello. Esso giacea nel fieno
del presepe, e sua madre, una straniera,

sopra la paglia. Era il suo primo, e il seno
le apriva; e non aveva ella né due
assi: all'albergo alcun le disse: È pieno.

Nella capanna povera le sue
lagrime sorridea sopra il suo nato,
su cui fiatava un asino ed un bue.

-Noi cercavamo Quei che vive… — entrato
disse Maath. Ed ella con un pio
dubbio: Il mio figlio vive per quel fiato…

the shepherds stood on the hills
and by tombs that
had turned into cradles

and by thundering springs.
An angel came with his arms open,
spread like one nailed to a cross.

He said: "Rejoice! God has
come to the Earth." And the heart
of the shepherds set out

to find the immortal God
of the immortal flock, the
Living One, the Shepherd

of a thousand taciturn stars.

IV

The skies sang hosannah and bloomed
with infinite stars. Bethlehem was
asleep as they came to a hut.

The angel pointed his finger:
a dark humble stable,
where a baby cried faintly.

The Son of Man, but more like
a little lamb in a manger.
His foreign mother lay there.

He was her firstborn, first to her
breasts, and nowhere to stay,
the inns being full.

Tears mixed with her smile
as she held her babe in that shack
with an ox and ass to keep them warm.

Maath said: "We seek the Living God."
And doubtful she said: "My son's
life hangs on a breath...."

-Quei che non muore... — Ed ella: Il figlio mio
morrà (disse, e piangeva su l'agnello
suo tremebondo) in una croce... — Dio...—

Rispose all'uomo l'Universo: È quello!

II. In Occidente

I

Grande, lungo le molte acque, al sussurro
del fiume eterno, sopra i sette monti,
bianca di marmo in mezzo al cielo azzurro,

Roma dormiva. Agli archi quadrifronti
battea la luna; e il Tevere sonoro
fiorìa di spuma percotendo ai ponti.

Alto fulgeva col suo tetto d'oro
il Capitolio: ma la notte mesta
adombrava la Via Sacra del Foro.

Nell'ombra un lume: il fuoco era di Vesta,
che tralucea. Nel tempio le Vestali
dormian ravvolte nella lor pretesta.

Era la notte dopo i Saturnali.
Nelle celle de' templi, sui lor troni,
taceano i numi, soli ed immortali.

Intorno alla Dea Madre i suoi leoni
giacean nel sonno. Gli ebbri Coribanti
dormian con nell'orecchio ululi e tuoni.

Rosso di sangue uno giaceva avanti
la Dea. Dischiuso il tempio era di Giano.
Esso attendeva, coi serrami infranti,

l'aquile che predavano lontano.

"We seek the Undying God."
"My son will die," said she,
"on a cross," and cried. "God…

It's Him!" The universe answered them.

II. In the West
I

Proud, by the great many waters
of the eternal river, on its seven hills,
marble-white against the blue sky,

Rome was asleep. The moon shone
on angular archways. In the roaring Tiber,
flowers of foam burst against bridges.

Tall stood the Capitol, its golden
roof bright, the mournful night
filled the Via Sacra with darkness.

A light in the shadow: Vesta's fire,
glowing in the temple, where maidens
slept in robes of purple and white.

The Saturnalia was over. Alone
in their temples and on their thrones,
the gods slept their immortal sleep.

The lions slept, surrounding
the goddess.[3] Her drunken priests
slept a slumber of rumble and thunder

in a pool of blood at her feet.
Janus's temple door was ajar, still,
its keys broken as the god awaited

the eagles preying abroad.

3.   Cybele.

II

Roma dormiva, ebbra di sangue. I ludi
eran finiti. In sogno le matrone
ora vedean gladiatori ignudi.

Ne' triclini ai dormenti le corone
eran cadute, e s'imbevean le rose
nel sangue che fluì dal mirmillone.

Dormivan su le umane ossa già rose,
le belve in fondo degli anfiteatri;
e gli schiavi tornati erano cose.

Dopo la breve libertà, negli atrï
giacean gli ostiari alla catena, quali
cani la cui leggera anima latri.

Era la notte dopo i Saturnali;
ed ogni schiavo dalla tarda sera
dormiva, udendo ventilar grandi ali,

e gracidare. Erano cigni a schiera
sul patrio fiume… No: su l'Esquilino
erano corvi in una nube nera…

Ei tesseva e stesseva il suo destino:
vedea sua madre; poi sentia la voce
del banditore: apriva al suo bambino

le braccia, e le sentia fitte alla croce.

III

Roma dormiva. Uno vegliava, un Geta
gladïatore. Egli era nuovo, appena
giunto: il suo piede, bianco era di creta.

L'avean, col raffio, tratto dall'arena
del circo; e nello spolïario immondo
alcun nel collo gli aprì poi la vena.

II

Drunk with blood, after the *ludi*,
Rome was asleep. Its ladies
dreamt of gladiators.

In the banquet halls, rose crowns,
fallen from the sleeping guests,
soaked up gladiators' blood.

Asleep on the bones they had chewed,
the beasts lay in their cages.
Slaves were things once again

after a short time of freedom,
the doorkeepers[4] back in their chains
like dogs whose souls bark and howl.

The Saturnalia was over. Slaves
in their sleep heard the sound
of great wings beating, the cawing

of crows, or was it swans on the river
of Rome, but no, it was ravens:
an unkindness like a dark cloud on the hills.

In his sleep, his fate passed him by:
his mother, his master, a child
he had hugged with outstretched arms,

arms that were nailed to a cross.

III

Rome was asleep, but one man was awake,
a Thracian gladiator, new to
the city, yet to be sold.

They had dragged him back
from the arena with their pointy gaff.
In the *spoliarium*, somebody opened his throat.

4.   The *ostiarii*, slaves who were in charge of the doors.

Rantolava: il silenzio era profondo:
il cader lento d'una goccia rossa
solo restava del fragor del mondo.

Ma d'uomini gremita era la fossa
in cui giaceva. All'occhio suo, tra un velo,
parea scoprirne e ricoprirne l'ossa.

Ed era solo, e l'uomo che col gelo
lo pungea di sua cute, più lontano
gli era del più lontano astro del cielo:

più della terra sua, più del suo piano
lunghesso l'Istro, e de' suoi bovi ch'ora
sdraiati ruminavano pian piano,

e de' suoi figli ch'attendean l'aurora,
piccoli nella lor nomade cuna,
e del suo plaustro, ch'era sua dimora,
là fermo e nero al lume della luna.

IV

E venne bianco nella notte azzurra
un angelo dal cielo di Giudea,
a nunzïar la pace; e la Suburra

non l'udiva; e nel tempio alto di Rhea
bandì la pace; e non alzò la testa
quell'uomo rosso ai piedi della Dea;

e vide, un fuoco, e disse, pace; e Vesta
ardeva, e le Vestali al focolare
sedeano avvolte nella lor pretesta;

e vide un tempio aperto, e dal sogliare
mormorò, pace; e non l'udì che il vento
che uscì gemendo e portò guerra al mare.

E l'angelo passò candido e lento
per i taciti trivi, e dicea, pace
sopra la terra!… Udì forse un lamento…

He was dying in silence, and the slow
dripping of that one red drop was
all that remained from the hubbub of the world.

He was dying in a pit full
of corpses whose bones
glistened white before his dying eyes.

But he was lonely, and the cold skin
of the corpse near him was further
from him than the furthest star,

than his land and his plain
on the Istros, and the cattle
he owned, peacefully grazing,

and his children waking at dawn
in their nomadic cradle
of his moveable home, a black chariot
motionless in the moonlight.

IV

White as a star in the blue night,
an angel came from Judaea
singing of peace, but the Suburra

was deaf to him. He sang of peace in the temple,
but the man at the goddess's feet
did not rise from his blood.

He saw a fire and said, "Peace."
Vesta's fire glowed, and the maidens
sat still in robes of purple and white.

At the threshold of an open temple,
he whispered, "Peace," to the wind,
who hissed and brought war to the seas.

White and slow the angel passed
the silent crossroads saying, "Peace
on Earth!" when he heard a whimper.

Vegliava, il Geta… Entrò l'angelo: pace!
disse. E nella infinita urbe de' forti
sol quegli intese. E chiuse gli occhi in pace.

Sol esso udì; ma lo ridisse ai morti,
e i morti ai morti, e le tombe alle tombe
e non sapeano i sette colli assorti,

ciò che voi sapevate, o catacombe.

ΚΕΔΕΣΙ ΤΕΠΘΜΗΝΟΙ

The Thracian slave was awake.… The angel said,
"Peace!" And in that great victorious city,
only one slave heard it and died.

He alone heard it, but he told the dead,
and the dead told the dead, from tomb to tomb,
and the seven hills didn't know what you knew, O tombs.

KEDESI TERPOMENOI[5]

<hr>

5.   Greek motto: "Taking comfort from our sorrows."

GLOSSARY

Abae, Euboea.

Achaeans, a collective name used by Homer for the Mycenaean Greeks who went to war against Troy.

Acheron, one of the five rivers in Hades, sometimes described as a swamp.

Achilles, the son of the sea goddess Tethys and of King Peleus of Pthia. He fought in Troy alongside the Greek army, and he is a central character in the *Illiad*.

Aeolus, the keeper of winds. He gifted Odysseus with a jar containing all the winds except Zephyr. Zephyr, a gentle breeze, was allowed to blow so that it would ensure a safe journey to Ithaca.

Aetolia, a region of Greece that sent warriors to the Trojan War. It is featured in the *Iliad*'s catalogue of ships (2.497–759).

Alala, a minor Greek goddess. She personified the war cry that Greek soldiers shouted when attacking their enemies.

Alexander, Alexander III of Macedonia, better known as Alexander the Great (356–323 BCE), a king, the son of King Philip II, whom he succeeded at the age of twenty, and Olympias. Alexander conducted an unprecedented military campaign, conquering Greece and the Persian Empire all the way to northwestern India. By the age of thirty, he had created the largest empire of antiquity. Many sources report Alexander's indomitable spirit and desire to advance further and explore uncharted territories. He was forced to interrupt his expedition when his troops revolted and probably assassinated him. The empire was then divided among his military leaders, or *diadochi*. In the *Quran* (18.86), Alexander is called Zul-Karnein, "the two-horned king."

Alpheios, a river in the center of the Peloponnesus in Greece.

Anthesteria, (literally the Feast or Festival of Flowers,) an ancient Greek festival in honour of DIONYSOS. It was celebrated from the 11th to the 13th of the month Anthesterion (between February and March). On this occasion, people drank the new wine and practiced rituals associated with mystery cults.

Dionysos, the Greek god of wine, fertility, theater, ritual madness, and religious ecstasy. His Roman counterpart was the god Bacchus.

Arne, a city in Boeotia.

Ascra, Hesiod's native village.

Ate, or Atë, the goddess embodying blind folly, rage and the uncontrolled impulses that often lead people to commit actions they would later regret. The word also refers to a state of mind that would cause one's downfall or death.

Aulis, an ancient town in Boeotia.

Bacchanals, rites in honor of the god Dionysus, involving music, drunkenness, intoxication, and sexual promiscuity. Euripides describes one in his tragedy *The Bacchae*.

Bacchylides (518–451 BCE), a Greek lyric poet born and based on KEA.

Bear, the constellation known as Ursa Major.

Briseis, a captive woman from Troy. She was initially given to ACHILLES but then taken by Agamemnon. Enraged and insulted, Achilles refused to continue fighting for the Greeks. Briseis was eventually returned to Achilles before he returned to battle to avenge Patroclus's death.

Calypso (Gk. "the hider"), a goddess, daughter of the Titan Atlas. She lived on the island of Ogygia. In *Odyssey* 5, Odysseus spends seven years detained on Ogygia where Calypso offers him immortality in the hope of marrying him. He never accepts, so the goddess eventually releases him.

Carmel / Carmelus, a chain of mountains in Israel.

Chalcis, a city in central Greece.

Charybdis, see SCYLLA AND CHARYBDIS.

Chios is a large island in the northern Aegean Sea. According to Thucydides (*Peloponnesian Wars* 3.104.5), Chios was the birthplace of Homer, whom he calls "a blind man from the rocky island of Chios."

Circe, referred to as the sorceress, was an enchantress and minor goddess on the island of Aeaea. She is famous for her knowledge of herbs and potions, as well as for her lovely singing. Her magic turns men into swine, which happens to Odysseus' crew when they land on Aeaea. Odysseus, who is protected by the herb moly, which Hermes has given him, eventually prevails over Circe, but stays with her for a year, becoming her lover, before setting out to Ithaca again.

Cithaeron, a mountain in central Greece.

Crow's Peak, a location on Ithaca mentioned in the *Odyssey*.

Cybele, an ancient goddess of fertility, who in Rome became known as Magna Mater. The mystery cult originated in Anatolia, and its followers believed in the afterlife as a return to Mother Earth.

Cyclopes, literally "round-eyes," were one-eyed giants. In the *Odyssey* (9), Odysseus recounts his encounter with the Cyclops Polyphemus, a shepherd living on a remote island. Polyphemus captures Odysseus and his companions, killing and devouring many of them. Eventually, Odysseus manages to escape by getting the giant drunk, piercing his only eye, and hiding himself and his men under the bellies of Polyphemus' sheep. As Odysseus tells the giant that his name is "Nobody," the enraged Polyphemus is unable to name his offender. However, once safe on his ship, Odysseus boastfully reveals his name to the giant, who prays to his father, the god Poseidon, to take revenge on the hero.

Cyme, a city in modern Turkey (Nemrut Limani).

Cynthus, a mountain on DELOS.

Deiphobos, son of Priam, third husband to HELEN.

Delias, the name of a young woman, inspired by the figure of Nausicaa in *Odyssey* 6. Delias is the lover of an old and blind poet clearly reminiscent of Homer. Her name is an indication of her provenance: the island of DELOS.

Delos a sacred island near the center of the Cyclades archipelago. It was a holy sanctuary and the birthplace of several deities. It was forbidden to bury the dead there so corpses had to be brought to the nearby island of Rhenea. For at least a millennium, until 100 CE, it was a major Panhellenic cult and pilgrimage center.

Dolopia, a region of Greece that sent warriors to the Trojan War. It is featured in the *Iliad*'s catalogue of ships (2.497–759).

Dryads, semi-divine creatures of Greek mythology. These nymphs inhabited trees and bushes.

Epirus, the northwestern region of Greece. Olympias, ALEXANDER's mother, came from there, and she retired there with some of ALEXANDER's sisters

Ergenekon, an inaccessible valley in the Altay mountains of central and east Asia. It features in the founding myth of Turkic and Mongolic peoples.

Euboea, a region of Greece that sent warriors to the Trojan War. It is featured in the *Iliad*'s catalogue of ships (2.497–759).

Eumaeus, Odysseus' loyal swineherd. He is the first to welcome Odysseus upon his return, although at first, he does not recognize him, since the hero is disguised as a beggar.

Gog and Magog, barbaric tribes who are referred to in several passages of the Bible and the Quran. ALEXANDER the Great prevented them from invading Israel by building a tall bronze door, also known as the Gates of Alexander. He devised a stratagem to keep them from being breached by putting trumpets on top of them, so that the wind would make the barbarians believe that there were armies guarding the wall.

Hades, the Greek god of death as well as the name of his kingdom in the afterlife.

Haemon, a mountain range in THRACE, now known as the Balkan Mountains.

Haliartus, a city in Boeotia.

Helen of Troy, the daughter of Leda and ZEUS. She was said to be the most beautiful woman who ever lived. She married Menelaus, king of Sparta. All her other suitors swore an oath to provide military assistance to him were Helen to be abducted. Paris, prince of Troy, abducted a willing or unwilling Helen and triggered the Trojan War. After the death of Paris, during the siege, Helen became the paramour or wife of Paris' brother DEIPHOBOS. When the Greeks conquered Troy, Helen returned to Sparta and lived there until her death.

Helicon, a mountain in Boeotia, celebrated in Greek mythology as the place where the Muses dwelled.

Helotes, the lowest rank in Spartan society. They were tasked with working the land.

Hens, refers to the constellation called the Pleiades or the Seven Sisters. In October, the Pleiades set in the sky, and farmers in Italy call these stars "the Hens" because they look like birds scattered by the arrows of an archer.

Inopus, a river on DELOS.

Ioulis, a city on KEA on the mountain known today as Hagios Elias.

Iris, the divine personification of the rainbow and the swift messenger of the gods. In the *Iliad*, she is always described with epithet "wind-footed."

Irus, a beggar who lived in Odysseus' house in his absence and served Penelope's suitors. When Odysseus returned, disguised as a beggar, the two engaged in a fight, which Odysseus won. He considered killing Irus but changed his mind and spared him.

Island of Rocks, the island of Laestrygonians. Odysseus visited it on his journey back to Ithaca (*Odyssey* 9). The Laestrygonians were giants fathered by Poseidon. As Odysseus' fleet sailed past the island, the giants threw rocks at them, destroying eleven of the hero's twelve ships.

Island of the Dead, the island where Odysseus descended to the Underworld, met many dead heroes from the Trojan War, and learned of his fate from the prophet TIRESIAS. (*Odyssey* 10–11).

Island of the Sun, Thrinacria, the mythical island where the cattle of Helios, the god of the Sun, pastured. One of Odysseus' sailors, Eurylochus, convinces the others to sacrifice the cattle in Odysseus'ship to the gods, thereby bringing about the death of his companions. Only Odysseus manages to swim safely to the island of CALYPSO. (*Odyssey* 12)

Island of Winds, the island ruled by AEOLUS, keeper of the winds.
Odysseus lands there and is gifted a jar containing all winds
except the west wind, which would make his ship sail fast
towards its destination. Pascoli's "The Sleep of Odysseus" tells
the story of the sailors who open the jar and wreak havoc.
(*Odyssey* 10)

Issus, the site of an ancient settlement on the coastal plain in southern
Turkey at its border with Syria, the site of ALEXANDER's famous
defeat (333 BCE) of the Persian King Darius III.

Isthmia, a sanctuary of Poseidon on the Isthmus of Corinth; the location of the ancient Isthmian Games.

Istros, the Greek name for the Danube.

Janus, the Roman god of beginnings and transitions, symbolized by
thresholds and doors. He is represented as having two faces.
The doors of his temples were opened in times of war and
closed in times of peace.

Karthaia, a city on KEA.

Kea, or Keos, a Greek island in the Cyclades Archipelago.

Laertes, king of Ithaca and father to Odysseus.

Leitus, one of the suitors of Helen of Troy, a leader of the Boeotians
and admiral of twelve ships that sailed against Troy.

Lethe, the river of oblivion at the entrance of HADES. Souls were forced
to drink its waters in order to forget their earthly lives and enter
a new dimension.

Locris, a region of Greece that sent warriors to the Trojan War. It features
in the *Iliad*'s catalogue of ships (2.497–759).

Lotus Island, the island of the lotus-eaters, a mythical race of people
living on an island where the lotus plant grew abundantly. Its
fruit was thought to be a narcotic, inducing in those who ate
it a peaceful apathy. In the *Odyssey* (9), Odysseus sends two
men to scout the island. The men eat the lotus fruit and forget
their journey, only wishing to stay. Odysseus eventually drags
them back to the ship.

Ludi, public games in ancient Rome involving horse races, sport
competitions, and theatrical performances.

Maath, a shepherd. His name is taken from Christ's genealogy (Luke
3.26).

Mecisteus, the name of a warrior in the *Iliad* (1.49). However, there
he is not recorded as being the son of Gorgo.

Memnon, son of the goddess Aurora and King Tyton. Memnon
fought with the Trojans in the Trojan War and was eventually
killed by Achilles. The Ptolemaic kings introduced the cult of
Memnon by building a temple near Thebes and a palace in

Abydos. Two statues in front of Amenophis II's temple were renamed "the colossi of Memnon." After the earthquake of 27 BCE, one of the statues began emitting a moaning sound, which was interpreted as a cry. According to Ovid's *Metamorphoses*, a flock of birds was born out of Memnon's ashes. They formed two rows and fought each other in a competition to honor the great hero.

Nereids, marine nymphs and daughters of Nereus. They were depicted on the Temple of Neptune in Rome, probably after a Greek sculpture.

Niobe. According to the myth reported by Ovid, Niobe boasted that she was more fertile than Latona, the divine mother of Apollo and Artemis. Latona asked Apollo and Artemis to punish Niobe for her hybris by killing her and her children (Ovid, *Metamorphoses* 6). Pliny attributed to Scopas a relief that depicted Niobe and her children.

Niritos, a mountain on Ithaca.

North's Breasts, *Ubera Aquilonis*, the chain of mountains which, according to the legend, separated the West from the East.

Odysseus (Gk name of Ulysses), the hero of the *Odyssey* and also an important character in the *Iliad*.

Orion, a constellation named after a hunter in Greek mythology.

Pan, the god of shepherds and herds as well as the inventor of music, traditionally a companion of nymphs and represented with goat-like features.

Patroclus, friend, companion, and lover of ACHILLES. After Achilles withdraws from the fighting in the Trojan War, Patroclus enters the battle wearing Achilles' armor. Hector kills him, which leads Achilles to rejoin the war.

Peleus, king of Phthia, father of Achilles.

Pelion, a mountain at the southeastern part of Thessaly in northern Greece. It extends as a peninsula between the Pagasetic Gulf and the Aegean Sea.

Pella, the capital of the ancient kingdom of Macedonia and the birthplace of ALEXANDER the Great.

Phemius, a poet who lived in Odysseus' palace in his absence and performed narrative songs for Penelope's suitors. When Odysseus returns home, he spares the life of the poet and keeps him in his household.

Pherae, a city in ancient Thessaly known for its horses.

Phocis, a region of Greece that sent warriors to the Trojan War. It features in the *Iliad*'s catalogue of ships (2.497–759).

Phorcys, a bay and harbor on the island of Ithaca. Mentioned in the *Odyssey* (Book 13).

Phthia, a district in ancient Thessaly where Achilles grew up. He was raised by the Centaur Chiron in the forests of Thessaly by the Spercheios River and in the vicinity of Mount Pelion.

Placos, a mountain near Thebes in ancient Anatolia.

Ploughman, Boötes, a constellation in the northern sky. Its name comes from Greek "Boótes," which literally means "the ox-driver" or "the ploughman." The constellation is also known as "the Big Dipper."

Polyphemus, see Cyclopes.

Poseidon, the god of the sea, brother of Zeus, father of the Cyclopes.

Psyche, a mortal woman whose names means "soul" as well as "butterfly" in ancient Greek. She was given in marriage to an unknown bridegroom who would visit her in the night. She was forbidden to see his face, but one night she raised her lamp and discovered he was Eros, son of Aphrodite. The goddess punished her for her curiosity and made her undergo several trials at the end of which she was able to reunite with her husband.

Sappho (circa 630–-570 BCE), an Archaic Greek poet from the island of Lesbos. She was known for her lyric poetry, which she accompanied on a stringed instrument, probably a lyre. She was regarded in her time as one of the greatest poets alive. Very little remains of her poetry, although what does remain has had a great influence on modern and contemporary verse.

Saturnalia, one of the most popular holidays in ancient Rome. It was celebrated every year from the 17th to the 23rd of December. During that time, to commemorate the mythical age of Saturn, the so-called Golden Age, slaves were given freedom of speech and their deeds forgiven. The celebrations included banquets and public games.

Scopas or Skopas (395–350 BCE), a sculptor in ancient Greece. Born in Paros, he then worked with Praxiteles and travelled extensively in the Hellenic world. Some of his most famous works include reliefs, now in the Museum of Halicarnassus, and the much-copied statue of Pothos (Desire).

Scylla and Charybdis, two mythological monsters described by Homer (*Odyssey* 12). They occupy either side of the strait of Messina between Sicily and Calabria. Scylla is a six-eyed sea monster, whereas Charybdis is a whirlpool. They probably personify the hazardous strait, where sailors had to sail close to either one side or the other, risking destruction either way. Odysseus passes close to Scylla, who kills several sailors, avoiding Charybdis, who would have sucked the entire fleet into its whirlpool.

Sigean Gates, the Trojan gates facing west toward Sigeum, the promontory in western Anatolia where the Greeks had landed.

Silenus, a mythical creature akin to satyrs, usually represented as half-human and half-goat. They accompanied the gods DIONYSUS and Pan. They are depicted as creatures of the forest with equine ears, hooves, and a tail. Despite their association with drunkenness and intoxication, *sileni* were also old and wise. According to Pliny (*Natural History* 36.4), a block of marble in one of the quarries on the island of Paros was once split into wedges and revealed the face of a *silenus*.

Sirens, mythical creatures represented as birds with women's heads, scaly feet, and feathers. They would sit on the rocky coast of their island (possibly Capreae or Cape Pelorum, both off the Italian coast) and with their enchanting voices lure the sailors to shipwreck. In the *Odyssey* (12), Odysseus is curious to hear their song, so he orders his crew to fill their ears with beeswax, tie him to the mast, and leave him there no matter how much he would beg. Thanks to this trick, which Circe had suggested to him, Odysseus escapes the lure of the Sirens.

Smylax, a plant similar to ivy.

Solon, an Athenian statesman, lawmaker, and poet (c. 638–558 BCE). He is also remembered as a poet, as well as for the reforms he introduced in the Athenian state. Only fragments of his poetry remain, mostly quoted by other poets. According to the Latin writer Aelianus, Solon seemed to have loved SAPPHO's poetry, and it is this connection that Pascoli focused on in the first of his *Convivial Poems*.

Spercheios River, a river in Phthia.

Spoliarium, a place in the amphitheater where mortally wounded gladiators would be stripped of their armor and killed.

Suburra, a poor neighborhood in ancient Rome between the Esquiline and the Viminal Hills.

Telemus, son of Eurymus, a prophet and a seer. He warned the CYCLOPS that he would be deprived of his sight by a man named Odysseus (*Odyssey* 9).

Tethys, a sea goddess, mother of Achilles, who foresaw the death of her son.

Thrace, a region in southeast Europe, which would have comprised southeast Bulgaria, northeast Greece, and northwest Turkey.

Tiberius, Tiberius Caesar Augustus (42 BCE–37 CE), the second Roman emperor. His father was Tiberius Claudius Nero and his mother was Livia Drusilla. Due to his rift with Octavian, Tiberius' father had been forced to flee Rome with his wife and child. Twice

the infant Tiberius put his parents at risk of being discovered
by Octavian's guards: the first time when he cried as the family
was secretly boarding a ship and the second time when Livia
had to rescue him from a fire in the woods of Greece.

Timotheus, probably the famous poet and musician who lived be-
tween the second half of the fifth century BCE and the first half
of the fourth. He was the author of many dithyrambs and *nomoi*
(a genre of ancient Greek music), one of which was famously
called "The Persians" and seems to have inspired Alexander
to conquer Persia. ALEXANDER may have heard Timotheus'
performances when he was a child at the Macedonian court.

Tiresias, a famous prophet. He predicted that Odysseus' journey home
from the Trojan War would be perilous but eventually success-
ful. He also added that once settled in Ithaca, Odysseus would
have to set out on an overland journey through continental
Greece towards populations that have never seen the seashore.
This journey would be complete only if a passer-by mistook
Odysseus' oar for a shovel. At that point, Odysseus had to
sacrifice to the god Poseidon, whose wrath had caused his
difficult return. Tiresias finally predicted that Odysseus' death
would be on the sea, but peaceful and in his old age.

Vesta, the goddess of hearth, home, and family. Her temple in Rome
was in the Forum, and it was the seat of the public hearth. En-
try to the temple was permitted only to the Vestals, the virgin
priestesses who tended the sacred fire.

Via Sacra, Sacred Street. In ancient Rome, it led from the Capitoline
Hill to the Forum and Coliseum.

Zeus, god of thunder and rain.

Zul-Karnein, see ALEXANDER.

*This Work Was Revised on 1 December,
2024 at Italica Press, Bristol UK.
It Was Set in ITC Giovanni
& Printed on 55-lb.
Natural Paper.*